NEW SPANISH SELF TAUGHT

Language Series titles available in
Barnes & Noble paperback editions

New French Self Taught
New German Self Taught
New Italian Self Taught
New Spanish Self Taught

THE QUICK, PRACTICAL WAY TO

READING • WRITING • SPEAKING • UNDERSTANDING

NEW SPANISH
SELF TAUGHT

Revised by

JUAN LÓPEZ-MORILLAS,
Brown University

Harper Perennial
A Division of HarperCollins*Publishers*

This work was originally published by Funk & Wagnalls Company.

NEW SPANISH SELF TAUGHT *(Revised)*. Copyright © 1952, 1959 by HarperCollins *Publishers*, Inc. All rights reserved. Printed in the United States of America. No part of this book may be used or reproduced in any manner whatsoever without written permission except in the case of brief quotations embodied in critical articles and reviews. For information address HarperCollins Publishers, 10 East 53rd Street, New York, N.Y. 10022.

First HarperPerennial edition published 1982.

ISBN: 0-06-463617-8

91 92 93 94 95 MPC 16 15 14 13 12 11

CONTENTS

FOREWORD

In the present revision, corrections and changes have been made throughout, and outmoded expressions have been brought up to date. Perhaps the most important feature of this revision, and certainly my chief contribution to it, is the new introduction to Spanish pronunciation prepared in accordance with the International Phonetic Alphabet (see inside front and back covers). This method of phonetic notation has been used throughout the new edition to indicate the pronunciation of many words and expressions. This new approach to pronunciation should facilitate the mastery of the authentic sound of the Spanish language.

Juan López-Morillas

Brown University
Providence, Rhode Island

The Method Explained

Every man and woman of intelligence realizes the imperative need of having command of a foreign language. The realization becomes more acute day by day as the fact is borne in on us that what once were known, in the old-fashioned phrase, as the "ends of the earth" are now, so to speak, practically our front lawn. Traveling by airplane we reach the remotest regions in flashes of time. By radio we know hour by hour what farthest distant peoples have on their minds and on their tongues. So it becomes increasingly necessary that we be able to tell them in their own language what we think and what we want to do.

Whether in professional, diplomatic, social, or commercial life, a sound and sure knowledge of our fellow man's language is the great essential of understanding among men and nations of the world.

The method used in this book is not new and has been successfully followed by thousands of students. By experiment and research, it was discovered many years ago that a thorough and workable command of a foreign language is not learned by long and arduous memorization of the grammatical rules of a language. Modern educational science now follows the far more efficient method that is presented in these pages. It is the most rational and simple method ever devised for learning a foreign language.

THE PRACTICAL MASTERY OF FOREIGN LANGUAGES

To think in a language not your mother tongue means that you will express yourself with sympathetic understanding of the people who speak that language. It means that you can converse easily and naturally as a good neighbor and a good friend. It is the great achievement of the method in this book that it enables its users easily and speedily to speak a foreign language just as fluently as their own. In doing this the student becomes accustomed to thinking in that language as well.

LANGUAGE AND GRAMMAR

are in no sense synonymous, although some school methods might lead us to suppose so.

Grammar is the science of language and, while necessary and desirable, is not so important as the ability to speak the language itself. Can anyone doubt this? Consider the majority of people you meet. Listen to their speech and examine it. Do they know the rules of English grammar? Do not even the very young children of educated persons express themselves correctly without ever having studied a single line of grammatical definitions? Yet,

THE STUDY OF GRAMMAR IS MADE EASY

"but it must be taught," as was said long ago by the great Erasmus, "at the proper time and kept within proper limits."

Colloquial mastery must precede it. Grammar will not then confuse, but will assist the pupil. It will cease to be a drudgery and will become a plain and simple explanation of forms and idioms already learned. It will no longer be an uncertain foundation, but will cap the edifice that has been reared by practical linguistic exercises. This is the true purpose of grammar, and in this sense it is taught throughout this book. A celebrated explorer and the master of many languages once wrote: "The only correct and scientific method by which a foreign language can be learned is to adopt

NATURE'S OWN WAY

by which all persons, whether children or adults, educated or otherwise, rapidly and correctly acquire the language which they constantly hear and which they are instinctively impelled to imitate when living in a foreign country."

It has often been observed that foreigners in the United States learn English seemingly with ease and surely with rapidity. Many of them know nothing of the principles of grammar. Some of them may be too young or may lack sufficient education to be able to read or write their native language. Despite such handicaps they master English sufficiently well within a few months to be able to make themselves understood. The quality of the English they acquire depends greatly on the kind of people they associate with. Judging by the facility with which foreigners in this country acquire English, it becomes obvious that when Americans live in a foreign country they must find some system which will enable them to obtain command of the language of that country in this same manner.

WHAT IS THE SYSTEM WHICH WE INSTINCTIVELY FOLLOW WHEN LIVING IN A FOREIGN COUNTRY?

At first the mind is confused by the multiplicity of foreign sounds heard. We try to grasp the ideas expressed in the strange tongue, and failing to do so we naturally are bewildered.

This state of mental confusion generally passes in about three or four weeks. The ear has become accustomed to some of these sounds and instinctively we begin to imitate the PHRASES we have heard most frequently pronounced by the persons surrounding us, and which, at the same time, are most necessary to our wants.

Now, what is our greatest necessity? Which of the needs of humanity is of paramount importance to young and old alike? It is nourishment—eating and drinking.

Consequently, the first sentences usually mastered are such as these: "*Please give me something to eat,*" or "*Please bring me the menu,*" or "*Please let me have a steak and some potatoes.*"

Such sentences are necessary to everyone; and it may be remarked that nature, through the mastery of these first simple sentences, points out

THE TRUE AND ONLY WAY

in which languages can be learned.

It is THROUGH SENTENCES, *and never through single, isolated words.* The verbs are the soul and backbone of all speech, and it is only by and through the proper study of verbs that mastery of a language can be attained.

To return to the sentence: "*Please bring me the menu.*" Not knowing any other expression, you cling to these words and use them again and again for your various needs.

For instance, when you want matches, or an umbrella, or some towels, instead of saying to the attendant: "*Please bring me the menu,*" you will point to the object and say to him: "*Please bring me ——— .*"

Consider here the simplicity of this mode of teaching. By mastering this first little phrase, you have been furnished with a "sentence-mold" by the use of which hundreds of correct sentences may be composed.

The attendant, understanding your abbreviated phrase and gesture, "*Please bring me* —— ," will give you the words "*matches*," "*umbrella*," or "*some towels*" in the language of the country in which you are living. You repeat these new words over and over again until they come quite naturally to you. In this way you go on from day to day, in fact from hour to hour, until after a few months you are able to express yourself readily and fluently. This is the process by which sounds become language. This is the mode in which any foreign language is learned when we live in a foreign country.

For those studying a foreign language here at home, it is necessary to use a text book containing practical idiomatic speech.

AN INDISPENSABLE VADE-MECUM

Language is divided into the Language of Literature and the Language of Every-day Life.

What part of English is used by the majority of people? The language of literature or the expressions of common life? What do our children speak when they enter school and receive their first lessons in spelling and reading? *The language of every-day life.* They understand and MUST be able to understand and follow their teachers before they can proceed to the study of English grammar. They MUST know common, every-day English before they can comprehend and appreciate the beauties of Shakespeare, Milton, and Tennyson.

Throughout this book the aim has been to give nothing but practical phrases and sentences which are used in the ordinary transactions of life. The proper selection of the vocabulary of practical life is the first distinguishing feature of the method according to which the lessons that follow have been prepared. Highly important as this part of the method is, it is a mere detail of the whole plan. The student must not overlook the fact that

DISCONNECTED, ISOLATED WORDS ARE NOT LANGUAGE

A person might learn a whole dictionary by heart and yet not be able to converse. As long as a child can use single words only, he cannot carry on a conversation. This book is based on the well tested theory that instead of beginning studies with little bits of baby sentences that no adult was ever known to use, the start should be made with connected, rational sentences, such as are employed in every-day language. Also, instead of learning phrases—the construction of which is the same as that of our native tongue—the student, from the beginning, should learn idiomatic sentences, the formation of which is utterly different from our mode of speaking. We must learn

TO THINK IN THE FOREIGN LANGUAGE ITSELF

No one can speak a foreign tongue properly who does not think in it. This is so old a maxim no one can doubt it. Yet the difficulty of learning to think in a foreign language seems at first insurmountable.

Is it possible to learn to think in a foreign language without actually living in the country of that language? Of course when we live in a foreign country and hear nothing but the foreign vernacular, it is easy to understand how we acquire the power of thinking in that foreign language.

But how can we hope to obtain the same results here in the United States where we cannot always associate with foreigners, where we speak nothing but English and think in English only, where the cares and duties of the day continually crowd in upon us, and where the little of a foreign language we learn today is almost forgotten by tomorrow? With all these drawbacks and disadvantages how can we learn to think in a foreign tongue?

No adult can learn as a child learns. In mastering its own tongue, the child reaches not only the power of expression but also the ability to think. From the perception of external facts he proceeds to mental conceptions. Each new word is a discovery to him. Each sound reveals to him a new world. Language is the basis of the child's whole mental development and underlies the acquisition of all his knowledge.

The adult, on the other hand, has passed beyond these preliminary stages. His intellect has been developed and trained. His memory is not nearly so fresh and retentive as that of an untutored child. He can already express his thoughts in one language, and in studying other tongues he aims solely at the acquirement of a new vehicle of sounds which will enable him to convey to natives of other countries the thoughts he expresses at home.

What is the meaning of the phrase, "to learn a foreign language"? It means to translate our thoughts into words and to express them in the foreign tongue. It must be accomplished by a sort of mental reconstruction. Life's scenes have to be represented anew in strange sounds which, constantly repeated, will become second nature to us. Again and again we have to *hear* and *repeat* these sounds. Again and again we must apply them until at last they are as familiar to us as the sounds of our native speech. The learner can, of course, *repeat* aloud over and over again and gain a great deal in this way. It is a valuable adjunct to this book to have also the International Phonetic Alphabet charts inside the front and back covers for ready reference.

Then there will no longer be talk of translation from one language into another. The words will have become so deeply impressed upon our memory that we shall utter them as unconsciously as we speak our mother tongue.

Language appeals, at first at least, chiefly to the *ear, tongue*, and *memory*, but though our intellect superintends the whole initiatory process, it cannot come into real action until the foreign sounds come just as unconsciously to us as the sounds of our mother tongue.

Remember also—the ear is the natural organ of language. If you desire to speak in a foreign language, listen to foreign speech and imitate what you have heard until the habit becomes second nature to you. This is The Method of Nature and this is

THE SECRET OF MASTERING A LANGUAGE

Thousands of persons have been successfully instructed by this method. Pupils as well as teachers of languages have testified to the splendid results that have been achieved by following this system. In the first place, all sentences are practical phrases based on the actual occurrences of every-day life.

After a few preliminary exercises, an advance is made with phrases that refer to speaking and understanding a language. Thereafter, as an introduction to life in a foreign land, the student continues his studies by entering a store to make some purchases. The next lesson takes him to the railway station. He buys railway tickets, checks his baggage, boards the train, arrives at his destination, takes a taxicab, drives to his hotel, engages a room, goes to the dining-room, gives his order to the waiter, eats his meal, and at the end of the day retires to his room.

Surely these are actual scenes in every-day life and occurrences with which every adult is familiar.

When such lessons have been thoroughly mastered, the next advance is to conversational exercises. English is now discarded and the foreign language alone is used. No new words are introduced and

EVERY SENTENCE IS BASED ON EXERCISES PREVIOUSLY LEARNED

By a conscientious use of this book the person who works with it will gain a mastery of foreign words, phrases, and sentences. Each phrase gradually presents conceptions and facts as clearly to the student as the English equivalents. Translation becomes unnecessary. The student's life is thus lived over again in the foreign language. His individuality is reconstructed and in this way the foreign language becomes in reality a "tongue" to the learner.

The study of it is no longer a laborious translation. The words cease to be meaningless printed signs and are immediately associated with living facts. The student no longer doubts and hesitates, but expresses his ideas as readily in the foreign language as in his own. He has acquired a new instrument of thought and action in his career. He is looking down a new vista of progress and achievement.

DIRECTIONS FOR PRIVATE STUDY

It has been made clear in the preceding pages that this book places its principal emphasis on the language of practical, every-day life. The words which the beginner is about to learn are therefore divided into the *necessary* and the *less necessary* ones. This is a simple, common-sense division. The necessary words, the expressions all men use and understand, must be mastered first.

How the necessary words were chosen can easily be illustrated. Consider, for instance, the three words, *money*, *fan*, and *chisel*. How do they compare with each other?

The word *money* is so important that no one can get on without the use of it—and, we might add, the substance of it. Everybody has to employ it and everyone must consequently know it. It is plainly a necessary word.

Fan belongs to a different class of expressions. Though no doubt necessary, the word, as well as the object itself, is by no means so imperatively necessary as *money;* it therefore belongs to another class, namely, the class of words which, though they ought to be learned, may be learned later.

Finally, there is the word *chisel.* One might live for twenty years in a foreign country without having any use for this word which to a carpenter is an absolute necessity. For the ordinary student the word belongs in the class of scarcely necessary expressions.

The user of this book must realize that what he is learning is basic. Every effort has been made to give only phrases and sentences used in the common transactions of life. The selection of the words used in this book is based on wide scientific research.

As the reader proceeds with the study of these pages and begins to acquire a vocabulary of essential terms, he should stop from time to time to test the various uses he can make of the words he has at his command. Lepsius, the famous Egyptologist, limited the number of words necessary for conversation on all general subjects to six hundred. Ogden and Richards' vocabulary for basic English is only eight hundred words. As his vocabulary grows from page to page, the student of this book will be surprised at the number of ideas it will enable him to express.

The learner may be puzzled at first by the long and sometimes complex sentences to which he is introduced, but he will soon realize that these are sentences we are in the habit of using in ordinary circumstances. This book rightly places an emphasis on idiomatic sentences constructed in a manner utterly foreign to our way of speaking.

The student must strive constantly to free himself from the habit of thinking in English. He must master each idiom to which he is introduced. These peculiar forms of expression common to every language are the lifeblood of language.

The complete mastery of a foreign tongue is best attained by training the eye, ear, tongue, and memory at one and the same time: the ear by giving the sound and intonation of every word and phrase; the eye by seeing the spelling; the tongue by pronouncing the words; and the memory by the continuous repetition of words and phrases so that the student no longer thinks *about* them but *in* them.

The person studying with this book should practice aloud as much as possible, for it is helpful to exercise the tongue and the ear at the same time. When he has read the English equivalent of a sentence and knows its meaning perfectly, he should read and pronounce the foreign sentence again and again until the words have become associated with their meaning.

After the main sentence has been mastered, the student will proceed with the variations given in the exercises. Study should be pursued without undue haste. One should be sure that he has thorough mastery of each section he studies before he proceeds to the next. In a few days the phrases will become second nature to the learner. He will no longer think *about* them but *in* them. He will begin to think in the foreign language itself, and will be able to form hundreds of new phrases by inserting a new noun here, a verb there, an adverb in another place, and so on.

The study of grammar is carried on with each sentence. The footnotes, which explain the grammatical peculiarities, *must* therefore be carefully studied. A full grammatical outline is found at the end of the book.

The vocabularies included in the book have been especially designed to increase the student's knowledge of *necessary* words and phrases.

The proverbs that have been included contain some of the basic folk wisdom common to so many nations. To learn the foreign equivalents of proverbs familiar to all of us is an easy and effective method of fixing words and phrases in the memory.

NEW SPANISH SELF TAUGHT

PART ONE

CONTENTS

THE SPANISH ALPHABET

A	a	ä in ah	N	n	ain'-ā
B	b	bā in bale	Ñ	ñ	ain'-yey
C	c	thā in thane	O	o	ŏ
Ch	ch	chā in chase	P	p	pā in paie
D	d	dā in dale	Q	q	coo in cool
E	e	ā in ale	R	r	ā'-rey
F	f	ā'-fey	Rr	rr	ā'-rrey
G	g	hā in hate	S	s	ā'-cey
H	h	ä'-tchey	T	t	tā in take
I	i	ē in eve	U	u	oo in ooze
J	j	hō'-tä	V	v	vā in vale
K	k	kah	X	x	ā'-keece
L	l	ā'-ley	Y	y	ē-grē'-ä-gä
Ll	ll	ail'-yey	Z	z	thä'-tä
M	m	ā'-mey			

PHONETICS AND PRONUNCIATION

Phonetic symbols

The phonetic symbols used in this text to indicate Spanish pronunciation are those of the International Phonetic Association (IPA). Each symbol stands for only one sound and each sound has only one symbol to represent it.

Although conventional spelling is more phonetic in Spanish than in any other languages, it does not represent pronunciation with any measure of accuracy.   Thus

(1) one letter may stand for more than one sound: cena, cosa.

(2) a combination of letters may represent only one sound: *que* has three letters, but only two sounds.

(3) the same sound may be spelled in more than one way: *vino,* Bueno.

Symbol	Conventional spelling	Phonetic transcription
i	v*i*	bi
e	d*e*	de
ɛ	ver	bɛr
a	p*a*n	pan
ɔ	p*o*r	pɔr
o	n*o*	no
u	t*u*	tu
j	b*i*en	bjen
w	f*ué*	fwe
p	*p*on	pɔn
b	*b*omba	ˈbɔmba
β	ca*b*o	ˈkaβo
m	*m*ano	ˈmano
f	*f*ama	ˈfama
θ	*z*ona	ˈθona
t	*t*an	tan
d	*d*onde	ˈdɔnde
ð	na*d*a	ˈnaða
s	*s*in	sin
z	des*d*e	ˈdezðe
n	*n*ota	ˈnota

Symbol	Conventional spelling	Phonetic transcription
ŋ	ta*n*go	ʹtaŋgo
l	*l*ado	ʹlaðo
r	ca*r*o	ʹkaro
r:	ca*rr*o	ʹkar:ɔ
tʃ	o*ch*o	ʹotʃo
dʒ	in*y*ección	indʒɛkʹɵjɔn
ɲ	ca*ñ*a	ʹkaɲa
ʎ	*ll*ave	ʹʎaβe
k	*c*on	kɔn
ɡ	*g*an*g*a	ʹgaŋga
γ	pa*g*o	ʹpaγo
x	ca*j*a	ʹkaxa

ʹ indicates that the following syllable is stressed.

: indicates that the preceding sound is long.

SPANISH PRONUNCIATION

I. VOWELS

It must be borne in mind that Spanish vowels are *pure, single* sounds, that is, that they maintain their distinct quality throughout the entire duration of their emission. Their correct articulation demands, therefore, a much greater tenseness of the speech organs than is necessary for the articulation of English vowels.

There are seven vowel sounds in Spanish.

Symbol	Tongue	Lips	Teeth	Examples
i	Tip pressed against lower teeth; front raised toward roof of mouth.	Spread, showing front teeth.	Open about ¼ inch.	ʹtʃiko aʹki biʹsita
e	Tip pressed against lower teeth; front raised toward roof of mouth, but less than for i.	Spread, but less than for i.	Open about ¼ inch.	ʹbeβe kanʹte beʹneno
ɛ	Tip pressed against lower teeth; front less raised than for e.	Spread, but less than for e.	Open about ½ inch.	ʹpɛrːɔ ʹθexa koʹmɛr
a	Tip pressed against lower teeth; front less raised than for ɛ.	In normal position.	Open about ¾ inch.	maʹɲana aʹβlar kɔʹrːal
ɔ	Tip slightly drawn back from lower teeth; back a little raised toward roof of mouth.	Slightly rounded.	Open about ½ inch.	kaʹlɔr ʹrːɔka ʹkɔxɔ
o	Tip farther back from lower teeth than for ɔ; back raised higher than for ɔ.	Rounded and protruding.	Open about ¼ inch.	ʹtoðo toʹmo moʹreno
u	Tip resting below lower teeth; back very high toward roof of mouth.	Tightly rounded.	Open about ¼ inch.	ʹluna ʹtriβu puʹɲaðo

II. SEMI-VOWELS

The sounds *u* and *i* often precede or follow each other or another vowel. In such cases they are noticeably weakened (hence the name semi-vowels; symbols *w* and *j*), while the accompanying vowel retains its full sound value. The resulting combination is called a diphthong and is counted as one syllable. When *i* and *u* are combined into a diphthong, whichever comes first becomes a semi-vowel.

A triphthong is a combination of the vowel sounds *a* or *ε* preceded by the semi-vowel *j* or *w* and followed by the semi-vowel *j*. A triphthong is counted as a single syllable.

Symbol	Conventional spelling	Phonetic transcription
w	c*u*ero	′kwero
	b*u*itre	′bwitre
	pa*u*sa	′pawsa
	b*u*ey	bwεj
j	vi*e*jo	′bjɛxɔ
	*y*ugo	′juɣo
	re*i*na	′rːɛjna
	camb*i*áis	kam′bjajs

III. CONSONANTS

The consonants are listed in the order of their place of articulation from the front to the back of the mouth (i.e., from lips to soft palate).

The following remarks should be carefully considered:

A. In the pronunciation of such English words as *pot, take, kit* a puff of breath is distinctly heard between the sounds *p, t, k* and the following vowel. Spanish *p, t, k* require considerably less expenditure of breath, so that between each of them and the following vowel there is no audible release of air.

B. *β, ð, γ* are weak forms of *b, d, g*, respectively. *β* is a *b* in the articulation of which the lips do not quite come together. *ð* is a *d* in which the tip of the tongue barely touches the edge of the upper teeth and does not interrupt the flow of air. *γ* is a *g* in which the back of the tongue approaches closely, but does not touch, the soft palate. *β, ð, γ* cannot be pronounced by themselves and are never found after a pause.

C. *s, z* are pronounced with the tongue curved upwards, so that the tip points toward the ridge above the upper teeth.

D. *r* is produced by tapping only once and very lightly the tip of the tongue against the ridge above the upper teeth. *r:* is produced in the same place, but with a minimum of three very rapid taps or trills.

E. ɲ is produced by placing the tip of the tongue against the lower teeth and trying at the same time to pronounce *n*. ʎ is produced by placing the tip of the tongue against the lower teeth and trying at the same time to pronounce *l*.

F. *x* is a "gargling" sound, produced by raising the back of the tongue toward the soft palate. It is similar to the sound found in Scotch *loch* and German *ach*.

Symbol	Conventional spelling	Phonetic transcription
p	*p*i*p*a	ʹpipa
	*p*a*p*el	paʹpɛl
	*p*re*p*arar	prepaʹrar
b	*b*anco	ʹbaŋko
	cam*b*io	ʹkambjo
	hom*b*re	ʹɔmbre
β	ca*b*eza	kaʹβeθa
	ro*b*le	ʹr:ɔβle
	el *v*ino	ɛlʹβino
m	*m*e*m*oria	meʹmorja
	ca*m*po	ʹkampo
	u*n* vaso	ʹum ʹbaso
f	*f*ino	ʹfino
	en*f*ermo	enʹfɛrmo
	con*f*iar	kɔnʹfjar
θ	ca*z*a	ʹkaθa
	ceni*z*a	θeʹnieθa
	ofre*c*er	ofreʹθɛr
t	*t*ela	ʹtela
	*t*ra*t*ar	traʹtar
	cos*t*a	ʹkɔsta
d	con*d*e	ʹkɔnde
	an*d*ar	anʹdar
	*d*inero	diʹnero

Symbol	Conventional spelling	Phonetic transcription
ð	seda	ˈseða
	madre	ˈmaðre
	la droga	laˈðroɣa
s	seco	ˈseko
	cosas	ˈkosas
	casto	ˈkasto
z	rasgo	ˈrːazɣo
	isla	ˈizla
	las manos	lazˈmanɔs
n	nada	ˈnaða
	canción	kanˈθjɔn
	carne	ˈkarne
ŋ	mango	ˈmaŋgo
	engaño	eŋˈgaɲo
	un gato	ˈuŋˈgato
l	lana	ˈlana
	alma	ˈalma
	laurel	lawˈrɛl
r	toro	ˈtoro
	drama	ˈdrama
	cortar	kɔrˈtar
rː	remo	ˈrːɛmo
	tierra	ˈtjɛrːa
	honra	ˈɔnrːa
tʃ	muchacho	muˈtʃatʃo
	leche	ˈletʃe
	corcho	ˈkɔrtʃo
dʒ	inyectar	indʒɛkˈtar
	con hielo	kɔnˈdʒelo
	el hierro	ɛlˈdʒɛrːɔ
ɲ	año	ˈaɲo
	sueño	ˈsweɲo
	reñir	rːɛˈɲir
ʎ	lleno	ˈʎeno
	gallo	ˈgaʎo
	Sevilla	seˈβiʎa

Symbol	Conventional spelling	Phonetic transcription
k	*c*áscara	′kaskara
	*k*ilo	′kilo
	pe*qu*eño	pe′keɲo
g	*g*oma	′goma
	*gu*inda	′ginda
	ven*g*anza	beŋ′ganθa
γ	la*g*o	′laγo
	se*gu*ir	se′γir
	car*g*a	′karγa
x	*j*arro	′xarːɔ
	*g*ente	′xente
	*g*itano	xi′tano

SYLLABIFICATION

The form of a syllable affects the nature of its component sounds. It is very important, therefore, to know how to separate a word into syllables, the more so since Spanish syllabification differs considerably from English.

A.   A single consonant appearing between vowels joins the vowel or vowels that follow:

ce-re-za	θe-′re-θa
ca-lle-jue-la	ka-ʎe-′xwe-la
i-na-ni-ma-do[1]	i-na-ni-′ma-ðo

B.   The consonants *l* and *r*, when they follow any consonant other than *s*, are joined to that consonant. This is called an "inseparable group:"

ha-blar	a-′βlar
re-cri-mi-na	rːɛ-kri-′mi-na
cua-dro	′kwa-ðro
ti-gre	′ti-γre
co-pla	′ko-pla

---

[1] This is a phonetic, not an orthographic, division into syllables. In writing, all prepositional prefixes (*ab, con, in, sub*, etc.), except when followed by *s* + consonant, form separate syllables. The word would, therefore, be divided: in-a-ni-ma-do.

C. In any other combination of two consonants, or of a consonant and an inseparable group, the first consonant joins the preceding vowel, and the second consonant or the inseparable group join the following vowel:

es-plen-dor   es-plen-'dɔr

her-ma-nas-tro   ɛr-ma-'nas-tro

D. In a combination of three consonants, or of two consonants and an inseparable group, the first two join the preceding vowel, and the third or the inseparable group join the following vowel:

pers-pi-caz   pɛrs-pi-'kaθ

ins-ta-lar   ins-ta-'lar

cons-tre-ñir   kɔns-tre-'ɲir

E. As previously indicated, diphthongs and triphthongs are counted as single syllables. The following list contains all the diphthongs and triphthongs in single Spanish words:

a*i*	b*ai*-le	'b*aj*-le
a*w*	c*au*-sa	'k*aw*-sa
ɛ*j*	p*ei*-ne	'p*ɛj*-ne
e*w*	d*eu*-da	'd*ew*-ða
*j*a	d*ia*-blo	'd*ja*-βlo
*j*ɛ	t*ie*-rra	't*jɛ*-rːa
*j*e	c*ie*-lo	'θ*je*-lo
*j*ɔ	D*io*s	d*jɔ*s
*j*o	v*ió*	b*jo*
*j*u	v*iu*-do	'b*ju*-ðo
ɔ*j*	es-t*oy*	es-'t*ɔj*
*w*a	c*ua*l	k*wa*l
*w*ɛ	c*ue*r-po	'k*wɛ*r-po
*w*e	h*ue*-vo	'w*e*-βo
*w*i	r*ui*-na	'r*wi*-na
*w*o	eva-c*uó*	e-βa-'k*wo*
*j*a*j*	cam-b*iái*s	kam-'b*jaj*s
*j*ɛ*j*	en-v*iéi*s	em-'b*jɛj*s
*w*a*j*	U-ru-g*uay*	u-ru-'ɣ*waj*
*w*ɛ*j*	b*uey*	b*wɛj*

STRESS

In words of two or more syllables, Spanish requires that one be pronounced with greater intensity than the others. This tonic intensity is called *stress*, represented in phonetic transcription by the symbol ['] placed before the syllable bearing the stress. In the written language stress is often represented by a mark (') called *accent* placed over the vowel of the stressed syllable. In most cases the accent is written to indicate that the word so marked is an exception to the general rules governing stress. These rules are two:

A. The majority of words ending in a vowel, a diphthong other than *ay* [aj], *ey* [ɛj], *oy* [ɔj], or the consonants *n* or *s* are stressed on the penultimate:

puente	'pwente
gracia	'graəja
origen	o'rixen
lunes	'lunes

B. The majority of words ending in the diphthongs *ay* [aj], *ey* [ɛj], *oy* [ɔj], or in a consonant other than *n* or *s* are stressed on the last syllable:

clavel	kla'βɛl
maguey	ma'ɣɛj
perdiz	pɛr'ðiə
verdad	bɛr'ðað
comer	ko'mɛr

All words not covered by these rules must be marked with an accent. Examples:

canté	kan'te
corrió	kɔ'r:jo
régimen	'r:ɛximen
cortés	kɔr'tes
mármol	'marmɔl
lápiz	'lapiə
áspid	'aspið
azúcar	a'əukar

CONNECTED SPEECH

In ordinary speech, sounds are uttered in a continuous flow interrupted by pauses of variable duration. The speaker may pause (1) to breathe, or (2) to arrange what he wishes to say in units of thought and render, thereby, his meaning clearer. Ideally, the intake of breath should come at the end of a unit of thought. That is why a unit of thought is spoken of as a *breath-group*. A breath-group is considered phonetically as a single word, and the rules of syllabification pertaining to single words are also applicable to it. Breath-groups are properly indicated in transcription by punctuation marks. Occasionally, however, the symbol [|] may be used to separate optional breath-groups.

In the following sentence there are eight words, but only one breath-group:

Esta tarde salgo para Sevilla en el expreso.
'esta'tarðe'salɣoparase'βiʎaeneles'preso.

The intimate linking of words within a breath-group brings about important sound changes which may be arranged into four main classes:

A.   Diphthongs and triphthongs may be formed between the final vowel or vowels of a word and the initial vowel or vowels of a word that follows. For example:

hijo [ixɔ] indócil [in'doeil]   'ixɔjn'doeil
aquí [a'ki] estuvo [es'tuβo]   a'kjes'tuβo
gracia ['graeja] y [i] fuerza ['fwɛrea]   'graejaj'fwɛrea

B.   Diphthongs and triphthongs may appear which are never encountered in single words:

vino ['bino] un [un] hombre ['ɔmbre]   'binow'nɔmbre
vida ['biða] u [u] honra ['ɔnrːa]   'biða'wɔnrːa
espacio [es'paejo] inútil [i'nutil]   es'paejoj'nutil

C.   The articulation of initial and final consonants of words may be modified:

ha [a] ganado [ga'naðo] dinero [di'nero]   'aɣa'naðoði'nero
con [kɔn] gusto ['gusto]   kɔn'gusto
estas ['estas] voces ['boees]   'estaz'βoees

D. The articulation of the last vowel in a word may change:

vestido [bes'tiðo] roto ['rːoto]	bes'tiðo̞'rːoto
calor [ka'lɔr] húmedo ['umeðo]	ka'lo'rumeðo
duque ['duke] joven ['xɔβen]	'dukɛ'xɔβen

INTONATION

Spanish, like any other language, has its peculiar melody or intonation, that is, its own range of variations of pitch which, although admittedly different for each speaker, remains, nevertheless, within boundaries which are constant for all native users of the language. Unhappily, no rules can be given which may help in the mastery of a correct Spanish intonation. Therefore, when you listen to your records pay as much attention to the intonation of breath-groups and sentences as to the articulation of sounds.

PUNCTUATION

Punctuation in Spanish is the same as in English, except in **questions** and **exclamations,** where the **inverted** marks are placed at the beginning of phrases, in addition to the regular signs at the end of such sentences, as:

¿Qué dice usted?	'ke'ðieews'te	What do you say?
¿Qué desea usted?	'keðe'seaws'te	What do you want?
¡Cómo llueve!	'komo'ʎweβe	How it rains!

FRASE FUNDAMENTAL

¿Qué quiere usted hacer esta mañana? Quisiera salir para Buenos Aires en el primer avión, pero no me es posible, porque espero a un amigo de Nueva York y debo quedarme en Miami hasta que él llegue en vapor, autobús o tren.

¿Qué quiere usted hacer esta mañana?

'ke'kjerews'tea'θe'restama'ɲana

Qué[1] /ke/

quiere V.[2] /'kjerews'te/

hacer /a'θɛr/

esta /'esta/

mañana /ma'ɲana/

EJERCICIOS GENERALES

1. ¿Qué quiere V.?
2. ¿Qué quiere V. hacer?
3. ¿Qué quiere V. hacer esta mañana?
4. ¿Qué quiere V. hacer mañana[3]?

---

[1] In questions qué (with the acute accent) means *what?* Que (without the accent) means that or which, or who.

[2] Usted /us'te/ is a contraction of vuestra merced /'bwestramɛr'θεð/ your Honor, your Lordship. This form is often written in an abbreviated manner, viz., V. or Vd. It is always used for *you* when *one* person is addressed, except in cases where familiarity exists when tú /tu/, *thou*, is used. Usted, however, is the only form taught in this system.

MAIN SENTENCE

What do you want to do this morning? I should like to leave for Buenos Aires by the first plane, but that is impossible; for I expect a friend from New York and must stay in Miami until he arrives by boat, bus or train.

PRONUNCIATION

'ke'kjerews'tea'ɵe'restama'ɲana? ki'sjerasa'lirparaβweno'sajres enɛlpri'mera'βiɔn, pero'nomespo'siβle, pɔrkes'peroawna'miɣoðe nweβa'jɔr | i'ðeβoke'ðarmem'miami | asta'kɛːl'ʎeɣemba'pɔr, awto'βus ⱡ o'tren.

What will you do this morning?

What

(do you want? do you wish?) (Questions in English are asked with the auxiliary verb **to do**. We say: What do you want? The Spaniards say simply: What want you? We say: Do you go? The Spaniards say: Go you?)

to do

this

morning?

GENERAL EXERCISES

1. What do you want?
2. What do you want to do?
3. What do you want to do this morning?
4. What do you wish to do to-morrow?

The plural **ustedes**, often written **Vds.**, is employed when several persons are addressed. This form is a contraction of **vuestras mercedes** /'bwestrazmer'ɵeðes/ your Lordships.

Naturally V. requires the verb in the **third person singular**, and Vds., the **third person plural**. Compare the conjugation and remarks on page 16.

[3] **Mañana** means *morning*, when used as a noun; la mañana, the morning When used as an adverb, **mañana** signifies to-morrow.

5. ¿Lo[1] quiere V. hacer? /lo'kjerews'tea'eɛr/. ¿Quiere V. hacerlo?[1] /us'tea'eɛrlo/

6. ¿Lo quiere V. hacer mañana? ¿Quiere V. hacerlo mañana?

7. ¿Lo quiere V. hacer hoy? /ɔj/ ¿Quiere V. hacerlo hoy?

Yo quiero	/'jo'kjero/
V. quiere[2]	/us'te'kjere/
él quiere	/'ɛl'kjere/
nosotros queremos	/no'sotrɔske'remɔs/
Vds. quieren[2]	/us'teðes'kjeren/
ellos quieren	/'eʎɔs'kjeren/

8. No[3] quiero[4] hacerlo esta[5] tarde. /'no'kjeroa'eɛrlo'esta'tarðe/
   No lo quiero hacer esta tarde.

9. ¿Por qué[6] no quiere V. hacerlo hoy?
   ¿Por qué no lo quiere V. hacer hoy?

10. ¿Cuándo quiere V. hacerlo? /'kwando/
    ¿Cuándo lo quiere V. hacer?

11. ¿Lo puede V. hacer esta tarde? /lo'pweðe/
    ¿Puede V. hacerlo esta tarde?

---

[1] The conjunctive personal pronouns *me, him, her, it, us, you, them* are placed **before the verb** in Spanish, except in *affirmative imperative sentences*, or if the verb stands in *the infinitive* or present participle.

In the latter three cases the pronouns are placed *after* the verb and merged into one word with it.

The pupil should commit these pronouns to memory:

me, me (to me)	**nos,** us (to us)
(**te**), (thee, to thee)	(**os**), (ye, to ye)
se, to you, or to him	**se,** to you, or to them
le, him (to him)	**les,** them (to them)
la, her	**las,** them (fem.)
lo, it	**los,** them (masc.)

We say in English: Will you do it? In Spanish: ¿Lo quiere V. hacer? *Or:* ¿Quiere V. hacerlo? (In the latter case we add *lo* directly to the infinitive *hacer* and write the two forms in *one* word.)

For further rules see Page 20, and Part X.

[2] In giving the conjugations the plan of *Professor Cándido Rosi* has been followed. The pronouns tú, *thou,* and vosotros, *ye,* are used only among relatives and intimate friends (also in Scripture and poetry).

5. Will you do it? (Literally: It [lo[1]] will you do? Or: Will you do it [hacerlo[1]])?

6. Do you want to do it to-morrow?

7. Do you wish to do it to-day [hoy]?

> I want
> you want[2]
> he wants
> we want
> you want[2]
> they want

8. I do not want [no[3] lo quiero hacer. Or: no quiero hacerlo] to do it this [esta[5]] afternoon.

9. Why [por qué[6]] do you not want to do it to-day?

10. When [cuándo] do you want to do it?

11. Can you [puede V.] do it this afternoon?

Mr. Rosi's plan not only simplifies the conjugations, but prevents the confusion which must necessarily arise in pupils' minds when told that *you* governs the third person in Spanish.

The pronouns are usually *omitted* in the conjugations, unless required on account of ambiguity or emphasis. In *questions*, however, they should always be used.

The personal pronouns **yo, él, ella, nosotros, ellos** and **ellas** are given here for the purpose of making the pupil familiar with them.

[3] The negation **no,** not, must always be placed *before* the verb. In English we use the auxiliary verb *to do* for negative statements. We say: I do not want to do it. In Spanish we express this by: No quiero hacerlo. We say: Don't you speak English? In Spanish: ¿No habla V. inglés?

[4] Instead of *quiero* the synonymous verb **deseo** /de'seo/, *I want, I wish, I desire,* is frequently used.

[5] **Tarde,** *afternoon,* is feminine, consequently **esta** must be employed. The masculine form is **este.** Compare Part X.

[6] Study remarks on punctuation, page 13, which explain the use of the inverted interrogation marks at the beginning of phrases.

12. No;[1] no puedo hacerlo esta tarde. /'pweðo/
No; no lo puedo hacer esta tarde.

Yo puedo	/'jo'pweðo/
V. puede	/us'te'pweðe/
él puede	/'ɛl'pweðe/
nosotros podemos	/no'sotrɔspo'ðemɔs/
Vds. pueden	/us'teðes'pweðen/
ellos pueden	/'eʎɔs'pweðen/

13. ¿Puede V. hacerlo mañana? Sí; puedo hacerlo mañana.
¿Lo puede V. hacer mañana? Sí; lo puedo hacer mañana.

Hablar
/a'βlar/

14. ¿Habla V. español?[2] /'aβlaws'tespa'ɲɔl?/

15. Lo hablo un poco. /lo'aβlown'poko/

16. ¿Lo habla V. bien? /lo'aβlaws'te'βjen?/

17. No, señor; no lo hablo muy bien. /'nose'ɲɔr; 'nolo'aβlo'mwi'βjenʃ

yo hablo[3]	/'jo'aβlo/
V. habla	/us'te'aβla/
él habla	/'e'laβla/
ella habla	/'e'ʎa:βla/
nosotros hablamos	/no'sotrosa'βlamɔs/
Vds. hablan	/us'teðe'saβlan/
ellos hablan	/'eʎo'saβlan/
ellas hablan	/'eʎa'saβlan/

18. ¿Puede V. expresarse en español? /espre'sarse/
¿Puede V. darse a entender[4] en español? /'darseaenten'deren-
espa'ɲɔl/

19. Lo hablo bastante para darme a entender.
/lo'aβloβas'tantepara'ðarmeaenten'dɛr/

---

[1] No means *no* as well as *not*.

[2] Adjectives referring to nationality are written with small letters, as: español,
Spanish; francés, French; alemán, German.

[3] Compare the remarks on verbs of the first conjugation, page 26.

[4] This phrase might be translated: Can you make yourself understood in
Spanish?

The two Spanish phrases given above mean exactly the same thing. Synony-

12. No, [no[1]], 1 cannot [no puedo] do it this afternoon.

> I can
> you can
> he can
> we can
> you can
> they can

13. Can you do it to-morrow? Yes, [sí], I can do it **to-morrow.**

To Speak

14. Do you speak [habla V.] Spanish? [español]?

15. I speak [hablo] it a [un] little [poco].

16. Do you speak it well? [bien]?

17. No, sir, [señor], I do not speak it very [muy] well.

> I speak
> you speak
> he speaks
> she speaks
> we speak
> you speak
> they speak (masc.)
> they speak (fem.)

18. Can you express yourself [expresarse] in [en] Spanish? **Or :** Can you give yourself [darse] to understand [a entender] in Spanish?

19. I speak it sufficiently to make myself understood. (Literally: It [I] speak sufficiently [bastante] in order to [para] give myself [darme] to understand.)

---

mous expressions are frequently introduced in order to accustom the student to a variety of diction. The most commonplace statement may be rendered in various ways, and the aim has been to give all the synonyms which are generally used.

The most polite way for: What do you want? is not: ¿Qué quiere V.? A polite Spaniard would prefer to say: ¿Qué se le ofrece a V.? *or*: ¿Qué desea V.?

puedo expresarme muy bien en español, pero lo hablo **bastante** darme a **entender or** : para darme a comprender. /kɔmpren'dɛr/

21. ¿Habla este caballero el español? /'estekaβa'ʎero/

22. Sí, lo habla con facilidad.

23. ¿Es él[1] español?[2] /'e'selespa'ɲɔl/

24. Sí señor; es español.[2] /'sise'ɲɔr/

Yo soy	/'jo'sɔj/	nosotros somos	/no'sotro'somɔs/
V. es	/us'teːs/	Vds. son	/us'teðe'sɔn/
él es	/'e'les/	ellos son	/'eʎo'sɔn/
ella es	/'eʎa'es/	ellas son	/'eʎa'sɔn/

25. ¿Y V., caballero,[3] es V. americano o español? /jus'te | kaβa'ʎero, 'esus'teameri'kanoːespa'ɲɔl?/

26. ¿Por qué[4] me lo[5] pregunta V.? /pɔr'kemelopre'ɣuntaws'te?/

27. Se lo[6] pregunto, porque[4] habla V. el inglés muy bien.
/selopre'ɣunto | pɔrke'aβlaws'teliŋ'glez'mwi'βjen/

---

[1] The personal pronoun must be used in questions.

[2] We say in English: Are you *a* Spaniard? In Spanish this is expressed by: *Are you Spanish?* ¿Es V. español? *This gentleman is a Frenchman*, este señor es francés.

[3] **Caballero** is used in the same way as **señor**.

[4] **Porque** (written without accent) means *because;* por qué, two words and the latter with an accent, means *why.*

[5] We have seen that the conjunctive pronouns are placed *before* the verb. (Compare note page 16.)

When a verb governs *two* conjunctive pronouns, the dative must *precede* the accusative (with the exception of the reflexive pronoun **se**, which always stands first, and which is fully explained in the next note).

As: *Why do you ask me?* (Literally: *Why to me it ask you?*)—¿Por qué me lo pregunta V.?

Will you give it to me? (Literally: *To me it will give you?*)—¿Me lo dará V.?

[6] The use of **le** and **se**—both meaning *you* in the dative and accusative singular—presents great difficulty to foreigners. The explanation will, of necessity, be somewhat long, but should, on account of its importance, be studied with great care.

a. **Usted** is inflected like any noun, viz.:

	SINGULAR		PLURAL	
Nom.	usted,	you	ustedes,	you
Gen.	de usted,	of you	de ustedes,	of you
Dat.	a usted,	to you	a ustedes,	to you
Acc.	(a) usted,	you	(a) ustedes,	you

20. I cannot express myself very well in Spanish, but [pero] I speak it sufficiently to get along.

21. Does this gentleman speak Spanish? (Literally: Speaks this gentleman [este caballero] Spanish?)

22. Yes, he speaks it fluently.

23. Is he [es él] a Spaniard?

24. Yes, sir, he is [es] a Spaniard.

I am	we are
you are	you are
he is	they are (masc.)
she is	they are (fem.)

25. And [y] you, sir, are you [es V.] an American or [o] a Spaniard?

26. Why do you ask that? (Literally: Why me it[5] ask you?)

27. I ask you (Literally: To you [se[6]] it I ask), because [porque] you speak English so well.

---

b. In the accusative, which is the case for the direct object, an **a** is placed before usted and ustedes.

The reason for this is that *active* verbs require **a** before the object, when a person, as: *I see this man*, veo **a** este hombre.—*Do you not know this lady?*—¿No conoce V. **a** esta señora?—*I ask you*, pregunto **a** V.—*I hear you*, oigo **a** V.

c. For the dative and accusative of **usted** Spaniards very frequently use **le** (dative and accusative, masculine) or **la** (accusative, feminine) in the singular, and **les** (dative, masculine) and **los, las** (accusative, masculine and feminine) in the plural.

This is often done to avoid repetition, but its use is almost universal.

Thus we say:

Oigo a V., mas no **le** veo,	*I hear you, but I do not see you.*
Vengo a ver a V. y a decirle,	*I came to see you and to tell you.*
Le digo,	*I tell you* (singular).
Les digo.	*I tell you* (plural).

d. The Spaniards never say *le lo, le la*, etc., when two conjunctive pronouns occur, but invariably change it for euphony's sake into **se lo, se la, se los, se las,** etc.

Thus in the above phrase:

Se lo pregunto   I *ask it of you*

For full rules and tables see Part X.

28. Soy español, pero mi madre era inglesa[1] y yo hablo fácilmente ambos idiomas, el inglés y el español. /peromi'maðrerajŋ'glesa | i'jo'aβlo'faeil'mente'ambosi'ðjomas/

29. ¿Es difícil el idioma español[2]? /'ezði'fieileli'ðjoma/

30. Nací en Madrid, y el español es mi lengua materna. /na'ejenma'ðrið/

31. ¿Es muy difícil la pronunciación española? /lapronuneja'ejonespa'ɲola/

32. La pronunciación española no es muy difícil; al contrario, es muy fácil. /alkɔn'trarjo 'faeil/

33. Me es muy difícil pronunciar correctamente frases españolas.[1] /pronun'ejarkə'r:ɛkta'mente'frasesespa'ɲolas/

34. Creo que la pronunciación española es muy difícil. /'kreoke/

35. Al contrario, la pronunciación inglesa es mucho más difícil que la nuestra. /alkɔn'trarjo 'ez'mutʃo'mazði'fieilkela'nwestra/

36. El inglés es mi[4] lengua materna.

---

[1] Adjectives agree in *gender* and *number* with the noun they qualify, as: el libro nuevo (masc. singular), *the new book;* libros nuevos (masc. plural), *new books;* una casa nueva (fem. singular), *a new house;* casas nuevas (fem. plural), *new houses.*

The feminine of adjectives is generally formed by changing the final o of the masculine form into a, as: bueno, buena, good; malo, mala, *bad.*

Adjectives referring to nationality and ending in a consonant, add a for the feminine, as: inglés, inglesa, *English;* francés, francesa, *French;* alemán, alemana, *German;* español, española, *Spanish.*

Adjectives not referring to nationality and ending in any other letter remain *unchanged* in the feminine, as:

un hombre cortés	*a polite man*
una mujer cortés	*a polite woman*
el trabajo es difícil	*the work is difficult*
la cosa es difícil	*the matter is difficult*

[2] The adjective stands generally after the noun qualified, as: una mujer hermosa, *a beautiful woman* (literally: a woman beautiful); una pintura española, *a Spanish picture;* una madre amada, *a beloved mother.*

There are, however, many cases where the adjectives are placed *before* the nouns. No satisfactory rule can be given; it is almost entirely a matter of style.

28. I am a Spaniard, but [pero] my mother was [era] an English-woman, and I speak both Spanish and English fluently.

29. Is Spanish a difficult language? (Literally: Is difficult [difícil] the language [el idioma] Spanish²?)

30. I was born [nací] in Madrid and Spanish is my mother-tongue.

31. Is the Spanish pronunciation [la pronunciación española] very difficult?

32. The Spanish pronunciation is not very difficult; on the contrary [al contrario] it is very easy. [fácil].

33. It is very difficult for me to pronounce [pronunciar] Spanish phrases [frases españolas³] correctly. [correctamente].

34. I believe [creo] that [que] the Spanish pronunciation is very difficult.

35. On the contrary, the English pronunciation is much [mucho] more [más] difficult than ours. [la nuestra].

36. English is my mother tongue.

Adjectives denoting *nationality*, *color* and *shape* are placed after the *noun*. For full rules see Part X.

³ The Spanish declension is very simple:

There are two articles: the definite **el**, *the*, for the masculine, **la**, *the*, for the feminine form, and the indefinite **un**, *a, an* (masculine), **una**, *a, an* (feminine).

DECLENSION OF THE ARTICLES

	Masculine		*Feminine*		
	SINGULAR	PLURAL	SINGULAR	PLURAL	
Nom.	el	los	la	las	the
Gen.	del	de los	de la	de las	of the, *or* from the
Dat.	al	a los	a la	a las	to the, *or* at the
Acc.	el	los	la	las	the

	Masculine	*Feminine*	
Nom.	un	una	a
Gen.	de un	de una	of a, *or* from a
Dat.	a un	a una	to, *or* at a
Acc.	un	una	a

Footnotes continued at bottom of page 24.

37. ¿Nació V. en Nueva York? No señor, nací en Chicago.

/na'ejows'tennweβa'jor? 'nose'ɲɔr, na'ejentʃi'kaɣo/

38. La pronunciación española es mucho más fácil que la de ustedes. Tenemos reglas fijas para la pronunciación.

/te'nemɔ'r:ɛɣlas'fixasparalapronuneja'ejɔn/

AFIRMATIVO

/afirma'tiβo/

Yo tengo	/'jo'tengo/
V. tiene	/us'te'tjene/
él tiene	/'ɛl'tjene/
ella tiene	/'eʎa'tjene/
nosotros tenemos	/no'sotrɔste'nemɔs/
Vds. tienen	/us'teðes'tjenen/
ellos tienen (masc.)	/'eʎɔs'tjenen/
ellas tienen (fem.)	/'eʎas'tjenen/

INTERROGATIVO

intɛr:ɔɣa'tiβo

¿Tengo yo?

¿tiene V.?

¿tiene él?

¿tiene ella?

¿tenemos nosotros?

¿tienen Vds.?

¿tienen ellos? (masc.)

¿tienen ellas? (fem.)

Footnotes continued from page 23.

Spanish nouns have *two genders,—masculine* and *feminine*.

The *gender* of a *noun* may be determined partly by its *signification*, and partly by its *ending*.

Nouns ending in **o** are generally *masculine*, and those ending in **a** are *feminine* (except those which designate males).

Nouns ending in an *unaccented* vowel form their plural by adding **s**, as:

el padre	*the father*	los padres	*the fathers*
la madre	*the mother*	las madres	*the mothers*

Nouns ending in a *consonant* or in an *accented* vowel (except **e**) add **es** in the plural, as:

el general	*the general*	los generales	*the generals*
la mujer	*the woman*	las mujeres	*the women*

For full rules see Part X.

[4] See note page 25.

37. Were you born [nació] in New York [Nueva York]? I born [nací] in Chicago.

38. The Spanish pronunciation is much easier than you ustedes]. We have [tenemos] definite rules [reglas fijas] for the pronunciation.

AFFIRMATIVE

I have
you have
he has
she has
we have
you have
they have (masc.)
they have (fem.)

INTERROGATIVE

Have I?
have you?
has he?
has she?
have we?
have you?
have they? (masc.)
have they? (fem.)

Special Note: The conjunctive possessive adjectives should be committed to memory. They are:

SINGULAR		PLURAL
my	mi	mis
thy	tu	tus
his, her, its, your	su	sus
our	nuestro, nuestra	nuestros, nuestras
(your)	vuestro, vuestra	vuestros, vuestras
their, your	su	sus

For full rules see Part X.

CONJUGACIÓN DEL TIEMPO PRESENTE

PRIMERA CONJUGACIÓN

Habl-ar

AFIRMATIVO	INTERROGATIVO
Yo habl-o	¿Hablo yo?
V. habl-a	¿habla V.?
él habl-a	¿habla él?
ella habl-a	¿habla ella?
nosotros habl-amos	¿hablamos nosotros?
Vds. habl-an	¿hablan Vds.?
ellos habl-an (masc.)	¿hablan ellos? (masc.)
ellas habl-an (fem.)	¿hablan ellas? (fem.)

Dese-ar

AFIRMATIVO	INTERROGATIVO
Yo dese-o	¿Deseo yo?
V. dese-a	¿desea V.?
él dese-a	¿desea él?
ella dese-a	¿desea ella?
nosotros dese-amos	¿deseamos nosotros?
Vds. dese-an	¿desean Vds.?
ellos dese-an (masc.)	¿desean ellos? (masc.)
ellas dese-an (fem.)	¿desean ellas? (fem.)

---

[1] There are three conjugations in Spanish.

The verbs of the first conjugation end in **ar** in the infinitive, as: habl*ar, to speak;* dese*ar, to wish;* pronunci*ar, to pronounce;* llam*ar, to call.*

The infinitive is the *ground form* of the verb on which its conjugation depends. **Ar** is called the ending. By striking off this **ar** we find the root or stem of the verb.

Thus *habl* is the stem of the verb hablar; *dese* the stem of desear; *pronunci,* the stem of pronunciar; *llam,* the stem of llamar.

The stem remains *unaltered* in all regular verbs.

To the stem various terminations are added by which persons, tenses and moods are distinguished, and which are common to all regular verbs of the same conjugation.

CONJUGATION OF THE PRESENT TENSE

FIRST CONJUGATION

To Speak[1]

AFFIRMATIVE	INTERROGATIVE
I speak	Do I speak?
you speak	do you speak?
he speaks	does he speak?
she speaks	does she speak?
we speak	do we speak?
you speak	do you speak?
they speak (masc.)	do they speak? (masc.)
they speak (fem.)	do they speak? (fem.)

To Wish

AFFIRMATIVE	INTERROGATIVE
I wish	Do I wish?
you wish	do you wish?
he wishes	does he wish?
she wishes	does she wish?
we wish	do we wish?
you wish	do you wish?
they wish (masc.)	do they wish? (masc.)
they wish (fem.)	do they wish? (fem.)

In the present tense of the first conjugation the following terminations are added:

yo	———o	nosotros	———amos
V.	———a	Vds.	———an
él	———a	ellos	———an
ella	———a	ellas	———an

The accompanying pronouns—with the exception of usted and ustedes—are generally omitted.

In *questions*, in cases of doubtful meaning and when specially emphasized the pronouns must *always* be expressed as: ¿Pago yo o paga él? *Do I pay or he?* El estudia y ella escribe, *he studies and she writes.*

CONJUGACIÓN DEL TIEMPO PRESENTE

SEGUNDA CONJUGACIÓN[1]

Vend-er[1]

AFIRMATIVO	INTERROGATIVO
Yo vend-o	¿Vendo yo?
V. vend-e	¿vende V.?
él vend-e	¿vende él?
nosotros vend-emos	¿vendemos nosotros?
Vds. vend-en	¿venden Vds.?
ellos vend-en	¿venden ellos?

TERCERA CONJUGACIÓN[2]

Recib-ir[2]

AFIRMATIVO	INTERROGATIVO
Yo recib-o	¿Recibo yo?
V. recib-e	¿recibe V.?
él recib-e	¿recibe él?
nosotros recib-imos	¿recibimos nosotros?
Vds. recib-en	¿reciben Vds.?
ellos recib-en	¿reciben ellos?

---

[1] Verbs of the second conjugation end in er in the infinitive.

It will be observed that the endings of the present tense of the first conjugation preserve the *a* of the infinitive; in fact *a* is the characteristic vowel of all verbs of the first conjugation.

In the second conjugation it is e.

[2] Verbs of the third conjugation end in ir in the infinitive.

The endings of the present tense are the same as those of the second conjugation, with the exception of the first person plural, which ends in imos.

There are, therefore, the following endings for the indicative of the present tense in the three conjugations:

CONJUGATION OF THE PRESENT TENSE

SECOND CONJUGATION

To Sell[1]

AFFIRMATIVE	INTERROGATIVE
I sell	Do I sell?
you sell	do you sell?
he sells	does he sell?
we sell	do we sell?
you sell	do you sell?
they sell	do they sell?

THIRD CONJUGATION[2]

To Receive[2]

AFFIRMATIVE	INTERROGATIVE
I receive	Do I receive?
you receive	do you receive?
he receives	does he receive?
we receive	do we receive?
you receive	do you receive?
they receive	do they receive?

PRESENT TENSE

1.	2.	3.
—o	—o	—o
—a	—e	—e
—a	—e	—e
—amos	—emos	—imos
—an	—en	—en
—an	—en	—en

By comparing this table carefully and conjugating the various verbs occurring in our phrases, the pupils will soon master the Spanish conjugations.

The irregular verbs will be taken up serially.

For full tables see Part X.

Ejercicio de conversación

1. ¿Tiene V. la bondad de[1] pronunciarme esta palabra?
/'tjenews'telaβɔn'daðepronun'ɵjarmestapa'laβra/

yo hago	/'aɣo/
V. hace	/'aɵe/
él hace	/'aɵe/
nosotros hacemos	/a'ɵemɔs/
Vds. hacen	/'aɵen/
ellos hacen	/'aɵen/

2. ¿Me haría[2] V. el favor de volver[3] a pronunciarla[4]?
/mea'riaws'tɛlfa'βɔrðeβɔl'βerapronun'ɵjarla/

3. ¿Cómo se[5] pronuncia esta palabra? /'komosepro'nunɵja/

4. No puedo pronunciar esta palabra. ¿Sería V. tan amable de volver a pronunciarla?

5. ¿Sabe V.[6] cómo se pronuncia esta palabra? /'saβews'te/

Yo sé	/se/
V. sabe	/'saβe/
él sabe	/'saβe/
nosotros sabemos	/sa'βemɔs/
Vds. saben	/'saβen/
ellos saben	/'saβen/

6. Sí; ya sé como se pronuncia. /'ja'se/

7. ¿Comprende V. el español? /kɔm'prende/

8. Lo comprendo muy poco. /'mwi'poko/

9. ¿Me comprende V. cuando hablo en español?

---

[1] After such expressions as: *"Will you have the kindness to do it?"* where we could say in English: *"Will you have the kindness* of *doing it,"* **de** must be used before the infinitive.

[2] **Hacer**, *to do, to make*, belongs to the irregular verbs. The indicative of the present tense is conjugated on the next page (the first person singular alone being irregular).

[3] **Volver** means literally, *to return*. The above phrase is, of course, idiomatic.

[4] **La** must be used here, because it refers to **palabra**, which is *feminine*.

Conversation Exercise

1. Will you please [¿Tiene V. la bondad de¹] pronounce this word [esta palabra] for me?

> I do (make)
> you do (make)
> he does (makes)
> we do (make)
> you do (make)
> they do (make)

2. Would you please [¿Me haría² V. el favor de¹] pronounce it once more? [volver³ a pronunciarla⁴?]

3. How is this word pronounced? (Literally: How [cómo] pronounces itself [se⁵] this word?)

4. I cannot pronounce this word. Would you be kind enough to pronounce it once more?

5. Do you know [¿Sabe V.⁶] how this word is pronounced?

> I know   we know
> you know   you know
> he knows   they know

6. Yes; now [ya] I know [sé] how it is pronounced.

7. Do you understand [comprende V.] Spanish?

8. I understand it very little.

9. Do you understand me when I speak Spanish?

---

⁵ *Active verbs* are often used passively with the pronoun **se** in the third person singular or plural, as:

El idioma español se habla en la América central.	*The Spanish language is spoken in Central America.*
No se puede ver nada.	*Nothing can be seen.*

⁶ **Saber,** *to know,* is an irregular verb. The indicative of the present **tense is** conjugated as above (the first person singular alone being irregular).

10. Le comprendo a V.¹ cuando V. habla despacio y claro.
/des'paθjoj'klaro/

11. ¿No me comprende V. cuando hablo de prisa? /'aβloðe'prisa/

12. No, señor; no le comprendo a V. cuando habla² tan de prisa.
/tande'prisa/

13. ¿Quiere V. hacerme el favor de hablar despacio y claro? Soy americano y no le comprendo cuando V. habla tan de prisa.

14. ¿Quiere V. hacerme el favor de repetir esta frase? No le comprendo a V. cuando habla tan aprisa. /rːepe'tir/

15. ¿Me comprende V. ahora? /a'ora/

16. Sí; ahora le entiendo perfectamente. /pɛr'fɛkta'mente/

17. ¿Qué dice V.³? /'ke'ðiθews'te?/

Yo digo	/'diɣo/
V. dice	/'diθe/
él dice	/'diθe/
nosotros decimos	/de'θimɔs/
Vds. dicen	/'diθen/
ellos dicen	/'diθen/

18. ¿Qué dice él?

19. ¿Qué dice este hombre? /'este'ɔmbre/

20. ¿Entiende V.⁴ lo que⁵ dice este hombre?
/en'tjendews'teloke'ðiθeste'ɔmbre/

Yo entiendo	/en'tjendo/
V. entiende	/en'tjende/
él entiende	/en'tjende/
nosotros entendemos	/enten'demɔs/
Vds. entienden	/en'tjenden/
ellos entienden	/en'tjenden/

---

¹ **Le comprendo a V.,** *I understand you.* The Spanish language has many pleonastic expressions. **Le,** it must be remembered, can mean either *him* or *you.* Consequently, in order to make it clearly understood that *you* is meant and not *him,* **a V.** is added. Wherever such a misunderstanding could not arise, **a V.** may be left out.

There are therefore three ways to express the phrase: *I understand you.*

a. Comprendo a V., (**a** has to be used before the personal object);

b. Le comprendo;

c. Le comprendo a V.

² **Usted** is left out here, because the meaning of the phrase is clear without it. In cases where any doubt might arise, **usted** *must* be used.

10. I understand you [Le[1] comprendo a V.[1]] when you speak slowly [despacio] and distinctly [claro].
11. Do you not understand me when I speak rapidly [de prisa]?
12. No, sir, I do not understand you when you speak so [tan] fast.

13. Will you please speak slowly and distinctly? I am an American and do not understand you when you speak so rapidly.
14. Will you please repeat [repetir] this phrase? I cannot understand you when you speak so fast.
15. Do you understand me now [ahora]?
16. Yes, now I understand you perfectly [perfectamente].
17. What do you say? (Literally: What say you [dice V.[3]]?)

> I say
> you say
> he says
> we say
> you say
> they say

18. What does he say? (Literally: What says he?)
19. What does this man say? (Literally: What says this man [este hombre]?)
20. Do you understand [entiende V.[4]] what [lo que[5]] this man says?

> I understand
> you understand
> he understands
> we understand
> you understand
> they understand

---

[3] **Decir**, *to say*, *to tell*, is an irregular verb. The indicative of the present tense is conjugated on page 32.

[4] **Entender**, *to understand*, is synonymous with comprender. *Entender* is slightly irregular. The e of the second syllable *ten* is changed into ie in the whole of the singular and in the third person plural of the present tense. A number of other verbs have similar irregularity. Compare Part X.

[5] *Which* (the relative pronoun) can never be omitted, as is frequently done in English. It must be expressed by lo que, *that which*, *what*, when it relates to an idea, *not a word*. All that (compare phrase 22) is expressed by todo lo que.

21. No; no le entiendo.

22. ¿Entiende V. todo lo que digo? /'toðoloke'ðiɣo/

23. Sí; yo entiendo todo lo que V. dice, si[1] habla despacio y claro.

24. No entiendo esta palabra; sírvase[2] repetirla. /'sirβaser:ɛpe'tirla/

25. ¿La entiende V. ahora? Sí; ya la entiendo.

26. ¿Qué quiere decir esta palabra? /'kjereðe'ɵir/

27. ¿Qué quiere decir esta palabra en inglés?

28. ¿Qué quiere decir?
¿Qué significa? /signi'fika/

29. ¿Quiere V. hacerme el favor de volver a repetirla? No entiendo lo que quiere decir.

30. Sírvase explicar esta palabra. /espli'kar/

31. ¿Me hace V. el favor de volver a explicarme esta palabra?

32. ¿Sabe V. lo que quiere decir en inglés esta palabra?

33. Sí, ahora sé lo que significa esta palabra.

34. ¿Tendría V. la bondad de explicarme esta frase española? No sé lo que quiere decir.

35. ¿Entiende V. ahora lo que significa ēsta frase?

36. Sí, ahora sé lo que significa esta frase y puedo repetirla en español y en inglés.

37. Me es muy difícil pronunciar todas estas frases. Creo que la pronunciación española es muy difícil. /'toðas/

38. Al contrario; la pronunciación española es muy fácil. Las palabras españolas se pronuncian según reglas definidas.
/se'ɣun'r:ɛɣlazðefi'niðas/

---

[1] Si (without the acute accent) means *if, whether;* sí (with the acute accent) means *yes.* Both words sound alike.

[2] Sírvase, or sírvase V. means *please.* It really is the imperative mood of the irregular verb servir, *to serve, to wait upon.*

21. No, I do not understand him.

22. Do you understand every thing [todo lo que] I say?

23. Yes, I understand every thing you say, if [si[1]] you speak slowly and distinctly.

24. I do not understand this word; please [sírvase[2]] repeat it once more.

25. Do you understand it now? Yes, now I understand it.

26. What does this word mean? (Literally: What wants to say [decir] this word?)

27. What is the meaning of this word in English?

28. What does this mean? (Literally: What wants to say? **Or:** What means [significa]?)

29. Will you please repeat that once more. I do not understand what it means.

30. Please explain [explicar] this word.

31. Will you please explain this word again to me?

32. Do you know what this word means in English?

33. Yes, now I know the meaning of this word.

34. Would you kindly explain this Spanish phrase to me? I do not know what it means.

35. Do you understand the meaning of this phrase now?

36. Yes, now I know what this phrase means and can repeat it in Spanish and in English.

37. It is very hard for me to pronounce all these phrases. I think the Spanish pronunciation is very difficult.

38. On the contrary, the Spanish pronunciation is very easy. Spanish words are pronounced [se pronuncian] in accordance with [según] definite rules [reglas definidas].

Sírvase, me hace V. el favor, quiere V. tener la bondad—are all phrases which practically mean the same thing.

For the conjugation of **servir** see Part X.

En una tienda

/e′nuna′tjenda/

_____

1. ¿Qué quiere V. hacer en esta tienda? Quiero comprar algo.
/kɔm′pra′ralɣɔ/

2. ¿Qué quiere V. comprar? Quiero comprar un sombrero.
/sɔm′brero/

3. Sírvase V. acompañarme. Quiero comprar un sombrero y no hablo bastante bien el español. /akɔmpa′ɲarme bas′tante/

4. Buenos días.[1] Mi amigo desea comprar un sombrero.
/′bwenɔz′ðias. mja′miɣoðe′sea/

5. ¿De qué clase quiere V. el sombrero?

6. Quiero uno de fieltro.

7. Pruébese V.[2] éste.[3] /′prweβesews′teːste/

8. Me está[4] muy chico. /meːs′ta′mwi′tʃiko/

9. También quiero un par de guantes. /tam′bjen ′um′parðe′ɣwantes/

10. ¿De qué clase los quiere V.? De cabritilla. /′klase kaβri′tiʎa/

11. ¿De qué tamaño? (Or: De qué número)? Del número seis.
/ta′maɲo ′numero′sɛjs/

_____

[1] The Spaniards never say "Good morning," but always **buenos días,** good day. *Good afternoon* or *good evening,* **buenas tardes. Buenas noches,** *good night.* All these forms are used only in the *plural.*

[2] This is the imperative of the (slightly) irregular verb **probar,** to prove. **Probar** belongs to a class of verbs which change the stem-vowel o into **ue** throughout the singular and in the third person plural of the present indicative and subjunctive, and in the same persons in the imperative. The conjugation of the present indicative is therefore:

Yo pruebo	*I prove*
V. prueba	*you prove*
él prueba	*he proves*
nosotros probamos	*we prove*
Vds. prueban	*you prove*
ellos prueban	*they prove*

[3] The English *one* in this and similar connections cannot be translated.

In a Store

___

1. What do you want to do in [en] this store [esta tienda]? I want to buy [comprar] something [algo].

2. What do you want to buy? I wish to purchase a hat [un sombrero].

3. Please [sírvase V.] accompany me [acompañarme]. I want to buy a hat and I do not speak Spanish well enough [bastante bien].

4. Good day [buenos días[1]]. My friend [mi amigo] wishes to buy a hat.

5. What kind of a hat do you want?

6. I want a felt one. (Literally: [I] want one of felt.)

7. Try on [pruébese V.[2]] this one [éste[3]].

8. It is[4] [está] too small [muy chico] for me.

9. I also [también] want a pair of gloves [un par de guantes].

10. What kind [clase] of gloves do you want? Kid [cabritilla] gloves.

11. What size [tamaño]? Number [número] six [seis].

___

[4] There are two verbs in Spanish for our verb *to be*, viz., **ser** and **estar**, the use of which offers peculiar difficulty to English speaking persons.

Ser—of which thus far the student has learned the indicative present—must be used, when the attribute is *permanent, inherent* or *essential*, as:

¿Es V. francés?	*Are you a Frenchman?*
Yo soy médico.	*I am a physician.*
La puerta es alta.	*The door is high.*

All these are inherent or permanent attributes: consequently **ser** must be used. **Estar** must be used, when the attribute is *temporary* or *accidental*, as:

Estoy bueno,	*I am well.*
La puerta está cerrada,	*The door is locked.*

The attributes here are temporary, consequently **estar** is used. For conjugation of **estar** see Part X.

See Part X for full particulars, rules and conjugations.

VOCABULARIO	VOCABULARY
El idioma; Los idiomas	**The Language; Languages**

LA PRONUNCIACIÓN — THE PRONUNCIATION

Tiene V. buena pronunciación. — You have a good pronunciation.

Su pronunciación es muy mala. — His pronunciation is very bad.

El acento /a'θento/ — The accent

Los acentos /a'θentɔs/ — The accents

No acentúa V. bien esta sílaba /'silaβa/ — You do not put the right accent on this syllable.

Acentúe V. bien esta sílaba. — Put the right accent on this syllable.

Pronunciar — To pronounce

Pronuncia V. bien. — You pronounce well.

Pronuncia V. mal. — You pronounce badly.

No pronuncia V. bien esta palabra. — You do not pronounce this word correctly.

Pronuncia V. mal esta palabra. — You pronounce this word incorrectly.

Corregir /kɔr:ɛ'xir/ — To correct

La equivocación /ekiβoka'θjɔn/ — The mistake

Las equivocaciones /ekiβoka'θjones/ — The mistakes

Hágame V. el favor de corregirme cuando me equivoque[1] en la pronunciación. /eki'βoke/ — Please correct me when I make mistakes in the pronunciation.

[1] This is the present tense of the subjunctive mood. Its use will be fully explained in a later lesson.

PART TWO

CONTENTS

CARDINAL NUMBERS[1]

Uno, una	/'uno 'una/	1
Dos	/dɔs/	2
Tres	/tres/	3
Cuatro	/'kwatro/	4
Cinco	/'θiŋko/	5
Seis	/sejs/	6
Siete	/'sjete/	7
Ocho	/'otʃo/	8
Nueve	/'nweβe/	9
Diez	/djeθ/	10
Once	/'ɔnθe/	11
Doce	/'doθe/	12
Trece	/'treθe/	13
Catorce	/ka'tɔrθe/	14
Quince	/'kinθe/	15
Diez y seis[2]	/djeθi'sejs/	16
Diez y siete		17
Diez y ocho		18
Diez y nueve		19
Veinte	/'bɛjnte/	20
Veintiuno	/bɛjnti'uno/	21
Veintidós		22
Veintitrés		23
Veinticuatro		24
Veinticinco		25
Veintiséis		26
Veintisiete		27
Veintiocho		28
Veintinueve		29

---

[1] The numerals are most important and ought to be mastered at once. The pupil must learn them so thoroughly that he can give any number at once and without hesitation.

[2] Observe that 16, 17, 18 and 19 are also rendered **dieciséis, diecisiete, dieciocho** and **diecinueve**.

CARDINAL NUMBERS — Continued

Treinta	/'trɛjnta/	30
Cuarenta	/kwa'renta/	40
Cincuenta	/ɵin'kwenta/	50
Sesenta	/se'senta/	60
Setenta	/se'tenta/	70
Ochenta	/o't∫enta/	80
Noventa	/no'βenta/	90
Ciento[3]	/'ɵjento/	100
Ciento uno		101
Ciento dos		102
Ciento tres		103
Ciento cuatro		104
Ciento cinco, etc.		105
Doscientos	/dɔs'ɵjentɔs/	200
Trescientos	/tres'ɵjentɔs/	300
Cuatrocientos		400
Quinientos	/ki'njentɔs/	500
Seiscientos		600
Setecientos	/sete'ɵjentɔs/	700
Ochocientos		800
Novecientos	/noβe'ɵjentɔs/	900
Mil[4]	/mil/	1,000
Diez mil		10,000
Cien mil	/ɵjen'mil/	100,000
Doscientos mil	/dɔsɵjentoz'mil/	200,000
Quinientos mil		500,000
Un millón	/'unmi'ʎɔn/	1,000,000
Dos millones	/'dɔzmi'ʎones/	2,000,000
Tres millones		3,000,000

---

[3] Ciento is changed into **cien** when standing before any noun or adjective (masculine as well as feminine) as: cien hombres, *one hundred men;* cien mujeres, *one hundred women.*

[4] Eleven hundred, twelve hundred, etc., can *not* be given as in English, but *must* be rendered by **mil,** as: mil ochocientos, 1800.

EN UNA TIENDA — Continuación

12. ¿Le sirven[1] a V. éstos? Sí, me sirven muy bien. /'sirβen/

13. ¿Y qué tal[2] le sirve este sombrero? Bien, muy bien.

Yo sirvo	/'sirβo/
V. sirve	/'sirβe/
él sirve	/'sirβe/
nosotros servimos	/sɛr'βimɔs/
Vds. sirven	/'sirβen/
ellos sirven	/'sirβen/

14. Sírvase enseñarme otros guantes; éstos no me gustan.
/ense'ɲarme'otrɔz'ɣwantes/

15. ¿Cuánto vale[3] este sombrero? Este vale diez pesos.[4] /'djeе'pesɔs/

16. ¿Y cuánto valen estos guantes? Tres pesos.

17. Eso es demasiado.

Eso es demasiado.	/'eso'ezðema'sjaðo/
Son muy caros.	/'sɔn'mwi'karɔs/
Yo estoy	/es'tɔj/
V. está	/es'ta/
él está	/es'ta/
nosotros estamos	/es'tamɔs/
Vds. están	/es'tan/
ellos están	/es'tan/

18. Ah no, señor, los guantes están ahora muy baratos. /ba'ratɔs/

19. ¿Desea V. pagar ahora por estos guantes?

---

[1] **Servir,** as stated before, is an irregular verb of which the indicative present is given above.

[2] How? is very frequently expressed by **qué tal.** In this connection its use is strictly idiomatic.

IN A STORE — Continuation

12. Do these gloves fit [sirven] you? Yes, these gloves fit me very well.

13. And how [qué tal] does this hat fit you? Well, very well.

> I serve
> you serve
> he serves
> we serve
> you serve
> they serve

14. Please show me [enseñarme] some other [otros] gloves; I do not like these. (Literally: these do not please me.)

15. How much is this hat worth? This hat is worth ten dollars. [pesos]. (Literally: How much is worth [vale] this hat?)

16. And what is the price of [cuánto valen] these gloves? Three dollars.

17. That is very expensive. (Literally: That is too much [demasiado]. Or: They are very expensive [muy caros].)

> I am
> you are
> he is
> we are
> you are
> they are

18. Oh! no, sir, gloves are now very cheap [baratos].

19. Do you want to pay [pagar] for these gloves now?

---

³ Valer, *to be worth*, is an irregular verb. The indicative present is conjugated:

Yo valgo	*I am worth*
V. vale	*you are worth*
él vale	*he (it) is worth*
nosotros valemos	*we are worth*
Vds. valen	*you are worth*
ellos valen	*they are worth*

⁴ Peso in South and Central America. Duro in Spain.

44

20. Sí, quiero pagarlos ahora. Aquí tiene V. el dinero. Muchas gracias. Mil gracias. /a′ki di′nero ′mutʃaz′ɣraejas ′mil′ɣraejas/

21. ¿Desea V. pagar ahora por este sombrero?

22. No, sírvase V. mandar al hotel este sombrero y la cuenta. Lo pagaré[1] allí.
/man′daralo′te′lestesɔm′brerɔjla′kwenta. lopaɣa′rea′ʎi/

23. No tengo aquí bastante dinero.

24. ¿Trae V. algún dinero en el bolsillo?
/′traews′teal′ɣundi′neroenelβɔl′siʎo/

Yo traigo	/′trajɣo/
V. trae	/′trae/
él trae	/′trae/
nosotros traemos	/tra′emɔs/
Vds. traen	/′traen/
ellos traen	/′traen/

25. ¿Cuánto dinero tiene V.?
¿Cuánto dinero trae V.?

26. ¿Trae V. mucho dinero en el bolsillo?

27. Traigo muy poco.

28. No traigo mucho dinero en el bolsillo. Mande (**or:** envíe) al hotel este sombrero. Lo pagaré allí.

---

[1] For information of the future tense and for rules as to its use see Part X.

20. Yes, I want to pay for them now. Here is your money [el dinero]. Many thanks [muchas gracias]. (**Or:** A thousand thanks [mil gracias].

21. Do you wish to pay for this hat now?

22. No, please send [mandar] this hat and your bill [la cuenta] to my hotel [al hotel]; I will pay [pagaré[1]] for it there [allí].

23. I have not money enough [bastante] with me.

24. Have you any money with you? (Literally: Carry you [trae V.] any [algún] money in the pocket [el bolsillo]?)

> I carry
> you carry
> he carries
> we carry
> you carry
> they carry

25. How much money have you with you?

26. Have you much money with you?

27. I have very little with me.

28. I have not much money with me. Send [mande; envíe] this hat to my hotel; I will pay [pagaré] for it there.

CONJUGACIÓN DEL TIEMPO FUTURO

PRIMERA CONJUGACIÓN[1]

Yo hablaré
V. hablará
él hablará
nosotros hablaremos
Vds. hablarán
ellos hablarán

Yo pagaré
V. pagará
él pagará
nosotros pagaremos
Vds. pagarán
ellos pagarán

SEGUNDA CONJUGACIÓN[1]

Yo venderé
V. venderá
él venderá
nosotros venderemos
Vds. venderán
ellos venderán

Yo comeré
V. comerá
él comerá
nosotros comeremos
Vds. comerán
ellos comerán

TERCERA CONJUGACIÓN[1]

Yo viviré
V. vivirá
él vivirá
nosotros viviremos
Vds. vivirán
ellos vivirán

Yo recibiré
V. recibirá
él recibirá
nosotros recibiremos
Vds. recibirán
ellos recibirán

---

[1] The future tense of all regular verbs is formed by adding the following endings to their stem:

1.	2.	3.
——aré	——eré	——iré
——ará	——erá	——irá
——ará	——erá	——irá
——aremos	——eremos	——iremos
——arán	——erán	——irán
——arán	——erán	——irán

CONJUGATION OF THE FUTURE TENSE

FIRST CONJUGATION[1]

I shall speak
you will speak
he will speak
we shall speak
you will speak
they will speak

I shall pay
you will pay
he will pay
we shall pay
you will pay
they will pay

SECOND CONJUGATION[1]

I shall sell
you will sell
he will sell
we shall sell
you will sell
they will sell

I shall dine
you will dine
he will dine
we shall dine
you will dine
they will dine

THIRD CONJUGATION[1]

I shall live
you will live
he will live
we shall live
you will live
they will live

I shall receive
you will receive
he will receive
we shall receive
you will receive
they will receive

It will be seen that **a** is the characteristic vowel of verbs of the first conjugation, **e** of the second, **i** of the third.

Form and conjugate the future tense of the following verbs. comprar, *to buy;* tomar, *to take;* representar, *to represent;* volver, *to return;* entender, *to understand;* perder, *to lose;* sentir, *to feel;* preferir, *to prefer.*

The future must be used in Spanish for the English "I will" or "I shall" when futurity is expressed, that is to say, whenever "I will" cannot be changed to "I want to, I wish, I desire," the future tense *must* be used as:

When will you do it? (= *When do you want to do it?*) ¿Cuándo quiere V. hacerlo?
But: *We will consider it.* Lo consideraremos.

La llegada — El hotel — Cuartos
/laʎe'ɣaða   elo'tɛl   'kwartɔs/

_____

1. ¿Qué desea V. hacer al llegar? /alʎe'ɣar/

2. Estoy[1] muy cansado. Quisiera ir inmediatamente a un buen hotel.
   /kan'saðo   ki'sjera'irinme'ðjata'menteawm'bweno'tɛl/

   Yo quisiera   /ki'sjera/
   V. quisiera
   él quisiera
   nosotros quisiéramos   /ki'sjeramɔs/
   Vds. quisieran   /ki'sjeran/
   ellos quisieran

3. ¿A qué hotel quiere V. ir? Al Hotel Continental.

4. ¿Va V. a pie? No, voy a tomar un taxi.
   /'baws'tea'pje?/ no, 'bɔjato'marun'taksi/

         Yo voy   /bɔj/
         V. va   /ba/
         él va
         nosotros vamos   /'bamɔs/
         Vds. van   /ban/
         ellos van

5. Estoy muy cansado. No puedo caminar[2] hasta[3] el hotel. Voy a
   tomar un taxi. /kami'narastaelo'tɛl/

6. ¿Va V. a pie hasta el hotel, o quiere V. tomar un taxi?

7. No estoy cansado; voy a caminar.

8. ¿Tiene V. equipaje[3]? /eki'paxɛ/

9. ¿Tiene V. mucho equipaje?

10. ¿Cuánto equipaje tiene V.?

_____

[1] Why must _estoy_ be used here? Compare page 37, note 4.

[2] **Caminar**, _to walk_, is synonymous with **ir a pie**. As stated before, synonymous expressions have frequently been introduced into the exercises for the sake of diversity.

The Arrival — The Hotel — Rooms

---

1. What do you want to do on arriving [al llegar]?

2. I am [estoy[1]] very tired [cansado]. I would like [quisiera] to go [ir] at once [inmediatamente] to a good hotel.

   I should like
   you would like
   he would like
   we should like
   you would like
   they would like

3. To which hotel do you want to go? To the Hotel Continental.

4. Are you going to walk (Are you going there on foot [va V. a pie])? No, I am going to take [tomar] a taxi.

I am going	or:	I go
you are going	"	you go
he is going	"	he goes
we are going	"	we go
you are going	"	you go
they are going	"	they go

5. I am very tired. I cannot walk [caminar[2]] to [hasta] the hotel. I am going to take a taxi.

6. Are you going to walk to your hotel or do you want to take a taxi?

7. I am not tired, I am going to walk.

8. Have you any baggage [equipaje]?

9. Have you much baggage?

10. How much baggage have you?

---

[3] **Hasta** means *to = as far as;* it also means *till, until.* In the latter case it denotes *time,* in the former *place,* as:

hasta mañana	*till to-morrow*
hasta la vista	*au revoir (auf wiedersehen) i. e., till we meet again*
voy hasta Madrid	*I go as far as Madrid*

[4] *Any* in this and similar connections need not be rendered.

… Tengo muy poco equipaje. Voy a tomar el tranvía. /tram'bia/

12. Tengo mucho equipaje. No puedo caminar hasta el hotel. Voy a tomar un taxi.

13. Chófer, al Hotel Continental. /'tʃofɛr/

14. Buenos días, ¿me puede V. dar un buen[1] cuarto?
/um'bwen'kwarto/

15. ¿Puede V. darme un buen cuarto en el primer piso[2]?
/pri'mɛr'piso/

16. Estoy muy cansado y deseo acostarme[3] en seguida.
/akɔs'tarmense'ɣiða/

17. Sírvase darme un buen cuarto en el primer piso.

18. Sírvase enseñarme un buen cuarto en el segundo piso. /se'ɣundo/

19. ¿Por cuánto puede V. darme este cuarto?

Yo doy[4]	/dɔj/
V. da	/da/
él da	/da/
nosotros damos	/'damɔs/
Vds. dan	/dan/
ellos dan	/dan/

---

[1] The following adjectives drop the final o before a masculine noun in the singular: **bueno**, good; **malo**, bad; **alguno**, anyone, someone, somebody; **nínguno**, no one, nobody, not any one; **primero**, first; **tercero**, third; **postrero**, last, as:

> Buen amo, *good master*
> ningún cuarto, *no room*
> el primer hombre, *the first man*

But if they stand *after* the noun the o is preserved as:

> Un hombre malo, *a bad man*   El libro tercero, *the third book*

The o is also preserved whenever the noun referring to the adjective is not expressed, as:

> Es bueno, *he is good*
> Alguno de estos señores, *one of these gentlemen*

[2] El primer piso in Spanish hotels corresponds to our second floor; the second to our third floor, etc.

[3] This verb is a *reflexive* or *pronominal* verb. Reflexive verbs are conjugated

11. I have very little baggage. I am going to take the street-car [el tranvía].

12. I have a great deal of baggage. I cannot walk to my hotel. I am going to take a taxi.

13. Driver, to the Hotel Continental.

14. Good morning, can you give me a good room [un buen[1] cuarto]?

15. Can you give me a good room on the first floor [el primer piso[2]]?

16. I am very tired and wish [deseo] to go to bed [acostarme[3]] at once [en seguida].

17. Please give me a good room on the first floor.

18. Please show me [enseñarme] a good room on the second [segundo] floor.

19. At what price [por cuánto] can you give me this room?

> I give
> you give
> he gives
> we give
> you give
> they give

with two personal pronouns, the first (expressed or understood) being the subject, and the second the object, as: él se engaña or se engaña, *he deceives himself.*

Almost any verb may be used reflexively in Spanish, which frequently occasions a modification of the meaning, as: dormir, to sleep; dormirse, to go to sleep; ir, to go; irse, to go away.

The pronouns used in connection with reflexive verbs are:

me, *myself*   **nos,** *ourselves*

se, ⎰ *himself, herself*   **se,** ⎰ *themselves*
           ⎱ *itself, yourself*   ⎱ *yourselves*

The conjugation presents no difficulties.

INDICATIVE PRESENT

(Yo) me equivoco	*I am mistaken*
V. se equivoca	*you are mistaken*
(él) se equivoca	*he is mistaken*
(nosotros) nos equivocamos	*we are mistaken*
Vds. se equivocan	*you are mistaken*
(ellos) se equivocan	*they are mistaken*

For full rules and conjugation see Part X.

[4] **Dar** is an irregular verb. See Part X.

20. ¿Cuánto es este cuarto por día? /pɔr'ðia/

21. ¿A cuánto por día es este cuarto?

22. Este cuarto es de a tres pesos por día.

23. Puedo darle este cuarto muy barato.

24. Este cuarto es muy caro. No lo quiero tomar. Sírvase enseñarme otro.

25. No tengo ningún[1] otro cuarto en este piso, pero puedo darle uno muy grande y barato en el tercero. /niŋ'gu'notro'kwarto tɛr'ɵero/

26. Este cuarto es grande[2] y hermoso. ¿Por cuánto me lo da V.?

27. Este cuarto es muy barato. No cuesta[3] sino dos pesos al día.

28. Muy bien, lo tomo.[4] Sírvase hacer subir el[5] equipaje y pagar al chófer.

29. ¿Desea V. comer ahora, caballero?

30. No, gracias. Estoy muy cansado y deseo acostarme inmediatamente.

31. ¿Desea V. algo más?—No gracias, tengo todo lo que necesito. /neɵe'sito/

---

[1] **No**, not, stands always—as we have seen already—*before* the verb, as: no lo quiero, *I don't want it*.

It will furthermore be observed that the Spaniards use a *double* negative. In English a *double* negative is equivalent to an affirmative, but this is not the case in Spanish, where **nada**, nothing, **ninguno**, no one, not any one, **jamás**, never, etc., are placed after **no**, as:

No quiero nada	*I don't want anything*
no lo he visto jamás	*I have never seen it*
no lo sabe nadie	*no one knows it*

The negative **no** is, however, omitted when the negative adjectives or adverbs stand at the beginning of the sentence, as:

Nada quiero	*I don't want anything*
jamás lo he visto	*I have never seen it*
nadie lo sabe	*nobody knows it*

20. What is the price of this room per day?

21. How much [a cuánto] is this room per day?

22. This room is three dollars per day.

23. I can give you this room very cheap.

24. This room is too expensive. I do not want to take [tomar] it. Please show me another one [otro].

25. I have no [ningún¹] other [otro] room on this floor, but I can give you a very large [grande] and inexpensive one [uno] on the third [el tercero] floor.

26. This room is large and beautiful [hermoso]. For how much can you give it to me?

27. This room is very cheap. It costs [cuesta³] only [sino] two dollars a day.

28. All right, I take [tomo⁴] it. Please send my baggage up [hacer subir el equipaje] and pay the [al] chauffeur. (Literally: Very well, it [I] take.)

29. Do you wish to dine [comer] now, sir?

30. No, thanks, I am very tired and want to retire at once.

31. Do you wish anything [algo] else?—No, thanks, I have everything I need [necesito].

---

² **Grande** loses its final syllable when standing before any noun beginning with a consonant, as: Una gran casa, a *large house;* un gran peligro, a *great peril.*

³ **Costar,** *to cost,* belongs to the class of verbs whose stem-vowel o is changed into ue throughout the singular and in the third person plural of the present indicative and subjunctive, and in the same persons in the imperative. See Part X.

⁴ The Present is used very frequently in Spanish, where we employ the Future, as:

Voy al instante,	*I will go at once.*
¿Me hace V. el favor?	*Will you do me the favor?*

⁵ The definite article is frequently employed in Spanish in place of our possessive pronoun. This is especially the case when *parts of the body* or *articles of dress* are mentioned, as:

¿Qué tiene V. en la mano?	*What have you in your hand?*
Me duele la cabeza,	*My head aches.*
Me quito los zapatos,	*I am taking off my shoes.*

32. No veo fósforos en el cuarto. Mozo, tráigame una caja de fósforos. /'no'βeo'fɔsforɔs 'trajɣamewna'kaxa/

33. Aquí están[1] los fósforos. ¿Quiere V. alguna otra cosa? /a'ki 'kosa/

34. No, gracias, nada más. Quiero acostarme inmediatamente.

35. Buenas noches,[2] señor. ¡Que pase V. buena noche! /ke'pa-sews'te'βwena'notʃe/

FRASE FUNDAMENTAL

Quisiera salir para Madrid en el primer

/ki'sjerasa'lirpara'maðriðenɛlpri'mɛr

tren, pero no me es posible

'tren, pero'no'me:spo'siβle/

Quisiera /ki'sjera/
salir /sa'lir/
para[3] /'para/
Madrid /ma'ðrið/
en[3] /en/
el /ɛl/
primer /pri'mɛr/
tren /tren/
pero /'pero/
no /no/
me /me/
es /es/
posible /po'siβle/

---

[1] **Estar** must always be used when temporary existence in a certain place or locality is expressed, as:

Yo estoy aquí,	I am here.
está en el café,	he is at the cafe.
estaba a la puerta,	he was at the door.

[2] *Good night, good day*, etc., must always be in the plural.

[3] The pupil should distinguish well between **para** and **por**.

Para means *for, to*, and denotes direction, destination, aim or purpose, as:

Estudio para aprender,	I study in order to learn.
Esta carta es para el señor Díaz,	This letter is for Mr. Díaz.
Pienso partir para Italia,	I think of starting for Italy.

Por means *for, by*, and is used like *par* in French, with passive verbs, denoting *bodily*, not mental, actions, as:

32. I do not see any matches [fósforos] in the room. Boy [mozo], bring me [tráigame] a box [una caja] of matches.

33. Here [aquí] are [están[1]] the matches. Do you wish anything else [alguna otra cosa]?

34. No, thanks, nothing else. I want to retire at once.

35. Good night [buenas noches[2]], sir, sleep well [que pase V. buena noche.].

MAIN SENTENCE

I should like to leave by the first train for Madrid,

but that is impossible

El mundo fué hecho por Dios,	*The world was created by God.*
Este cuadro fué pintado por Murillo,	*This picture was painted by Murillo.*

Por denotes motive, aim, and is also used in connection with the *price* of things, as:

Lo hace por temor,	*He does it from fear.*
Lo hago por favorecerle,	*I do it to favor him.*
¿Por cuánto?	*For how much? At what price?*
Daré la casa por dos mil pesos,	*I shall give [sell] the house for two thousand dollars.*

In other words:

Por signifies:	**Para signifies:**
Origin, Cause, Motion.	*Destination, Aim, Intention.*
¿Por qué? *Why?*	¿Para qué? *For what purpose?*
¿Por quién? *By whom?*	¿Para quién? *For whom?*
Voy a Madrid por París, *I travel to Madrid by way of Paris.*	Quiero salir para París, *I want to leave for Paris.*
Por la mañana, *In the morning.*	Para mañana, *Till to-morrow.*

Un viaje
/'um'bjaxɛ/

1. ¿Qué desea V. hacer mañana por la mañana? Desearía[1] salir para Sevilla en el primer tren. /desea'ria se'βiʎa/

2. Dispense V., caballero, desearía ir[2] a Barcelona. Hágame el favor de decirme dónde está[3] la estación[4] del ferrocarril.
/dis'pensews'te barθe'lona fa'βɔrðeðe'θirme esta'ejɔndɛlfɛrːɔ-ka'rːil/

3. Dispense V., ¿dónde está la estación central? /θen'tral/

4. Dispense V., ¿por dónde se va a la estación central?

5. Dispense V., ¿cuál es la sala de espera?

6. Dispense V., ¿dónde está el despacho de billetes?
/des'patʃoðeβiʎetes/

7. Dispense V., quiero ir a Barcelona. ¿Dónde está el despacho de billetes (**or**: el despacho de boletos). /des'patʃoðeβoletɔs/

---

[1] **Desearía** is the Conditional of desear, to wish, to desire.

If, therefore, we take the verbs **hablar**, to speak; **vender**, to sell, **and vivir**, to live, as paradigms, the Conditional is formed thus:

1.	2.	3.
yo hablar*ía*	vender*ía*	vivir*ía*
V. hablar*ía*	vender*ía*	vivir*ía*
él hablar*ía*	vender*ía*	vivir*ía*
nosotros hablar*íamos*	vender*íamos*	vivir*íamos*
Vds. hablar*ían*	vender*ían*	vivir*ían*
ellos hablar*ían*	vender*ían*	vivir*ían*

It will be apparent that a is the characteristic vowel of the first conjugation, e of the second and i of the third. Of course, this would be rendered: *I should speak, you would speak*, etc.

A Journey

1. What do you want to do to-morrow morning [mañana por la mañana]? I should like [desearía[1]] to leave by the first train for Seville.

2. Excuse me [dispense V.], sir, I should like to go [ir] to [a] Barcelona. Please tell me where the railroad station [estación del ferrocarril] is.

3. Excuse me, where is the Central Station?

4. Pardon me, which is the way [por dónde se va] to the Central Station?

5. Excuse me, which [cuál] is the waiting room [la sala de espera]?

6. I beg your pardon; where is the ticket-office [despacho de billetes]?

7. I beg your pardon; I want to go to Barcelona. Where is the ticket-office?

To the stem of the regular verbs the following terminations are added in

THE CONDITIONAL

1.	2.	3.
——aría	——ería	——iría
——aría	——ería	——iría
——aría	——ería	——iría
——aríamos	——eríamos	——iríamos
——arían	——erían	——irían
——arían	——erían	——irían

[2] Ir, to go, is generally followed by a.
[3] Estar is used in reference to localities.
[4] The *station* is called la estación, while el ferrocarril means the *railroad*.

8. Dispense V., quisiera salir en el tren expreso para Barcelona. ¿Podría V.[1] decirme dónde está el despacho de billetes? /'trenes'preso po'ðria/

9. Siga V.[2] derecho. /'siɣawsteðe'retʃo/
   Por ahí derecho. /pora'iðe'retʃo/

10. El despacho de billetes[3] está a la derecha. /alaðe'retʃa/

11. Dispense V., ¿me podría V. decir a qué lado está el despacho de billetes? /'laðo/

12. ¿A qué lado está el despacho de billetes? A la derecha. A la izquierda. /alajɵ'kjɛrða/

13. Sírvase darme un billete para Barcelona.

14. ¿De qué clase? De segunda.

15. Sírvase darme un billete de segunda para Barcelona.

16. De ida o de ida y vuelta? /'dɛjða | o'ðɛjðaj'βwelta?/

17. Sírvase darme uno de ida y vuelta.

18. ¿Cuánto vale el billete para Barcelona?

19. ¿Cuánto es el billete de segunda clase para Barcelona?

20. ¿Cuánto vale un billete de ida y vuelta de tercera clase? /tɛr'ɵera'klase/

21. Doscientas cincuenta pesetas. Aquí los tiene V. y aquí tiene V. el billete y el cambio. /dɔs'ɵjentasɵiŋ'kwentape'setas 'kambjo/

22. ¿Tiene V. equipaje? Sí, tengo un baúl. /ba'ul/

---

[1] **Podría** is the conditional of the verb **poder**, *to be able.* The student has previously learned the present tense *puedo.* The future and conditional are conjugated thus:

FUTURE	CONDITIONAL
yo podré	podría
V. podrá	podría
él podrá	podría
nosotros podremos	podríamos
Vds. podrán	podrían
ellos podrán	podrían

8. Pardon me; I would like to leave by the **express-train** [expreso] for Barcelona. Could you [podría V.] please tell me where the ticket-office is?

9. Go straight ahead. (Literally: Follow you [siga V.] straight. **Or:** Through there straight.)

10. The ticket-office is on the right side [a la derecha].

11. I beg your pardon, could you please tell me on which side [a qué lado] the ticket-office is?

12. On which side is the ticket-office?—On the right. On the left [a la izquierda].

13. Please give me a ticket to Barcelona.

14. Which class [clase]?—Second.

15. Please give me a second class ticket to Barcelona

16. Single [de ida] or return [de ida y vuelta]?

17. Please give me a round-trip ticket.

18. How much is [vale] a ticket to Barcelona?

19. How much is [es] a second class ticket to Barcelona?

20. How much is a return-ticket third class [de tercera clase]?

21. Two hundred and fifty pesetas.—Here you are.—And here is your ticket and your change [el cambio].

22. Have you any baggage? Yes, I have a trunk [un baúl].

---

[2] Siga V. is the imperative of the irregular verb **seguir**, *to follow*. The indicative present is conjugated thus:

Yo sigo	*I follow*
V. sigue	*you follow*
él sigue	*he follows*
nosotros seguimos	*we follow*
Vds. siguen	*you follow*
ellos siguen	*they follow*

[3] A ticket is either **un billete, un boleto, una boleta** or **una papeleta.**

VOCABULARIO

Continuación

Se ha equivocado V.
/se'aekiβo'kaðows'te/

¿Qué quiere decir eso?

El sentido /sen'tiðo/

Usar, emplear /u'sar emple'ar/

Esta palabra no se usa en ese sentido.

¿Cómo se emplea esta palabra?

La frase; las frases

La oración; las oraciones

VOCABULARY

Continuation

You have made a mistake.

What does that mean?

The sense

To use; to employ

This word is not used in that sense.

How is this word used?

The phrase; the phrases

The sentence; the sentences.

Para hacer compras

Quisiera hacer unas compras.

¿Cuánto vale eso?

¿Cuánto es esto?

¿Es eso lo más barato?

No se lo puedo dar más barato.

La cuenta /'kwenta/

El recibo /rːɛ'θiβo/

Sírvase mandar al hotel estos efectos y con ellos la cuenta recibida.

To Make Purchases; to do some shopping

I would like to do some shopping.

How much does that cost?

What is the price of this?

Is that the cheapest price?

I cannot give it to you any cheaper.

The bill

The receipt

Please send these goods with a receipted bill to the hotel (please to send to the hotel these goods and with them the bill receipted).

PART THREE

CONTENTS

Un viaje

(*Continuación*)

23. Quisiera facturar mi baúl. ¿Dónde está el despacho de equipajes?

24. ¿Podría V. decirme dónde está el despacho de equipajes? Quisiera facturar este baúl.

25. Llamaré al portero; él se lo facturará. /pɔr'tero faktura'ra/

26. Portero, este caballero desearía facturar su baúl.

27. Está muy bien. ¿A dónde va V., caballero?

28. Voy para Lima.

29. ¿Tiene V. ya su billete? Por supuesto. Hélo aquí. **Or:** Aquí lo tiene V.[1] /pɔrsu'pwesto 'eloa'ki/

30. Sírvase dármelo. Sírvase ir a la sala de espera. Yo facturaré el equipaje y le traeré a V. el talón. /trae're ta'lɔn/

31. Aquí tiene V. su talón. Hay que[2] pagar exceso por el equipaje. /'ajkepa'ɣares'θeso/

32. Muchas gracias. Aquí tiene V. el dinero para el exceso. ¿Y cuánto le debo a V.?

---

[1] Of the imperative mood of **haber**, *to have,* only one person is used, viz.: **hé** (accented to distinguish it from **he**, I have). It is used in the sense of *to possess, to be* and *to see.* As:

hélo aquí	*here it is*	hélo allí	*there it is*
héla aquí		héla allí	
hélos aquí	*here they are*	hélos allí	*there they are*
hélas aquí		hélas allí	
héme aquí, *here I am*		hé allí su libro, *there is your book*	

For rules see Part X.

A Journey
Continued

23. I would like to check [facturar] my trunk. Where is the baggage room [despacho de equipajes]?

24. Could you please inform me where the baggage room is? I would like to check this trunk.

25. I will call the [al] porter [portero]; he will check your trunk for you.

26. Porter, this gentleman would like to have his trunk checked.

27. All right; where are you going, sir?

28. I am going to [para] Lima.

29. Have you your ticket? Certainly [por supuesto]; here it is [hélo aquí].

30. Please give it to me. Go into the waiting-room. I will check your baggage and bring you the check [el recibo].

31. Here is your check, sir. There is [hay que²] some overweight [exceso] to pay.

32. Many thanks. Here is the money for [para] the overweight. And how much do I owe [debo] you?

---

² **Haber,** *to have,* is often used impersonally, *i. e.,* in the third person singular (even when referring to the plural), as:

Hay un hombre a la puerta,	*There is a man at the door.*
Hay dos hombres abajo,	*There are two men downstairs.*

When followed by **que** and the infinitive of some other verb, it expresses obligation or necessity, and is rendered by *to be necessary,* or its equivalents, as:

Hoy hay mucho que hacer,	*There is a great deal to be done to-day.*
¿Qué hay que hacer?	*What is to be done?*
Mañana habrá mucho que hacer,	*There will be much to be done to-morrow.*

Haber is used to form a great variety of idiomatic expressions; they will be taught gradually. For conjugation and full rules see Part X.

33. No tenemos tarifa. Dé V.[1] lo que le plazca.[2] /ta'rifa 'dews'te 'plaɵka/

34. ¡Ya ya! eso es una propina, ¿no es así? /'ja'ja | 'esoesunapro'pina, 'noesa'si?/

35. Sí señor.—Mil gracias. Los americanos son generosɔs pues dan buenas propinas. /xɛne'rosɔspwez'ðam'bwenaspro'pinas/

36. ¿A qué hora sale este tren? /a'keɔra/

37. Este tren sale dentro de cinco minutos. /'dentro mi'nutɔs/

38. ¿Hay vagón de fumar? /'ajba'ɣɔndefu'mar/

39. ¡Sí! Aquí está y hay bastantes asientos vacíos.

40. ¿Sabe V. cuándo llega este tren a Quito? A las ocho de ia noche. Aquí tiene V. un itinerario. /itine'rarjo/

---

[1] **Dé V.** is the imperative of **dar**, *to give*.

[2] **Plazca** is the subjunctive mood of **placer**, *to please*.

Verbs ending in **cer** or **cir** preceded by a *vowel*, insert before the stem ending a z whenever the stem meets an **a** or an **o**, as:

INDICATIVE PRESENT	SUBJUNCTIVE
Yo plazco	que yo plazca
V. place	que V. plazca
él place	que él plazca
nosostros placemos	que nosotros plazcamos
Vds. placen	que Vds. plazcan
ellos placen	que ellos plazcan

The terminations of the present subjunctive are exceedingly simple.

SUBJUNCTIVE MOOD

Present

1.	2.	3.
——e	——a	——a
——e	——a	——a
——e	——a	——a
——emos	——amos	——amos
——en	——an	——an
——en	——an	——an

33. We have no price [tarifa]. You may give what you like [dé V.[1]] [plazca[2]].

34. Oh, yes [ya ya]! That's [eso es] a tip [una propina], isn't it [no es así]?

35. Yes, sir.—Ever so much obliged to you [mil gracias]! Americans are generous [generosos] since they [pues] give good tips [buenas propinas].

36. At what time [a qué hora] does this train leave?

37. This train leaves in [dentro de] five minutes [minutos].

38. Is there [hay] a smoking-car [vagón de fumar]?

39. Yes, here it is and there are plenty of empty seats.

40. Do you know when this train arrives in Quito? At eight P.M. Here is a time-table [un itinerario].

If, therefore, we take the verbs **hablar**, *to speak;* **vender**, *to sell;* **vivir**, *to live*, as paradigms, the following is:

THE SUBJUNCTIVE MOOD

Present

1.	2.	3.
Yo hable	venda	viva
V. hable	venda	viva
él hable	venda	viva
nosotros hablemos	vendamos	vivamos
Vds. hablen	vendan	vivan
ellos hablen	vendan	vivan

Of course, this form would be rendered: *I may speak, you may speak, he may speak*, etc.

The subjunctive is rarely used in English conversation; in Spanish the opposite is the case. English-speaking persons experience, therefore, great difficulty in understanding this mood, for which no proper equivalents exist in their tongue.

As a general rule, it may be stated that the subjunctive mood is used in clauses dependent on a verb expressing *possibility*, *wish*, *doubt*, *apprehension*, *command*, or broadly speaking, *emotions*

The two clauses are connected by the conjunction que, as:

¿Qué quiere V. que yo haga?   *What do you want me to do?*
Quiero que V. escriba a su amigo.   *I wish you would write to your friend.*

In the above sentence the subjunctive mood is used, because *wish* is implied.
These general hints must suffice for the present. For full rules see Part X.

THE ORDINAL NUMBERS[1]

Primero,[1] a	/pri'mero/	1st
Segundo, a	/se'ɣundo/	2nd
Tercero, a	/tɛr'θero/	3rd
Cuarto, a	/'kwarto/	4th
Quinto, a	/'kinto/	5th
Sexto, a	/'sesto/	6th
Séptimo, a	/'sɛptimo/	7th
Octavo, a	/ɔk'taβo/	8th
Nono, a	/'nono/	
Noveno, a	/no'βeno/	9th
Décimo, a[2]	/'deθimo/	10th
Undécimo, a	/un'deθimo/	11th
Duodécimo, a	/dwo'ðeθimo/	12th
Décimo tercio, etc.	/'deθimo'tɛreɔjo/	13th
Vigésimo, a	/bi'xesimo/	20th
Vigésimo primo		21st
Vigésimo segundo		22nd
Vigésimo tercio, etc.		23rd
Trigésimo, a	/tri'xesimo/	30th
Cuadragésimo, a	/kwaðra'xesimo/	40th
Quincuagésimo, a	/kiŋkwa'xesimo/	50th
Sexagésimo, a	/sɛksa'xesimo/	60th
Septuagésimo, a	/sɛptwa'xesimo/	70th
Octagésimo, a	/ɔkta'xesimo/	80th
Nonagésimo, a	/nona'xesimo/	90th
Centésimo, a	/θen'tesimo/	100th
Milésimo, a	/mi'lesimo/	1000th
Millonésimo, a	/miʎo'nesimo/	1,000,000th
Postrero, a	/pɔs'trero/	
Ultimo, a	/'ultimo/	the last

---

[1] Ordinal numbers are treated like adjectives and agree in gender and number with the noun to which they refer, as:

Este muchacho es el primero,	*This boy is the first.*
La Quinta Avenida	*Fifth Avenue*

Primero, first, **tercero**, third, and **postrero**, last in order, drop the final o in the singular before a noun, as:

el primer día	*the first day*
el tercer libro	*th. third book*
el postrer discípulo	*the last pupil*

CONVERSATIONAL EXERCISES
What they are and how they should be studied

Having thoroughly mastered the foregoing sentences the student must now familiarize himself with the Conversational Exercises.

They consist of practical phrases, such as we are in the habit of using in every-day life. But as every person employs his own peculiar mode of diction,

Diversity of Expression

must be acquired from the very start.

The most commonplace thought can be expressed in numerous ways, and therefore, throughout these textbooks, and especially in the Conversational Parts, a vast number of sentences are given, which, though worded differently, are almost identical in their meaning.

The Advantages of this Plan

are evident. The pupil is no longer confined to a single phrase, but becomes familiar with a variety of expressions. He does not learn only **one** sentence by which he may state his wants, but has at his disposal **the whole colloquial vocabulary on any one subject,** and is thus enabled to carry on a conversation with anyone.

At the same time

The Conversations are Graded

in such a manner, that only such constructions, idioms, moods and tenses are given as have been previously mastered by the student.

All phrases used are

Sentence Patterns

They are intended to teach the pupil to **think** in Spanish, and with **this** end in view, they must always be studied **aloud** and rendered frequently in Spanish until the pupil can utter them smoothly **and** rapidly.

Primo and **tercio** are used in place of *primero* and *tercero* after another **ordinal** number, as:

> vigésimo primo, *twenty-first*   trigésimo tercio, *thirty-third*

With the exception of **primero,** the first, the Spaniards use the cardinal **numbers** for dates, as:

> ¿Qué día del mes tenemos hoy?   *What day of the month is to-day?*
> Tenemos el quince de junio.   *It is the 15th of June.*

[2] Ordinal numbers above *décimo* are rarely used.

CONVERSACIÓN
/kɔmbɛrsa'θjɔn/

Para hacer preguntas acerca del camino
/para'θɛrpre'ɣuntasa'θɛrkaðɛlka'mino/

1. Dispense V., caballero. ¿Podría V. decirme dónde está el mejor cine de la ciudad?

2. ¿Me hace V. el favor de enseñarme (or: de decirme), por dónde queda la calle Rivadavia?

3. Dispense V. ¿Por dónde se va a la Calle Belgrano?

4. Disculpe V. ¿Está por aquí el Hotel Continental?

5. Dispense V. ¿Por dónde queda el Teatro de la Comedia?

6. Disculpe V. ¿Por dónde está el Teatro de Variedades?
   /te'atroðeβarje'ðaðes/

7. ¿Sería V. tan amable de indicarme por dónde puedo ir a la estación del ferrocarril?

8. ¿Me hace V. el favor de decirme si puedo ir por esta calle al teatro?

9. Sí, señor, siga V. derecho por ella hasta que llegue[1] a la Plaza Constitución.

10. Doble V. a la derecha[2] por la segunda calle y siga V derecho hasta que llegue a una plaza. /'doβlews'te 'plaθa/

11. Pase V. el puente y entonces cruce la plaza. No puede V. equivocarse (or: equivocar el camino). /en'tɔnθes'kruθe/

12. ¿Está lejos de aquí? No, no está lejos. /'lexɔs/

13. ¿Quiere V. que le acompañe? Me hará V. un gran favor.
    /akɔm'paɲe mea'raws'te/

---

[1] After the following conjunctions the subjunctive mood must be used, when uncertainty or doubt is expressed or implied:

a fin de que	*in order that*	lejos de que	*far from*
a menos que	*unless*	por poco que	*however little*
aunque	} *although*	por mucho que	} *however*
aun cuando		por más que	

CONVERSATION

To Inquire One's Way

1. Excuse me, sir; could you please tell me where the best motion-picture house in the city is?

2. Will you please show me [enseñarme] the way to [por dónde queda] Rivadavia Street?

3. I beg your pardon, which is the way to Belgrano Street?

4. Pardon me, is this the way to the Hotel Continental?

5. Pardon me, how do I go to the Comedy Theatre?

6. Pardon me, which is the way to the Variety Theatre [el Teatro de Variedades]?

7. Would you be kind enough [sería V. tan amable] to tell me [de indicarme] the way to the railroad station?

8. Will you please tell me whether this street leads to the theatre?

9. Yes, go straight ahead [derecho] till you come to Constitution Square.

10. Take [doble V.] the second street on the right [a la derecha] and go straight ahead till you come to a square.

11. Go across [pase V.] the bridge [el puente], then [entonces] diagonally across [cruce V.] the square. You cannot miss your way [equivocarse] [equivocar el camino].

12. Is it far from here? No, it is not far [lejos].

13. Shall I accompany you? Yes, please.

---

bien que	*though*	para que	*in order that*
en caso que	*in case that*	siempre que	*whenever*
con tal que	*provided that*	supuesto que	*supposing that*
hasta que	*until*	¡ojalá!	*would to God!*

[2] A la derecha, *to the right;* a la izquierda, *to the left.*

Para hacer compras

1. ¿Qué quiere V. hacer esta mañana?

2. Deseo salir para hacer unas compras. /unas'kɔmpras/

3. ¿Y en dónde quiere V. hacer las compras?

4. Verdaderamente no lo sé. V. que ha estado en Buenos **Aires** varias veces,[1] ¿quiere V. decirme en dónde puedo comprar buenos guantes? /berða''ðera'mente 'aes'taðo 'barjaz'βeθes/

AFIRMATIVO

Yo he estado[2]	/'eːs'taðo/
V. ha estado	/'aes'taðo/
él ha estado	/'aes'taðo/
nosotros hemos estado	/'emoses'taðo/
Vds. han estado	/'anes'taðo/
ellos han estado	/'anes'taðo/

INTERROGATIVO:

¿he estado yo?[3]
¿ha estado V.?
¿ha estado él?
¿hemos estado nosotros?
¿han estado Vds.?[4]
¿han estado ellos?

---

[1] With **vez,** *time, turn,* **veces,** *times, turns,* the multiplicative numbers are formed:

una vez	*once*	algunas veces	*sometimes*
dos veces	*twice*	la primera vez	*the first time*
tres veces	*three times*	la última vez	*the last time*
esta vez	*this time*	cada vez	*each time*
aquella vez	*that time*	muchas veces	*many times*
todas las veces	*every time*	otra vez	*another time*
varias veces	*several times*	a veces	*by turns, sometimes*

[2] There are two verbs in Spanish for *to have,* viz., **haber** and **tener.**
The difference between them is this:

Haber is used exclusively in the formation of *compound tenses,* while **tener** is used as an *active* verb indicating *possession* (in which case *to have* may generally be replaced by *to hold* or *to possess* without affecting the meaning of the sentence).

He comprado unos guantes.	*I have bought some gloves* (compound tense).
No tengo guantes.	*I have no gloves* (*I do not possess any*).

Both verbs have peculiar idiomatic uses. (See Part X.)

Purchases — Shopping

1. What do you want to do this morning?

2. I would like to go out to do some shopping [para hacer unas compras].

3. And where do you want to make your purchases?

4. I really [verdaderamente] do not know. You have been [ha estado] several [varias] times [veces[1]], in Buenos Aires. Can you not tell me where I can get some good gloves?

AFFIRMATIVE

I have been
you have been
he has been
we have been
you have been
they have been

INTERROGATIVE:

have I been?
have you been?
has he been?
have we been?
have you been?
have they been?

---

[3] The *Past Participle*, which is used for the formation of compound tenses, ends in the first conjugation in **ado,** and in the second and third conjugation in **ido.**

If, therefore, we take **hablar, vender** and **vivir** as paradigms, the past participles are **hablado,** spoken; **vendido,** sold; **vivido,** lived.

The compound tenses are: he hablado, *I have spoken;* he vendido, *I have sold;* he vivido, *I have lived.*

[4] **Usted** and **ustedes,** like the other pronouns, used in interrogative sentences with compound tenses, stand directly after the participle.

¿Ha recibido V. la carta?	*Have you received the letter?*
¿No me ha entendido V.?	*Did you not understand me?* / *Have you not understood me?*
¿Qué ha perdido V.?	*What have you lost?*
¿Ha leído V. los periódicos?	*Have you read the papers?*

5. ¿Es eso todo lo que necesita? /neɵe'sita/

6. No, tengo[1] también que[1] comprar algunas frioleras para mi esposa. /frio'leras/

7. Ella necesita unas horquillas para el pelo, un cepillo de cabeza, un cepillo para dientes, un peine y otras chucherías. /or'kiʎas ɵe'piʎo ka'βeɵa 'djentes 'pɛjne tʃutʃe'rias/

8. Sírvase V. venir conmigo,[2] pues no sé en donde se pueden conseguir todas estas cosas. /kɔn'miɣo kɔnse'ɣir/

9. V. puede encontrarlas[3] cerca de[4] aquí. ¿Quiere V. salir immediatamente? /eŋkɔn'trarlas'ɵerkaðea'ki/

10. Sí, inmediatamente. Mi señora quiere salir y necesita todas esas cosas.

11. Está bien; aquí en⌃frente hay una buena tienda en donde V. puede conseguir todo lo que necesita.

---

[1] There is no verb in Spanish corresponding to the English *I must*. All expressions with *I must*, or "I have to," or "I am obliged to" are expressed by **tener que** with the verb in the infinitive, as:

Tengo que escribir cartas.	*I have letters to write.*
Tenemos que salir.	*We must go out.*
¿Tiene V. que enviar un telegrama?	*Are you obliged to send a telegram?*

There are a number of other constructions for the English *must, to be obliged to*, as **haber de** or **hay que**, as:

He de hacer la correspondencia,	*I have to attend to the correspondence.*
¿Qué hay que hacer?	*What is there to be done?*

Compare Part X.

[2] The preposition **con**, *with*, is used in a peculiar manner with the personal pronouns **mí**, *me;* **ti**, *thee;* **sí**, *to him*, viz., **conmigo**, *with me;* **contigo**, *with thee;* **consigo**, *with him*.

[3] **Encontrar**, *to meet*, belongs to the same class of irregular verbs which change the **o** of the second syllable into **ue** in the whole of the singular and third person plural of the indicative and subjunctive present, and in the corresponding persons in the imperative.

PRESENT

Indicative	*Subjunctive*
Yo encuentro	encuentre
V. encuentra	encuentre
él encuentra	encuentre
nosotros encontramos	encontremos
Vds. encuentran	encuentren
ellos encuentran	encuentren

5. Is that [eso] all you need [necesita]?

6. No, I have to buy some small things [algunas frioleras] for my wife.

7. She needs hairpins [unas horquillas para el pelo], a hair-brush [un cepillo de cabeza], a tooth-brush [un cepillo para dientes], a comb [un peine] and some other trifles [otras chucherías].

8. Please come along with me [venir conmigo²] as [pues] I do not know where to get [conseguir] all these things.

9. You can get them quite near [cerca de⁴ aquí]. Do you want to go at once?

10. Certainly, at once. My wife wishes to go out and needs all these articles.

11. All right; directly opposite [enfrente] is a very good shop, where you can get everything you need.

---

⁴ The following prepositions require **de** after them:

acerca de	*concerning, about*	dentro de	*within, in, into*
además de	*beside*	después de	*after (time or order)*
alrededor de	*around*	detrás de	*behind*
antes de	*before (time or order)*	encima de	*on, over*
		fuera de	*outside, beyond*
cerca de	*near, about*	lejos de	*far from*
debajo de	*under (place)*		
delante de	*before (place)*		

The simple prepositions are:

a	*at, to*	hacia	*toward*
ante	*before*	hasta	*until*
bajo	*under*	mediante	*by means of*
con	*with*	menos	*but, except*
contra	*against*	no obstante	*notwithstanding*
de	*of, from*	para	*for, to*
desde	*from*	por	*by, for, through*
durante	*during*	según	*according to*
en	*in, on, at*	sin	*without*
entre	*between, among*	sobre	*on, upon*
excepto	*except*	tras	*behind*

12. ¿Es una tienda barata?

13. Sí, bastante barata. V. sabe muy bien que todos esos artículos para tocador son aquí mucho más[1] baratos que en los Estados Unidos /toka'ðɔr es'taðosu'niðɔs/

14. Aquí tiene V. la tienda; algo grande, ¿no es verdad?[2] Sí, bastante grande y bonita. /'noezβɛr'ðað? bo'nita/

15. ¿Qué desea V. comprar primero? Guantes.

16. Quiero dos pares de guantes, uno negro y otro oscuro.[3] Sírvase enseñarme unos guantes de cabritilla buenos. /'pares 'neɣro ɔs'kuro kaβri'tiʎa/

17. ¿Los quiere V. muy claros? /'klarɔs/

18. No muy claros. Déme un color que no sea[4] muy claro.

19. ¿De qué precio los quiere V.?—No muy caros.

20. Por cincuenta pesos le puedo dar unos muy buenos.

21. ¿Cuánto es eso en moneda de los Estados Unidos? /mo'neða/

22. Un peso es veinte centavos. Un peso tiene cien centavos. /θen'taβɔs/

---

[1] The *comparative* is formed by placing **más**, *more*, or **menos**, *less*, before the adjectives, as:

    caro, *dear*   más caro, *dearer*   menos caro, *less dear*

The *superlative* is formed either by placing **el, lo, la, más** or **menos** before the adjective, or by adding **ísimo, ísima** to the adjective whose last vowel is then elided, as:

    caro, *dear*   el más caro, *the dearest*
        muy caro or carísimo, *very dear*

The former is called the *relative superlative*, and the latter the *absolute superlative*. The comparative is usually followed by **que**, *than*, as:

    Es más hábil que su hermano   *he is more skilful than his brother*
    él tiene más dinero que yo   *he has more money than I*

For further rules see Part X.

[2] The Spanish mode of expression: "¿No es verdad?" is peculiar. It resembles the German "nicht wahr?", or the French "n'est-ce pas?"

[3] *The principal colors are*—Los colores principales son:

12. Is it an inexpensive shop?

13. Yes, quite [bastante] inexpensive. You know that toilet [tocador] articles are much cheaper here than in the United States.

14. Here is the shop; fairly [algo] large, isn't it [no es verdad]? Yes, quite large and attractive [bonita].

15. What do you want to buy first? Gloves.

16. I want two pairs [pares] of gloves, a pair of black ones and a pair of brown ones. Please show me some [unos] good kid gloves.

17. Do you want a light tan [claros]?

18. Not too light; give me [déme] a good medium shade.

19. What price do you wish to pay?—Not too expensive, please.

20. For fifty pesos I can give you very good gloves.

21. How much is that in United States money [en moneda de los Estados Unidos]?

22. A peso is 20 cents [centavos]. A peso is worth one hundred centavos.

Black	negro	*Pink*	rosado *or* color de rosa
blue	azul	*red*	rojo
pale blue	azul claro	*purple*	púrpura
dark blue	azul oscuro	*lilac*	lila
brown	castaño	*violet*	violeta
crimson	carmín	*yellow*	amarillo
green	verde	*white*	blanco
olive green	verde olivo	*flesh color*	encarnado
orange	naranja	*ultramarine*	ultramarino

⁴ The subjunctive mood must be employed here, as *a wish* and consequently *a possibility* is implied. The subjunctive present of ser, *to be*, is conjugated:

Yo sea	*I may be*
V. sea	*you may be*
él sea	*he may be*
nosotros seamos	*we may be*
Vds. sean	*you may be*
ellos sean	*they may be*

23. Cinco pesos son un dólar en moneda de los Estados Unidos. ¿No le parecen[1] a V. baratos? /pa'reɵen/

24. Sí, me parecen muy baratos. Por un dólar no tenemos guantes como ésos en los Estados Unidos.

25. ¿Quiere V. probárselos? /pro'βarselɔs/

26. Estos guantes no me sirven; me quedan muy estrechos;—me están muy grandes. /es'tretʃɔs/

27. ¿Cuánto importa todo? /im'pɔrta/

28. Todo importa quince pesos.

Saludos
/sa'luðɔs/

1. Buenos días, ¿cómo está V.?[2]

2. Estoy muy bien, gracias. ¿Qué tal? /'ke'tal/

3. ¿Y cómo está su señora? /se'ɲora/

4. Mi señora está muy bien, gracias.

5. Y V., ¿qué tal?[3]—Perfectamente bien; gracias. (Also: Para servir a V., gracias[4]).

6. Y su hermano, ¿cómo sigue[5]? /'siɣe/

---

[1] *It seems to me*, is expressed by me parece, as:

That seems very dear to me.	Me parece demasiado caro.
It seems all right.	Me parece bien.

In a similar way we say for: "*Doesn't it seem to you?*" or: "*Don't you think?*" **¿No le parece a V.?**

Don't you think the weather is going to clear?	¿No le parece a V. que el tiempo se va a aclarar?
No, I don't think so.	No, no me parece así.
Don't you think it is going to rain?	¿No le parece a V. que va a llover?

[2] As **estar**, *to be*, is used to describe the *temporal* or *accidental* state of persons or things, *i. e.*, when a change is likely to occur at any time, it follows logically that it must be used to denote the *state of health*, as:

How are you?	¿Cómo está V.?
I am well.	Estoy bien.
How is your partner?	¿Cómo está su socio?
He is better.	Está mejor.
This young man is ill.	Este joven está enfermo.

23. Five pesos are equal to a dollar in United States money. Don't you think that they are cheap [no le parecen a V. baratos]?

24. Yes, that's very inexpensive. For a dollar we can't get gloves like [como] those in the United States.

25. Will you try them on [probárselos]?

26. These gloves do not fit me; they are too tight [estrechos];—too large [grandes].

27. How much does that amount [importa] to in all? (Literally: How much amounts to all?)

28. That amounts to 15 pesos in all.

Salutations

1. Good morning, how are you?[2]

2. Thanks, I am pretty well. How are you?

3. And how is your wife [su señora]?

4. My wife is quite well, thank you.

5. And how are you, yourself?—Quite well, thanks.

6. And how is your brother?

---

[3] A strictly idiomatic expression, but very generally used.

[4] **Para servir a V.**, *at your service* (literally: in order to serve you), an idiomatic phrase used as an expression of politeness.

[5] Another mode of expression used in inquiries in regard to health. **Seguir** means literally *to continue* or *to follow*. It is conjugated thus:

PRESENT

Indicative	*Subjunctive*
Yo sigo	siga
V. sigue	siga
él sigue	siga
nosotros seguimos	sigamos
Vds. siguen	sigan
ellos siguen	sigan

7. Espero que esté[1] ya bueno.

8. Yo estoy muy bien, gracias, pero mi pobre hermano, siento[2] decir, no puede salir aún. Todavía está muy débil. /'poβɪɐ 'sjentoðe'ɵir toða'βia 'mwi'ðeβil/

9. Lo siento mucho.[3] ¿Tiene V. un buen médico? /'meðiko/

10. Sí, nuestro médico es muy bueno, pero mi hermano estuvo[4] muy grave y, como le dije[5] a V., está aún muy débil. /es'tuβo'mwi'ɣraβe komole'ðixɛaws'te/

11. Pero pronto se pondrá[6] bueno. Es muy joven, su constitución es buena y a su edad se recobra fácilmente la salud. /pɔn'dra 'xɔβen kɔnstitu'ɵjɔn e'ðað/

---

[1] The subjunctive **esté** must be employed here, as a wish and possibility is implied. *The subjunctive of the present tense of* **estar** *is conjugated:*

Yo esté	*I may be*
V. esté	*you may be*
él esté	*he may be*
nosotros estemos	*we may be*
Vds. estén	*you may be*
ellos estén	*they may be*

[2] **Siento** from sentir, *to feel* or *to be sorry. I am very sorry*, lo siento mucho. It is conjugated thus in the

PRESENT

Indicative	*Subjunctive*
Yo siento	sienta
V. siente	sienta
él siente	sienta
nosotros sentimos	sintamos
Vds. sienten	sientan
ellos sienten	sientan

[3] The use of the adverbs **muy** and **mucho** must be noted by the student. *Muy* can never qualify a verb and cannot stand alone. *Mucho*, on the other hand, can be used with verbs only and stands by itself. *Mucho* is always used in connection with **hacer** when referring to the weather.

Hace mucho frío.	*It is very cold.*
Hace mucho calor.	*It is very warm.*
Hace mucho sol.	*It is very sunny.*
¿Hace mucho frío hoy? Sí, mucho.	*Is it very cold to-day? Yes, very.*
¿Habla muy bien? Sí, muy bien.	*Does he speak very well? Yes, very well.*

7. I hope [espero] he has quite recovered [esté ya bueno].

8. I am very well, thanks, but my poor [pobre] brother, I am sorry [siento[2]] to say, cannot yet [aún] go out. He is still [todavía] very weak [débil].

9. I am very sorry for that [lo siento mucho[3]]. Have you a good physician? [médico]?

10. Yes, our physician is very good, but my brother was [estuvo[4]] very ill [grave] and is, as I told [dije[5]] you, very weak as yet.

11. But he will surely get [se pondrá[6]] well soon [pronto]. He is quite young [joven], his constitution [su constitución] is good, and at his age [edad] health is recovered easily [fácilmente].

---

[4] The **Pretérito** (past definite tense) denotes what occurred on a certain occasion wholly past, whether it happened yesterday, a few weeks before, or ages ago. It is, therefore, called *the historical tense* and is used especially in narration. **Estuve,** *I was,* is conjugated:

Yo estuve	*I was*
V. estuvo	*you were*
él estuvo	*he was*
nosotros estuvimos	*we were*
Vds. estuvieron	*you were*
ellos estuvieron	*they were*

Compare Part X.

[5] **Dije** is the Pretérito of the irregular verb **decir,** *to say, to tell.* It is conjugated:

Yo dije	*I said*
V. dijo	*you said*
él dijo	*he said*
nosotros dijimos	*we said*
Vds. dijeron	*you said*
ellos dijeron	*they said*

[6] **Pondrá** is the future of the irregular verb **poner,** *to put, to place.* **Ponerse** means *to become.* The Future is conjugated:

Yo pondré	*I shall put*
V. pondrá	*you will put*
él pondrá	*he will put*
nosotros pondremos	*we shall put*
Vds. pondrán	*you will put*
ellos pondrán	*they will put*

12. ¡Dios lo quiera!
¡Ojalá!

13. Mañana volveré a verle a V., pues deseo saber cómo sigue su hermano. Mientras tanto déle V. mis recuerdos.

14. ¡Hasta la vista!

12. Let us hope so. (Literally: May God [Dios] will [quiera] it. **Or:** Would to God [ojalá]!)

13. To-morrow I will call on you again [volveré a verle a V.]. I must see how your brother is getting along [sigue]. Meanwhile [mientras tanto] give him my regards [mis recuerdos].

14. Good-bye [hasta la vista]!

VOCABULARIO	VOCABULARY
Una autopista /awto'pista/	A super-highway
La carretera /karːɛ'tera/	The highway
El camino	The road
La curva /'kurβa/	The curve
Una cuesta /'kwesta/	A hill
Cuesta arriba, abajo	Uphill, downhill
El paso a nivel /'pasoani'βel/	The level crossing
El cruce /'kruθe/	The crossroads
La cuneta	The ditch
Un automóvil /awto'moβil/ Un coche /'kotʃe/ Un carro /'karːɔ/	A motor car
El camión /ka'mjɔn/	The truck
El autobús /awto'βus/	The bus
Una motocicleta /motoθi'kleta/	A motorcycle
Una bicicleta /biθi'kleta/	A bicycle
Conducir[1] /kɔndu'θir/ Manejar /maneɛ'xar/	To drive
De prisa	Fast
Despacio	Slowly
Arrancar /arːaŋ'kar/	To start (a vehicle)
Frenar	To brake
El freno	The brake
Parar	To stop

---

[1] For the conjugation of this verb see p. 280.

PART FOUR

CONTENTS

Conversación

1. ¿Entiende V. el español?

2. Lo entiendo un poco, pero no muy bien.

3. ¿Me entiende V. cuando hablo de prisa? /de'prisa/

4. Le entiendo cuando V. habla despacio y claro, pero cuando V.
empieza[1] a[2] hablar de prisa, o mejor[3] dicho, cuando habla con
naturalidad, no entiendo casi una palabra. /em'pjeθa'βlar
me'xɔr'ðitʃo kɔnnaturali'ðaδ/

5. ¡Qué lástima!
Eso es una lástima. /'lastima/

6. A su oído de V.[4] le falta práctica. /o'iðo 'falta 'praktika/

7. V. debe escuchar más a los españoles cuando hablan entre sí.
/esku'tʃar entre'si/

---

[1] **Empezar**, *to begin*, belongs to that large class of irregular verbs which insert
i before the stem-vowel e—ie throughout the singular and in the third person
plural of the present indicative and the subjunctive and in the same persons
in the imperative.

PRESENT

Indicative	*Subjunctive*
Yo empiezo	empiece
V. empieza	empiece
él empieza	empiece
nosotros empezamos	empecemos
Vds. empiezan	empiecen
ellos empiezan	empiecen

The subjunctive is written with a **c**, because all verbs ending in **zar** change **z**
into **c** before **e**

[2] Verbs of motion, destination, encouragement, inclination or habit, or reflexive
verbs indicating strong moral decision or effort require the preposition **a** before
the infinitive of the verb they govern. Make note of the following verbs:

animar a	*to encourage to*	enviar a	*to send to*
aprender a	*to learn to*	habituar a	*to accustom to*
aspirar a	*to aspire to*	inclinar a	*to incline to*
comenzar a	⎫	ir a	*to go to*
echar a	⎬ *to begin to*	ponerse a	*to begin to*
empezar a	⎭	tender a	*to aim to*
enseñar a	*to teach to*	volver a	*to return to*
			to—again

For full list and examples see Part X.

Conversation

1. Do you understand Spanish?

2. I can understand Spanish a little, but not very well.

3. Do you understand me when I speak rapidly?

4. I understand you when you talk slowly and distinctly; but when you begin [empieza] to [a][2] speak rapidly or, perhaps I ought to say [mejor[3] dicho], when you talk naturally, I can scarcely [casi] understand a word.

5. That's a great pity [lástima]!

6. Your ear [oído] lacks [falta] training [práctica].

7. You ought to listen [escuchar] more to Spanish-speaking people when they converse with one another [entre sí].

---

[3] The following adjectives are compared irregularly:

Grande	*large*	mayor	*larger*	el, la, lo mayor	*the largest*
pequeño	*small*	menor	*smaller*	el, la, lo menor	*the smallest*
bueno	*good*	mejor	*better*	el, la, lo mejor	*the best*
malo	*bad*	peor	*worse*	el, la, lo peor	*the worst*

The following adverbs have also an irregular comparative and superlative:

bien	*well*		mejor	*better*
mal	*badly*		peor	*worse*
mucho	*much*		más	*more*
poco	*little*		menos	*less*
lo mejor, muy bien			*best, very well*	
lo peor, muy mal			*worst, very badly*	
lo más, muchísimo			*most*	
lo menos, poquísimo			*least*	

See Part X.

[4] Usted is—as we have noticed before—frequently used in connection with its substitute le in the pleonastic construction, when joined to the *same* verb:

Le diré a V.	*I shall tell you.*
¿Qué le pasa a V.?	*What is the matter with you?*
Le busco a V.	*I am looking for you.*
¿Le he servido a V. a su gusto?	*Have I served you to your satisfaction?*

Le and se are often used in Spanish, not only with **usted,** but with a noun:

| A mi padre le pareció muy caro. | *It seemed very dear to my father.* |
| A mi hermana se lo había dicho. | *He had told it to my sister.* |

8. Lo he tratado de[1] hacer, pero me parece que los españoles **hablan** mucho más de prisa que nosotros.

9. Eso le parece a V. Con tiempo y práctica se acostumbrará[2] el oído y ya verá V.[3] lo fácil que es entender cualquiera[4] conversación. /'tjempo seakɔstumbra'raelo'iðo kwal'kjera/

10. ¡Ojalá! Pero dispense, acaba de[5] usar una expresión que me es nueva. ¿Qué quiere decir literalmente "Ya verá V."?

11. "Ya verá V." quiere decir literalmente: "Already you will see." ¿Entiende V. ya lo que quiere decir: "Ya verá V."?

12. Sí, ya lo entiendo y deseo que me dé V. siempre la traducción literal. /keme'ðews'te'sjemprelatraðuk'ejɔnlite'ral/

13. Las traducciones literales, amigo mío,[6] son imposibles en muchos casos. /impo'siβles 'kasɔs/

---

[1] The following verbs require **de** before the infinitive:

acabar de	*to have just*
acordarse de	*to remember to*
alegrarse de	*to be glad*
cesar de	*to cease to*
dejar de	*to fail to*
desistir de	*to cease from*
disuadir de	*to dissuade from*
encargar de	*to commission to*
excusar de	*to excuse from*
eximir de	*to free from*
haber de	*to have to*
ocuparse de	*to busy oneself with*
olvidarse de	*to forget to*
tratar de	*to try to*

Ejemplos

Acabo de llegar.	*I have just arrived*
No me acuerdo de haberlo dicho.	*I do not remember saying so.*
Se me olvidó de decirlo.	*I forgot to tell it.*
No deja de estudiar.	*He does not cease studying.*
Trataré de hacerlo.	*I shall try to do it.*

[2] **Acostumbrar** means *to accustom;* **acostumbrarse** (reflexive), *to get accustomed to.*
[3] Future of **ver,** *to see.*
[4] **Cualquiera,** plural **cualesquiera,** *any* (*whatever*), is used both as an adjective or as a pronoun, relating to persons or things.

8. I have tried [tratado] to [de] do that, but it seems to me that t⟨ Spanish people talk a great deal faster than we.

9. That only seems so to you. In time and by practice your ear will get accustomed [se acostumbrará] to it and you will find it quite easy [ya verá V. lo fácil que es] to understand almost any [cualquiera] conversation.

10. I hope so [ojalá]! But pardon me, you have just used [acaba V. de usar] an expression which is new to me. What is the literal meaning of: "Ya verá V."?

11. "Ya verá V." means literally: "Already [then] you will see." Do you understand now what "Ya verá V." means?

12. Yes, now I understand it and I wish that you would always give [dé] me literal translations [la traducción literal].

13. Literal translations, my dear friend [amigo mío[6]] are in many cases [en muchos casos] an impossibility.

---

[5] **Acabar de** corresponds to the French *venir de* and expresses our *just, just now*, as:

Acabo de recibir su carta.	*I have just received your letter.*
Acabo de oír de su llegada.	*I have just heard of his arrival.*
Acaban de dar las cuatro.	*It has just struck four (o'clock).*

[6] The absolute possessive adjectives are:

Singular	*Plural*	
mío, mía	míos, mías	*my*
tuyo, tuya	tuyos, tuyas	*thy*
suyo, suya	suyos, suyas	{ *his her its your*
nuestro, nuestra	nuestros, nuestras	*our*
vuestro, vuestra	vuestros, vuestras	*your*
suyo, suya	suyos, suyas	{ *their your*

These absolute forms are employed in direct address, but without the definite article:

amigo mío	*my friend (my dear friend)*
hijo mío	*my son (my dear son)*
muy señores míos	*Gentlemen (Dear Sirs [in letters])*

Compare Part X.

14. ¿Y por qué?

15. Porque cada idioma tiene sus peculiaridades, sus modismos y formas de expresión que nunca se pueden traducir literalmente.[1]
/'kaðaj 'ðjoma pekuljari'ðaðes mo'ðizmɔs espre'sjɔn traðu'eir/

16. ¿Hay muchos modismos en español?

IMPORTANCIA DEL IDIOMA ESPAÑOL

17. El idioma español, amigo mío, es uno de los más ricos del mundo. Entre[2] los idiomas modernos el francés y el español son muy ricos en expresiones y por lo tanto tienen muchos modismos.

18. ¿Tendría V. la bondad de citar algunos de los modismos más usados? Quiero decir de los que se usan en la conversación diaria.
/ei'tar u'saðɔs/

19. Con mucho gusto. ¿Se acuerda V. del verbo "tener" que estudiamos[3] en el primer libro? /a'kwɛrða/

20. Sí, me acuerdo[4] perfectamente, pero no estudiamos sino el presente del indicativo. /'sinoɛlpre'senteðelindika'tiβo/

---

[1] Adverbs are formed from adjectives by adding **mente** to the feminine form of the adjective, as:

antiguo	*old*	antiguamente	*in olden times*
común	*common*	comúnmente	*commonly*
fácil	*easy*	fácilmente	*easily*
fuerte	*strong*	fuertemente	*strongly*
franco	*frank*	francamente	*frankly*

[2] **Entre**, *between, among*, belongs to the simple prepositions which govern the accusative. Compare Part X.

[3] The Pretérito, the use of which has already been explained, is formed by adding the following endings to the stem of regular verbs:

1.	2 and 3.
——é	——í
——ó	——ió
——ó	——ió
——amos	——imos
——aron	——ieron
——aron	——ieron

The regular verbs of the second and third conjugation have the same endings. If, therefore, we take **hablar**, *to speak;* **vender**, *to sell*, and **vivir**, *to live*, as paradigms we have the following conjugations for the

14. And why?

15. Because every [cada] language possesses its own peculiarities [peculiaridades], its own idioms and modes [formas] of expression which can never [nunca] be translated [traducir] literally.

16. Are there [hay] many idiomatic expressions in Spanish?

IMPORTANCE OF THE SPANISH LANGUAGE

17. The Spanish language, my dear friend, is one of the richest [uno de los más ricos] tongues in the world [del mundo]. Among modern [modernos] tongues French and Spanish are very rich in expressions and, as a matter of course [por lo tanto], contain many idioms.

18. Would you have the kindness [la bondad] to mention [citar] some of the most generally used [usados] idioms? I mean those which are used in every-day [diaria] conversation.

19. With much pleasure [gusto]. You remember [se acuerda V.] the verb "tener" which we studied [estudiamos³] in our first book?

20. Yes, I remember it perfectly, but we studied only [sino] the indicative present [el presente del indicativo].

PRETÉRITO

1.	2.	3.
Yo hablé	vendí	viví
V. habló	vendió	vivió
él habló	vendió	vivió
nosotros hablamos	vendimos	vivimos
Vds. hablaron	vendieron	vivieron
ellos hablaron	vendieron	vivieron

Of course, this would be rendered: I spoke, you spoke, he spoke, we spoke, you spoke, they spoke, etc., etc.

⁴ **Acordarse,** *to remember*, is a reflexive verb. It belongs to that numerous class of slightly irregular verbs which change the o of the stem-vowel into **ue** throughout the whole singular and in the second and third person plural of the present indicative and subjunctive, and in the same persons in the imperative mood:

PRESENT

Indicative	*Subjunctive*
Yo me acuerdo	me acuerde
V. se acuerda	se acuerde
él se acuerda	se acuerde
nosotros nos acordamos	nos acordemos
Vds. se acuerdan	se acuerden
ellos se acuerdan	se acuerden

21. Pues bien, V. debe estudiar todo el verbo,[1] pues su uso es muy común y presenta muchas dificultades a las personas de habla inglesa. /ˈtoðoɛlˈβɛrβo koˈmun preˈsenta difikulˈtaðes/

22. Primeramente, tenemos dos verbos correspondientes a "to have," a saber: "tener" y "haber."

USO DE "HABER" Y "TENER"

23. Lo sé. Eso fué explicado antes.

24. Por consiguiente V. sabe que "haber" se usa sólo para formar los tiempos compuestos; por ejemplo: "Le he mandado a V. un telegrama." "Se lo he explicado a V. la última vez." "Nunca he oído tal cosa." /pɔrkɔnsiˈɣiente porɛˈxemplo teleˈɣrama/

25. Sí, lo veo muy claro, y también sé que "tener" es un verbo activo que se puede usar en lugar del verbo "poseer" sin alterar en nada el significado de la oración. /akˈtiβo poˈseːr siɣnifiˈkaðoðela ɔraˈθjɔn/

26. Me alegro de que V. lo vea[2] tan claro. ¿Ha aprendido V. toda la conjugación de "tener"? /kɔnxuɣaˈθjɔn/

27. No, todavía no.

28. Pues V. debe estudiarla. V. la encuentra[3] en el libro número diez, en el cual está la gramática del idioma español. /enˈkwentra ˈliβroˈnumeroˈðjeθ graˈmatika/

---

[1] Todo, toda, *all, whole, every,* when used as an adjective, is followed by the definite article, as:

todo el día	*the whole day, all day*
toda la noche	*the whole night, all night*
todos los meses	*every month*
todas las mañanas	*every morning*
todas las tardes	*every afternoon*
todas las semanas	*every week*
todos los años	*every year*

[2] The subjunctive is used after verbs denoting joy, grief, vexation, surprise, etc., as:

I am glad you know it.	Me alegro de que lo sepa V.
I am glad it rains.	Me alegro de que llueva.
It is too bad he will not come.	Es una lástima que no venga.

21. Well, then [pues bien], you ought to study the whole verb, as the use of it is very common [común] and presents many difficulties [muchas dificultades] to English-speaking persons.

22. To begin with [primeramente], we have two verbs corresponding to "to have," viz.: [a saber[2]] "tener" and "haber."

USE OF "HABER" AND OF "TENER"

23. I know that; that was explained before. (Literally: It [I] know.)

24. Consequently [por consiguiente] you know that "haber" is used mainly for the formation of [para formar] compound tenses [los tiempos compuestos], as for instance [por ejemplo]: "I have sent [mandado] you a telegram [telegrama]." "I have explained this to you the last time [la última vez]." "I have never heard [oído] anything like it [tal cosa]."

25. Yes, all this is clear to me and I also know that "tener" is an active [activo] verb and can generally be used instead of "to possess" [poseer] without [sin] affecting [alterar] the meaning [el significado] of the sentence [la oración].

26. I am glad that this is clear to you [V. lo vea[2] tan claro]. Have you learned the whole conjugation [la conjugación] of "tener"?

27. No, not yet.

28. Well, you must study it. You will find [encuentra] it in the tenth book [libro número diez] which contains [en el cual está] the grammar [la gramática] of the Spanish language.

---

[2] Encontrar, *to meet*, belongs to that numerous class of slightly irregular verbs which change the stem-vowel o into ue in the whole singular, and the second and third person plural in the present indicative and subjunctive and in the same persons in the imperative.

PRESENT

Indicative	Subjunctive
Yo encuentro	encuentre
V. encuentra	encuentre
él encuentra	encuentre
nosotros encontramos	encontremos
Vds. encuentran	encuentren
ellos encuentran	encuentren

29. Estúdiela V. bien, y en la próxima lección le enseñaré a V. algunos modismos en los que se emplea el verbo "tener." Por ahora, adiós. /es'tuðjela 'prɔksimalek'ejɔn a'ðjɔs/

30. ¡Vaya V.[1] con Dios! /'bajaws'tekɔn'djɔs/

LAS ESTACIONES DEL AÑO

1. Buenos días, amigo mío. ¡Cuánto me alegro de verle a V.! ¿Cómo está V.?

2. Muy bien, gracias. Y V., ¿qué tal se siente[2] hoy?

3. Estoy muy bien, gracias. Este delicioso tiempo de primavera me gusta[3] mucho. /deli'ejoso prima'ßera me'ɣusta/

4. "¿Tiempo de primavera?" — Dispense V. que repita[4] esas palabras, pero como me son desconocidas no sé lo que quieren decir. /rːɛ'pita deskono'eiðas/

---

[1] **Vaya V.** is the subjunctive (or imperative) of the irregular verb **ir.** The present tense is conjugated:

PRESENT

Indicative	Subjunctive
Yo voy	vaya
V. va	vaya
él va	vaya
nosotros vamos	vayamos
Vds. van	vayan
ellos van	vayan

For full conjugation see Part X.

[2] **Sentir,** *to feel, to perceive,* is an irregular verb. The conjugation of the present tense is:

PRESENT

Indicative		Subjunctive	
Yo siento	nosotros sentimos	sienta	sintamos
V. siente	Vds. sienten	sienta	sientan
él siente	ellos sienten	sienta	sientan

Compare Part X.

29. Study it well and in our next lesson I will teach [enseñaré] you some idioms in which [en los que] the verb "tener" is used [se emplea]. Good-bye [Adiós] for the present.

30. Good-bye, sir. (Literally: May you go [vaya V.¹] with God [con Dios].)

THE SEASONS OF THE YEAR

1. Good morning, my dear friend! I am delighted to see you. How are you? (Literally: How much [cuánto] I rejoice [me alegro] to [de] see you.)

2. Thanks, I am quite well. And how [qué tal] do **you** feel [se siente²] to-day?

3. I am very well, thank you. This beautiful [delicioso] spring [primavera] weather [tiempo] just suits [gusta³] me.

4. "Spring weather?" Pardon me for repeating [dispense V. que repita] these words after you, but they are unknown [desconocidas] to me and I don't quite know what they mean.

---

³ Gustar, *to please, to like,* is nearly always used as an impersonal verb. In Spanish, therefore, a person does not like a thing, but the thing *is pleasing* to the person. ¿Le gusta a V.? means literally: *Does it please you?*

In the same way we say:

¿Le gusta a V. la lengua castellana?	*Do you like the Spanish language?*
Sí señor, a mí me gusta más que ningún otro idioma.	*Yes, sir, I like it better than any other language.*
¿Le gusta a V.?	*Do you like it?*
¿Qué le gusta a V. más, panecillos, tostadas o pan?	*What do you like best: rolls, toast or bread?*

⁴ Repetir, *to repeat,* is an irregular verb. The conjugation of the present tense is:

PRESENT

Indicative	*Subjunctive*
Yo repito	repita
V. repite	repita
él repite	repita
nosotros repetimos	repitamos
Vds. repiten	repitan
ellos repiten	repitan

5. V. sabe, por supuesto, que tenemos cuatro estaciones, a saber: la primavera, el verano, el otoño y el invierno, pero supongo[1] que sus nombres en español le son a V. nuevos. /pɔrsu'pwesto esta'ejones be'rano o'toɲo im'bjɛrno su'pɔŋgo/

6. Lo son. Déjeme repetirlos con V.: la primavera, el verano, el otoño y el invierno. /'dɛxeme/

7. Bien dicho.[2] Su pronunciación es excelente.

8. Me lisonjea V., señor profesor. Vds. los españoles son muy amantes de cumplimientos. /lisɔn'xɛa a'mantezðekumpli'mjentɔs/

9. No lisonjeros, sino[3] corteses. Se conoce tan poco en este país nuestro carácter, que algunas veces se dice que la cortesía de la gente de habla española es algo superficial. Nada de eso. La cortesía de nuestra gente es innata, pues generalmente se encuentra lo mismo entra la clase pobre que entre la más alta. /kɔr'teses pa'is ka'raktɛr/

10. Ojalá se pudiese[4] decir otro[5] tanto de todas las gentes. Temo que los modales de algunas personas deben parecerles a ustedes algo bruscos. /pu'ðjese 'temo mo'ðales 'bruskɔs/

---

[1] **Suponer,** *to suppose,* is an irregular verb. The verb from which it is derived, is **poner,** *to put, to place.* The present tense is conjugated:

PRESENT

Indicative	Subjunctive
Yo pongo	ponga
V. pone	ponga
él pone	ponga
nosotros ponemos	pongamos
Vds. ponen	pongan
ellos ponen	pongan

For full conjugation see Part X.

[2] **Dicho,** *said,* is the irregular past participle of **decir,** *to say, to tell.* The present tense is conjugated:

PRESENT

Indicative	Subjunctive
Yo digo	diga
V. dice	diga
él dice	diga
nosotros decimos	digamos
Vds. dicen	digan
ellos dicen	digan

5. You know, of course [por supuesto], that we have four seasons [estaciones], viz. [a saber]: spring [la primavera], summer [el verano], autumn [el otoño] and winter [el invierno], but I suppose [supongo] that their Spanish names [nombres] are new to you.

6. They are. Please let me [déjeme] repeat them after you: Spring, summer, autumn and winter.

7. That was very good [bien dicho²]! Your pronunciation is excellent [excelente]!

8. You flatter [lisonjea] me, professor [profesor]. You Spanish people are always so complimentary [amantes de cumplimientos].

9. Not complimentary, but polite. Our character is so little known in this country, that it is sometimes said that the Spanish-speaking people's courtesy is somewhat superficial. Nothing of the kind! Our people's courtesy is inborn, since it is generally found among the poorer classes as well as among the highest.

10. I wish [ojalá] I could say [se pudiese⁴] just as much [otro⁵ tanto] about all people. I am afraid [temo] that the manners [modales] of some persons must appear [parecerles] rather rude [algo bruscos] to you.

---

³ There are three words in Spanish for *but*, viz.: **Pero, mas** and **sino. Pero** and **mas** are placed at the beginning of adversative sentences, as:

Quisiera salir, pero no puedo. *I should like to go out, but I can not.* Sino can be employed only when preceded by a *negative* clause (no verb being expressed after *but*), as:

No es blanco, sino pardo.	*It is not white, but gray.*
No tengo hambre, sino sed.	*I am not hungry, but thirsty.*

⁴ The subjunctive mood must be used here, as a desire is expressed. **Pudiese** is the second form of the subjunctive of the imperfect of the irregular verb **poder,** to be able. It is conjugated:

Yo pudiese	*I might be able*
V. pudiese	*you might be able*
él pudiese	*he might be able*
nosotros pudiésemos	*we might be able*
Vds. pudiesen	*you might be able*
ellos pudiesen	*they might be able*

⁵ **Otro, otra,** *another, other* (plural *others*), is used of persons and things and
Footnotes continued on page 96.

11. Hablando[1] con franqueza, creo que algunas personas podrían aprender un poco de nosotros en este particular; pero también nosotros podríamos aprender de otros muchas cosas, que son mucho más importantes que la urbanidad. Pero volviendo a nuestra conversación. /kɔnfran'keəa partiku'lar bɔl'bjendo/

12. He olvidado de lo que hablábamos.[2] /ɔlβi'ðaðo a'βlaβamɔs/

13. Hablábamos de las estaciones del año, y yo acababa de citarle a V. sus nombres. ¿Se acuerda V. de ellos? /aka'βaβa əi'tarle/

14. Perfectamente: la primavera, el verano, el otoño, y el invierno.

Footnotes continued from page 95.

may be employed as a pronoun or an adjective. The indefinite article cannot be used with it, as in English. The definite article must be employed whenever a distinct person or thing is to be specified.

Déme V. otro libro.	*Give me another book.*

The following expressions with **otro** are idiomatic:

otro tanto	*the same thing*
Yo haría otro tanto	*I would do the same thing*
una y otra vez	*repeatedly*
el otro día	*the other day*
al otro día	*the next day*
otro día	*another day*

[1] **Hablando** is the Gerund of hablar, to speak.
The Gerund ends in

1.	2.	3.
——ando	——iendo	——iendo

We have, therefore, for our paradigms: hablando, *speaking;* vendiendo, *selling;* viviendo, *living.*

The Gerund is used in connection with **estar,** *to be,* similar to the progressive conjugation in English, and expresses the action of the verb as continuing or unfinished:

Estoy leyendo.	*I am reading.*
Estaba escribiendo.	*He was writing.*
Está lloviendo.	*It is raining.*
¿Qué está V. haciendo?	*What are you doing?*

The Gerund is frequently used, as in phrase 11, for the sake of euphony or brevity, where we employ *while, whilst, as, since, if, although,* etc., as:

Deseando ver a V. he venido a Madrid.	*As I wished to see you I came to Madrid.*
Viendo que su socio no venía, se fué.	*When he saw that his partner did not come, he went away.*

For further rules see Part X.

11. Frankly speaking [hablando[1] con franqueza], I think [creo] that some people could [podría] learn a little from us in this particular [este particular]; but we also could learn many things from others [otros] which are much more important than courtesy. But, returning [volviendo] to our conversation.

12. Now I have quite forgotten [olvidado] what we were talking [hablábamos[2]] about.

13. We were talking about the seasons and I had just mentioned their names to you [acababa de citarle a V. sus nombres]. Do you remember [se acuerda V.] them?

14. Perfectly: spring, summer, autumn and winter.

---

[2] The Imperfect adds the following endings to the stem:

1.	2.	3.
——aba	——ía	——ía
——aba	——ía	——ía
——aba	——ía	——ía
——ábamos	——íamos	——íamos
——aban	——ían	——ían
——aban	——ían	——ían

It will be seen that verbs of the second and third conjugations add the same endings. For our three paradigms, *hablar*, *vender* and *vivir*, we have therefore the following conjugation in

THE IMPERFECT

1.	2.	3.
Yo hablaba	vendía	vivía
V. hablaba	vendía	vivía
él hablaba	vendía	vivía
nosotros hablábamos	vendíamos	vivíamos
Vds. hablaban	vendían	vivían
ellos hablaban	vendían	vivían

This in English is: "I was speaking," "you were speaking," "he was speaking," etc.

This tense ought to be called the *descriptive* tense in Spanish. It is used to describe the qualities of persons or things and the state, disposition or place in which they were, as:

Las muchachas estaban vestidas de *The girls were dressed in white and had*
blanco, y tenían flores en los cabellos. *flowers in their hair.*

For full rules in regard to the use of the Imperfect see Part X.

15. Muy bien. ¿Qué tiempo hace hoy?

16. Dispense que le interrumpa;[1] pero por qué dice V. "hace"?

VOCABULARIO **VOCABULARY**

(*Continued*)

El despacho	The office
El cajero /ka'xɛro/	The cashier
El despacho del cajero	The cashier's desk
Pagar /pa'ɣar/	To pay
¿Cuánto importa eso?	How much does that amount (come) to?
El dinero /di'nero/	The money
El cambio /'kambjo/	The change
No tengo cambio.	I have no change.
¿Tiene V. cambio?	Have you any change?
No me dió V. todo el cambio. /djo/	You did not give me all the change.
Cambiar /kam'bjar/	To change, to exchange
¿Puede V. cambiar un billete de cien pesos?	Can you change a hundred dollar bill for me?
El billete	The bill
El papel moneda	The paper money
¿Quiere V. plata o billetes?	Do you want silver or paper?
Vender /ben'dɛr/	To sell
El vendedor /bende'ðɔr/	The salesman
¿A qué precio vende V. esto?	At what price do you sell this?

---

[1] The Subjunctive is employed after verbs expressing entreaty, permission, command, etc., as in phrase 16.

Permítame V. que le haga una pregunta.   *Allow me to ask you a question.*

15. Very good! How is the weather to-day?

16. Pardon me for interrupting you [que le interrumpa[1]]; but why do you say "makes"?

VOCABULARIO	VOCABULARY
¿Cuánto pide V. por esto? /'pide/	How much do you charge for this?
¿Cuánto cobra V. por esto?	How much do you ask for this?
Es demasiado caro. No lo quiero a ese precio. /dema'sjado/	That is too dear; I don't want to take it at that price.
La calidad /kali'dad/	The quality
No me gusta esta calidad. /'gusta/	I don't like this quality. (= not me pleases this quality)
¿Qué tal le gusta a V. ésta?	How do you like this one?
Me gusta más.	I like it better.
El paño /'paɲo/	The cloth
La seda /'seda/	The silk
La lana /'lana/	The wool
El algodón /alɣo'dɔn/	Cotton
El vestido /bes'tido/	The dress
Los vestidos	The dresses
Un vestido de seda	A silk dress
Un vestido de lana	A woolen dress
Un vestido de algodón	A cotton dress
Usar; durar /u'sar du'rar/	To wear
Estos géneros duran mucho.} Dura mucho este género.	These goods wear very well.
Los negocios /ne'ɣoejɔs/	The business
La tienda /'tjenda/	The store; the shop.
La tienda de ropas	The dry goods store.
El sombrero	The hat

VOCABULARIO	VOCABULARY
El sombrerero	The hatter
La modista /mo'ðista/	The milliner
El taller de la modista /ta'ʎer/	The millinery shop
La librería /liβre'ria/	The bookstore
El librero /li'βrero/	The bookseller
El papel; los papeles /pa'pɛl/	The paper; the papers
La papelería /papele'ria/	The stationery store
El zapato /θa'pato/	The shoe
El zapatero /θapa'tero/	The shoemaker
La zapatería /θapate'ria/	The shoestore
El reloj /rːɛ'lo/	The watch
El relojero /rːɛlɔ'xero/	The watchmaker
El comerciante /komɛr'θjante/	The merchant
El pan	The bread
El panadero /pana'ðero/	The baker
La panadería /panaðe'ria/	The bakery
El bollo /'boʎo/	The roll
El pastel	The cake
El carnicero /karni'θero/	The butcher
La carne	The meat
La carnicería /karniθe'ria/	The butcher-shop
El metro /'metro/	The metre
El kilo /'kilo/	The kilo
Una libra /'liβra/	A pound

PART FIVE

CONTENTS

"Hacer" y "tener"

(Continuación)

17. Porque para hablar del tiempo se usa el verbo "hacer."

18. ¡Qué raro! Pero no me debe extrañar eso pues en otras lenguas se usa el mismo verbo.

19. V. tiene razón[1] y para acostumbrarnos al uso de este verbo formemos[2] unas cuantas frases con él. /rːaˈθɔn fɔrˈmemɔs/

20. ¿Me deja V. hacerle una pregunta, señor profesor?

21. Todas las que V. guste.[3] /ˈguste/

22. ¿De qué idioma se deriva el verbo "hacer"? ¿Es árabe? De seguro que no es del latín. /deˈriβa ˈaraβe laˈtin/

23. ¿Y por qué no? Quítele V. la **h** y póngale[4] en su lugar una **f** y dígame[5] después lo que puede ser si no es latín. /ˈkitele ˈatʃe ˈpɔŋgale luˈɣar ˈefe ˈdiɣame/

24. Ya veo su origen latino; pero no quiero interrumpirle más, pues deseo formar frases acerca del tiempo para aprender a usar correctamente ese verbo. /oˈrixen/

---

[1] An idiomatic expression. Other examples and complete rules are to be found in the next lesson.

[2] The imperative mood has, as a matter of fact, only two forms of its own, viz.: the second person singular and plural; all the others are taken from the subjunctive mood.

"Hacer" and "Tener"

(Continuation—from p. 99)

17. Because "hacer" is used [se usa] in reference to the weather.

18. How very peculiar [raro]! And yet it ought not to surprise [extrañar] me, for other languages use the same verb.

19. Precisely so [V. tiene razón[1]]. Now in order that [para] you may become familiar with this verb, let us form [formemos[2]] a number of sentences [unas cuantas frases] with it.

20. May I ask you a question [una pregunta], professor?

21. As many as [todas las que] you like [guste[3]].

22. From which language is "hacer" derived [se deriva]? Is it Arabic [árabe]? It surely [de seguro] does not come from the Latin [latín].

23. And why not? Take away [quítele V.] the *h*, put [póngale] an *f* in its place [su lugar] and then [después] tell me [dígame] what else this word is but [sino] Latin.

24. Now I see its Latin origin [origen] but I will not interrupt you [interrumpirle] any more as I am anxious to form some phrases about [acerca] the weather so that [para] I may learn to [a] use that verb correctly.

---

[3] The subjunctive is used in relative sentences when the relative refers to persons, objects or ideas which are mentioned in an indefinite or uncertain sense, as:

Hay pocos que lo hagan.	*There are but few who do it.*
Venga lo que viniera.	*Come what will!*

[4] Irregular imperative of **poner.**

[5] Irregular imperative of **decir.**

1. Buenos días, amigo mío. ¡Cuánto me alegro de verle! ¿Qué tal le va[1] desde que tuve el gusto de verle a V.? La última vez que le vi[2] V. tenía dolor de cabeza. Espero que V. se halle[3] hoy mejor. /'tuβe bi 'aʎe/

Yo tuve	/'tuβe/
V. tuvo	/'tuβo/
él tuvo	
nosotros tuvimos	/tu'βimɔs/
Vds. tuvieron	/tu'βjerɔn/
ellos tuvieron	

2. Gracias, ya estoy mejor, mejor dicho, bueno y dispuesto a continuar nuestra lección. /dis'pwesto kɔntinu'ar/

3. Me alegro mucho, pero quítese el sobretodo y siéntese.[4] /'kitese soβre'toðo 'sjentese/

4. ¿En dónde[5] me siento, señor profesor?

5. Siéntese en esta silla, y ahora empecemos. ¿De qué hablamos la última vez? /'siʎa/

---

[1] Another mode of expression, similar to the German: "Wie geht es Ihnen?" Thus:

¿Qué tal (*or* cómo) le va a V.?	*How do you do?*
¿Cómo le va a V. en los negocios?	*How are you getting on in business?*
¿Cómo va de salud?	*How is your health?*

[2] Vi is the preterite tense of the irregular verb **ver**, *to see*. It is conjugated:

Yo vi	*I saw*
V. vió	*you saw*
él vió	*he saw*
nosotros vimos	*we saw*
Vds. vieron	*you saw*
ellos vieron	*they saw*

[3] The subjunctive must be used here because possibility is implied.

[4] Sentarse, *to be seated*, belongs to that numerous class of verbs which are reflexive in Spanish. In English these are for the most part passive verbs, as: **equivocarse**, *to be mistaken;* **engañarse**, *to be deceived;* **disgustarse**, *to be displeased*,

1. Good morning, my dear friend. Delighted to see you! How have you been since I had [tuve] the pleasure of seeing you? The last time I saw [vi] you you had a headache [dolor de cabeza]. I trust you feel [se halle V.] better to-day.

> I had
> you had
> he had
> we had
> you had
> they had

2. Thanks, I am a great deal better; that is, I am quite well and ready [dispuesto] to [a] go on [continuar] with our lesson.

3. I am very glad of that, but please take off [quítese] your overcoat [el sobretodo] and sit down [siéntese⁴].

4. Where shall I sit, professor?

5. On this chair [esta silla], please. And now let us begin [empecemos]. What were we talking about the last time?

---

etc. Verbs compounded in English with *to get* or *to become* are also used reflexively in Spanish, as: **enfermarse,** *to get ill (to fall ill)*; **enriquecerse,** *to become rich,* etc.

Sentar (and of course, **sentarse**) changes the stem-vowel into ie throughout the singular and the third person plural of the present indicative and subjunctive, and in the same persons in the imperative.

PRESENT

Indicative		*Subjunctive*	
Yo me siento			me siente
V. se sienta			se siente
él se sienta			se siente
nosotros nos sentamos			nos sentemos
Vds. se sientan			se sienten
ellos se sientan			se sienten

⁵ **En,** *in,* when placed before **donde,** *where,* means *within, inside of.* When motion is expressed or implied *where* should be expressed by **a donde,** *where, whereto, whither,* and **de donde,** *wherefrom, whence,* as:

¿A dónde va V.?	*Where are you going?*
¿De dónde viene V.?	*Where do you come from?*

6. V. me había[1] explicado el uso del verbo "hacer" con referencia al tiempo.

7. ¡Ah! sí, ya me acuerdo. ¿Y ha aprendido V. de memoria la conjugación del verbo "hacer"? /deme'morja kɔnxuɣa'ejɔn/

8. Sí señor. "Hacer" es muy irregular, pero creo que sé toda la conjugación. /irːɛɣu'lar/

9. ¡Veamos! Conjugue V. el indicativo presente. /kɔn'xuɣe/

Yo hago	/'aɣo/
V. hace	/'aɵe/
él hace	
nos.[2] hacemos	/a'ɵemɔs/
Vds. hacen	/'aɵen/
ellos hacen	

10. Bien, muy bien. Y el subjuntivo presente.

Yo haga	/'aɣa/
V. haga	
él haga	
nos. hagamos	/a'ɣamɔs/
Vds. hagan	/a'ɣan/
ellos hagan	

---

[1] The pupil should study the whole conjugation of "haber" in Part X.

Modo indicativo del verbo "haber"

(To have)

	Yo	*Usted*	*Él*	*Nosotros*	*Ustedes*	*Ellos*
Presente:	he	ha	ha	hemos	han	han
Imperfecto:	había	había	había	habíamos	habían	habían
Pretérito:	hube	hubo	hubo	hubimos	hubieron	hubieron
Futuro:	habré	habrá	habrá	habremos	habrán	habrán
Condicional:	habría	habría	habría	habríamos	habrían	habrían

Gerundio:	habiendo
Participio:	habido

6. You had [había] explained [explicado] the use of "hacer" in reference to the weather.

7. Ah! yes, I remember. And have you learned the conjugation [la conjugación] of "hacer" by heart [de memoria]?

8. Yes, sir. "Hacer" is very irregular, but I think I know the whole conjugation.

9. Well, let us see [veamos]! Conjugate the indicative present.

> I make
> you make
> he makes
> we make
> you make
> they make

10. Good, very good. And now the present of the subjunctive.

> I may make
> you may make
> he may make
> we may make
> you may make
> they may make

---

[2] In future we shall abbreviate **nosotros** into **nos.**

11. ¡Bravo! Y ahora el pretérito.

Yo hice	/'iɵe/
V. hizo	/'iɵo/
él hizo	
nos. hicimos	/i'ɵimɔs/
Vds. hicieron	/i'ɵjerɔn/
ellos hicieron	

12. Bien, muy bien. Y ahora el futuro. /fu'turo/

Yo haré	/a're/
V. hará	/a'ra/
él hará	
nos. haremos	/a'remɔs/
Vds. harán	/a'ran/
ellos harán	

13. ¡Bravo! Y el condicional. /kɔndiɵjo'nal/

Yo haría	/a'ria/
V. haría	
él haría	
nos. haríamos	/a'riamɔs/
Vds. harían	/a'rian/
ellos harían	

14. ¡Es V. un buen estudiante! Conjugue V. el subjuntivo imperfecto, la primera forma.[1]

Yo hiciera	/i'ɵjera/
V. hiciera	
él hiciera	
nos. hiciéramos	/i'ɵjeramɔs/
Vds. hicieran	/i'ɵjeran/
ellos hicieran	

---

[1] There is no material difference between the first and second forms of the imperfect of the subjunctive.

In either form it is employed after verbs in any past tense in the indicative, and after the conditional, as:

11. Excellent! And now the past.

> I made
> you made
> he made
> we made
> you made
> they made

12. Good, very good. And now the future.

> I shall make
> you will make
> he will make
> we shall make
> you will make
> they will make

13. Excellent! And the conditional.

> I should make
> you would make
> he would make
> we should make
> you would make
> they would make

14. You are indeed a diligent student [un buen estudiante]! Conjugate now the first form[1] of the imperfect of the subjunctive.

> I might make
> you might make
> he might make
> we might make
> you might make
> they might make

Desearía que V. me hiciera (*or* hiciese) ese favor.   *I wish you would do me that favor.*

Le mandaron que fuese (*or* fuera) a Veracruz.   *They ordered him to go to Veracruz.*

15. Muy bien. Y la segunda forma.

Yo hiciese   /i'ejese/

V. hiciese

él hiciese

nos. hiciésemos   /i'ejesemɔs/

Vds. hiciesen   /i'ejesen/

ellos hiciesen

16. ¡Bravo! No tengo duda de que V. vencerá muy pronto todas las dificultades del idioma español. /'duða benee'ra/

17. V. no puede imaginarse lo mucho que quiero aprenderlo. No hay idioma que sea[1] más importante para el hombre de negocios que el hermoso idioma de Cervantes. /impɔr'tante 'ɔmbreðene'ɣoejɔs eer'ßantes/

18. V. tiene mucha razón. El mercado natural de este país está en el sur, y con la excepción del Brasil en donde se habla el portugués, en todo el continente americano al sur del Río Grande se habla el español. /mɛr'kaðonatu'ral sur bra'sil pɔrtu'ɣes kɔnti'nente rjo'ɣrande/

19. Los hombres de estado de este país y muchos hombres de negocios empiezan a ver esto, y para obtener los mercados sudamericanos debemos conocer[2] el idioma y las necesidades comerciales de esos países. /em'pjeean suðameri'kanɔs kono'eer neeesi'ðaðes komer'ejales/

EL TIEMPO

20. Sin duda alguna. Pero ahora formemos algunas oraciones idiomáticas con el verbo "hacer." ¿Cómo diría V.:[3] "The weather was very bad yesterday"? /ora'ejonesiðjo'matikas di'ria/

21. Oh, eso es muy fácil. Ayer hizo muy mal tiempo. /a'jɛr/

---

[1] The subjunctive mood is employed after *impersonal* expressions, unless they denote positive certainty:

Es extraño que V. no lo sepa.	*It is strange that you do not know it.*
Es lástima que no venga.	*It is a pity that he does not come.*
Es necesario que lo haga V.	*You must do it.*

[2] There are two verbs in Spanish for the English verb *to know*, viz.: **saber** and **conocer**. Conocer denotes *to be acquainted with*, to know by sight or from experience; **saber** means *to know by study*, to have a knowledge of something.

[3] The pupil should now study the irregular verb **decir** in Part X. At any rate he should master the indicative mood as given on the next page.

15. Very good. And the second form!

> I might make
> you might make
> he might make
> we might make
> you might make
> they might make

16. Bravo! I have no doubt [duda] that you will soon master [vencerá V.] the difficulties of the Spanish language.

17. You can't imagine how anxious I am to learn it. No other tongue is [sea[1]] so important [importante] for business men [el hombre de negocios] as the beautiful [hermoso] language of Cervantes.

18. You are quite right. The natural market [el mercado natural] for the United States is to the south [el sur], and with the exception [la excepción] of [del] Brazil, where Portuguese [portugués] is spoken, Spanish is the language of the whole American Continent [continente], south of the Rio Grande.

19. American statesmen [hombres de estado] and many business people realize this fact, and in order to [para] gain [obtener] the South American markets, we must know [conocer] the Spanish language and understand the commercial needs [las necesidades comerciales] of those countries.

THE WEATHER

20. No doubt about it [sin duda alguna]! But now let us form some [algunas] idiomatic [idiomáticas] phrases with "hacer." How would you say [diría V.[3]]: The weather was very bad yesterday?

21. Oh, that [eso] is very easy. Yesterday [ayer] the weather was very bad.

Modo indicativo del verbo "decir"
(To say, to tell)

	Yo	Usted	Él	Nosotros	Ustedes	Ellos
Presente:	digo	dice	dice	decimos	dicen	dicen
Imperfecto:	decía	decía	decía	decíamos	decían	decían
Pretérito:	dije	dijo	dijo	dijimos	dijeron	dijeron
Futuro:	diré	dirá	dirá	diremos	dirán	dirán
Condicional:	diría	diría	diría	diríamos	dirían	dirían

Gerundio: diciendo
Participio pasado: dicho

22. Muy bien. Y ahora dígame algo del tiempo de hoy. /ɔj/

23. Ayer hizo muy mal tiempo, pero hoy lo hace muy bueno. Está muy agradable; hace calor, pero no mucho. /aɣra'ðaβle/

24. ¿Hace viento? /'bjento/

25. Anoche,[1] hizo mucho viento pero hoy no hace casi nada. /a'notʃe 'kasi/

26. ¿Ha leído V. el periódico? ¿Qué dicen del observatorio sobre el tiempo para mañana? /pe'rjoðiko ɔβserβa'torjo/

27. Aquí traigo[2] el periódico. Déjeme ver; ¡aquí está! Las probabilidades para mañana son que tendremos fuertes vientos del oeste y chubascos. /proβaβili'ðaðes o'este tʃu'βaskɔs/

28. V. tradujo[3] eso muy bien. Ahora voy a darle a V. algunas frases sobre el tiempo con el verbo "hacer." /tra'ðuxɔ/

29. ¿Qué clase de tiempo hace hoy?

---

[1] **Anoche** is rendered by *last night;* **esta noche,** by *to-night.*
[2] The student should learn the whole conjugation of **traer,** *to bring.*

Modo indicativo del verbo "traer"

(*To bring*)

	Yo	*Usted*	*Él*	*Nosotros*	*Ustedes*	*Ellos*
Presente:	traigo	trae	trae	traemos	traen	traen
Imperfecto:	traía	traía	traía	traíamos	traían	traían
Pretérito:	traje	trajo	trajo	trajimos	trajeron	trajeron
Futuro:	traeré	traerá	traerá	traeremos	traerán	traerán
Cond:	traería	traería	traería	traeríamos	traerían	traerían

Modo subjuntivo

Pres:	traiga	traiga	traiga	traigamos	traigan	traigan
Imp: 1.	trajera	trajera	trajera	trajéramos	trajeran	trajeran
Imp: 2.	trajese	trajese	trajese	trajésemos	trajesen	trajesen
Fut:	trajere	trajere	trajere	trajéremos	trajeren	trajeren

Gerundio: trayendo

Participio pasado: traído

22. Very good, and now tell me something [algo] about to-day's [hoy] weather.

23. Yesterday the weather was very bad, but to-day it is very fine. It is pleasant [agradable] and warm [hace calor], and yet not too warm.

24. Is it windy [hace viento]?

25. It was quite windy last evening [anoche], but to-day there is scarcely [casi] any breeze.

26. Have you read the paper [el periódico]? What does the weather bureau [observatorio] say about [sobre] weather probabilities for to-morrow?

27. I have [traigo] the paper here. Let me [déjeme] see; here it is: The probabilities [las probabilidades] for to-morrow are that we shall have [tendremos] strong westerly [del oeste] winds with showers [chubascos].

28. You translated [tradujo V.] that very well. I will now give you [voy a darle a V.] some phrases in regard to the weather with "hacer."

29. What kind [clase] of weather is it to-day?

---

[3] Tradujo V. is the Pretérito of the irregular verb **traducir**, *to translate*. The indicative is as follows:

Modo indicativo del verbo "traducir"

(*To translate*)

	Yo	Usted	Él	Nosotros	Ustedes	Ellos
Pres:	traduzco	traduce	traduce	traducimos	traducen	traducen
Imp:	traducía	—ía	—ía	—íamos	—ían	—ían
Pret:	traduje	tradujo	tradujo	tradujimos	tradujeron	tradujeron
Futuro:	traduc-iré	—irá	—irá	—iremos	—irán	—irán
Condicional:	traduc-iría	—iría	—iría	—iríamos	—irían	—irían

30. Hace un tiempo delicioso. El tiempo está hermosísimo. /deliˈɵjoso ɛrmoˈsisimo/

31. Abra V. la ventana y mire cómo está el tiempo. /ˈaβra benˈtana ˈmire/

32. Hace un sol espléndido, pero hace mucho frío. /esˈplendiðo/

33. Me parece que vamos a tener mal tiempo; el barómetro señala lluvia. /baˈrometroseˈɲalaˈʎuβja/

34. V. tiene razón; el barómetro ha bajado;[1] temo que tengamos[2] agua. /baˈxaðo/

35. Muy bien! Veo que V. entiende perfectamente estos modismos.

36. ¿Son estos todos los modismos en los que[3] se usa el verbo "hacer"?

37. Oh, no, usamos el verbo "hacer" impersonalmente en la tercera persona del singular en frases como las siguientes: "Hace dos años, Hace dos horas," etc. V. me entiende, ¿no es verdad? /siˈɣjentes/

38. Perfectamente.

39. Entonces forme V. una oración. /oraˈɵjɔn/

40. Hace dos horas hacía buen tiempo, pero ahora ha cambiado el viento y está desagradable. /kamˈbjaðo desaɣraˈðaβle/

41. Very good. I see you understand these idioms perfectly, and now let us consider [pasemos] the verb "tener." Have you learned this verb by heart [de memoria]?

42. I think I know it, but I wish you would ask me some questions.

43. Give me the Past of the Indicative and the Imperfect of the Subjunctive.

---

[1] *The thermometer has risen*, el termómetro ha subido. *The thermometer has fallen*, el termómetro ha bajado.

[2] After verbs of doubt, fear and apprehension the subjunctive mood must be used:

Temo que no vengan a tiempo.   *I am afraid they will not arrive in time.*
Dudaba que le hubiesen hecho esa   *I doubted whether they should have asked*
pregunta.   *him this question.*

[3] The relative pronoun que is accompanied by the article **el, la, los, las, lo,** according to gender and number in the following cases:

30. Splendid, the weather is delightful [delicioso]. The weather is [está] most beautiful [hermosísimo].

31. Open [abra V.] the window [la ventana] and see [mire] how the weather is.

32. The sun [sol] is shining gloriously, but it is quite cold.

33. It seems to me that we are going to have bad weather; the barometer [el barómetro] points [señala] to rain [lluvia].

34. You are quite right; the barometer has fallen [bajado]; I am afraid it is going to rain.

35. Excellent! I see you understand these idioms perfectly.

36. Are these all the idiomatic expressions in which [en los que] "hacer" is employed?

37. Oh, no, we use the verb "hacer" impersonally [impersonalmente] in the third person singular with phrases like these [como las siguientes]: "Two years ago, Two hours ago," etc. You understand me, don't you?

38. Perfectly.

39. Then form a sentence.

40. Two hours ago the weather was fine, but now the wind has changed [cambiado] and it is quite disagreeable [desagradable].

41. Muy bien. Veo que V. entiende perfectamente estos modismos, y ahora pasemos al verbo "tener." ¿Aprendió V. de memoria este verbo? /pa'semɔs apren'djo/

42. Creo que lo sé; pero deseo que me haga V. algunas preguntas.

43. Dígame el pretérito del indicativo y el imperfecto del subjuntivo. /suβxun'tiβo/

---

a. When the relative is accompanied by a preposition, as:

Me ha pagado, con lo que estoy contento.   *He has paid me and I am pleased with it (literally: with which I am pleased).*

b. When the relative refers to a whole sentence, as:

He estado en el campo, lo que me ha hecho bien.   *I have been in the country and it did me good (literally: which had done me good).*

c. To avoid ambiguity, *i. e.*, when the relative is separated from the noun to which it refers, as:

Pidió la libertad de su hijo, la que consiguió   *He asked for his son's liberty and obtained it (literally: which he obtained).*

PRETÉRITO (Modo indicativo)

Yo tuve	/'tuβe/
V. tuvo	/'tuβo/
él tuvo	
nos. tuvimos	/tu'βimɔs/
Vds. tuvieron	/tu'βjerɔn/
ellos tuvieron	

IMPERFECTO (Modo subjuntivo)
Primera forma

Yo tuviera	/tu'βjera/
V. tuviera	
él tuviera	
nos. tuviéramos	/tu'βjeramɔs/
Vds. tuvieran	/tu'βjeran/
ellos tuvieran	

Segunda forma

Yo tuviese	/tu'βjese/
V. tuviese	
él tuviese	
nos. tuviésemos	/tu'βjesemɔs/
Vds. tuviesen	/tu'βjesen/
eilos tuviesen	

43. ¡Bravo! Y el futuro—

Yo tendré	/ten'dre/
V. tendrá	/ten'dra/
él tendrá	
nos. tendremos	/ten'dremɔs/
Vds. tendrán	/ten'dran/
ellos tendrán	

PAST (Indicative Mood)

I had
you had
he had
we had
you had
they had

IMPERFECT (Subjunctive Mood)
First Form

I might have
you might have
he might have
we might have
you might have
they might have

Second Form

I might have
you might have
he might have
we might have
you might have
they might have

43. Excellent! And the Future?

I shall have
you will have
he will have
we shall have
you will have
they will have

44. Muy bien. Y el condicional—

Yo tendría	/ten'dria/
V. tendría	
él tendría	
nos. tendríamos	/ten'driamɔs/
Vds. tendrían	/ten'drian/
ellos tendrían	

45. ¡Bravo! Y ahora el presente del subjuntivo—

Yo tenga	/'teŋga/
V. tenga	
él tenga	
nos. tengamos	/teŋ'gamɔs/
Vds. tengan	/'teŋgan/
ellos tengan	

46. ¡Bien, muy bien! Ahora déjeme darle algunas reglas sobre el uso idiomático del verbo "tener." /'usɔjðjo'matiko/

47. Ya le he explicado a V. que "tener" indica posesión. /in'dikapose'sjɔn/

48. Sí, me acuerdo de esta regla perfectamente, pero déjeme hacerle una pregunta. /mea'kwɛrðo'ðesta'rːɛɣla 'dɛxɛme/

49. Las que V. quiera.[1] /'kjera/

50. ¿Se usa así el verbo "tener" en todos sus tiempos y modos? /a'si/

---

[1] The pupil should now master the whole conjugation of **querer, to wish, to be willing.**

Modo indicativo del verbo "querer"

(*To be willing; to wish*)

Pres:	quiero	quiere	quiere	queremos	quieren	quieren
Imp:	quería	quería	quería	queríamos	querían	querían
Pret:	quise	quiso	quiso	quisimos	quisieron	quisieron
Fut:	querré	querrá	querrá	querremos	querrán	querrán
Cond:	querría	querría	querría	querríamos	querrían	querrían

44. Very good. And the Conditional?

> I should have
> you would have
> he would have
> we should have
> you would have
> they would have

45. Excellent! And now the Present Subjunctive?

> I may have
> you may have
> he may have
> we may have
> you may have
> they may have

46. Very good indeed! Now let me give you some rules in regard to [sobre] the idiomatic use of "tener."

47. I have already explained [explicado] to you that "tener" indicates [indica] possession [posesión].

48. Yes, I remember this rule perfectly, but let me ask you a question.

49. As many as you like [quiera[1]].

50. Is "tener" used in this way [así] in all tenses and moods [modos]?

Modo subjuntivo

Presente:	quiera	quiera	quiera
Imperfecto:	quisiera	quisiera	quisiera
Imperfecto:	quisiese	quisiese	quisiese
Futuro:	quisiere	quisiere	quisiere
	queramos	quieran	quieran
	quisiéramos	quisieran	quisieran
	quisiésemos	quisiesen	quisiesen
	quisiéremos	quisieren	quisieren

Gerundio: queriendo
Participio: querido

51. Sin duda alguna; en toda su conjugación, por ejemplo: He tenido la desgracia de perder mucho dinero en la quiebra del Banco de Colombia. /sin'duðal'ɣuna porɛ'xemplo laðes'ɣraθja ðeper'ðɛr 'kjeβra ko'lɔmbja/

52. Gracias, esto me lo explica perfectamente. /es'plika/

53. Ahora sírvase V. continuar y decirme la otra regla acerca del uso idiomático del verbo "tener." /kɔntinu'ar a'θɛrka/

VOCABULARIO	VOCABULARY
Comidas y bebidas	**Eating and Drinking**
/ko'miðasiβe'βiðas/	

Comer /ko'mɛr/	To eat; to dine
Beber /be'βɛr/	To drink
Cenar /θe'nar/	To sup
El apetito /ape'tito/	The appetite
No tengo apetito.	I have no appetite.
Tener hambre /'ambre/	To be hungry
¿Tiene V. hambre?	Are you hungry?
Sí, tengo hambre.	Yes, I am hungry.
Tener sed /sɛð/	To be thirsty
¿Tiene V. sed?	Are you thirsty?
No, no tengo sed.	No, I am not thirsty.

El almuerzo	**The Breakfast**
/al'mwɛrθo/	

El desayuno /desa'juno/	The (light) breakfast
La merienda /me'rjenda/	The afternoon snack
El café /ka'fe/	The coffee
Una taza de café /'taθa/	A cup of coffee
El té /te/	The tea

51. Undoubtedly, throughout the whole conjugation, as for instance: I have had the misfortune [la desgracia] of losing [perder] a great deal of money by the failure [la quiebra] of the Colombia Bank [Banco].

52. Thanks; this makes everything clear and plain to me.

53. Now please go on [continuar] and give me the next rule in regard to [acerca del] the idiomatic use of "tener."

VOCABULARIO	VOCABULARY
Una taza de té	A cup of tea
El chocolate /tʃokoˈlate/	The chocolate
Almorzar[1] /almɔrˈθar/	To breakfast
¿Qué almuerza V.? Café, té o chocolate?	What do you take for breakfast? Coffee, tea or chocolate?
Tomo café, pero mi señora toma té.	I drink coffee, but my wife takes tea.
¡No le gusta a V. el té?	Don't you like tea?
Prefiero café. /preˈfjero/	I prefer coffee.
Pedir /peˈðir/	To order
¿Pidió V.?	Did you order?
¿Qué desea V. pedir?	What do you wish to order?
El biftec	The beefsteak
Bien cocido /koˈθiðo/	Well done
Mozo, tráigame un biftec y una taza de café. /ˈtrajɣame/	Waiter, bring me a steak and a cup of coffee.
¿Lo quiere V. bien cocido?	Do you want it well done?
No, a la inglesa[2]	No, rare, please.

---

[1]**Almorzar** belongs to the class of verbs which change o of the stem syllable into ue throughout the singular and third person plural in the present indicative and subjunctive and in the same persons in the imperative.

[2]Idiomatic expression.

VOCABULARIO	VOCABULARY
La chuleta /tʃu'leta/	The chop
La chuleta de carnero /kar'nero/	The mutton chop
La chuleta de ternera	The veal chop
La chuleta de cerdo /'θεrðo/	The pork chop
Las patatas /pa'tatas/ Las papas /'papas/ }	The potatoes
Patatas fritas /'fritas/	Fried potatoes
Tráigame una chuleta de carnero y patatas fritas.	Bring me a mutton chop and fried potatoes.
El huevo; los huevos /'weβo/	The egg; the eggs
Huevos pasados por agua /'aɣwa/	Soft boiled eggs
Huevos revueltos /rːɛ'βweltɔs/	Scrambled eggs
Huevos duros /'durɔs/	Hard boiled eggs
Huevos fritos /'fritɔs/	Fried eggs
Huevos escalfados /eskal'faðɔs/	Poached eggs
Huevos frescos /'freskɔs/	Fresh eggs
Una tortilla /tɔr'tiʎa/	An omelette
¿Cómo quiere V. los huevos, pasados por agua o duros?	How do you want the eggs, soft boiled or hard?
Hervidos tres minutos. /ɛr'βiðɔs mi'nutɔs/	Let them boil three minutes.
La sal /sal/	The salt
La pimienta /pi'mjenta/	The pepper
El azúcar /a'θukar/	The sugar
La leche /'letʃe/	The milk
La nata /'nata/ La crema /'krema/ }	The cream

VOCABULARIO	VOCABULARY
El vinagre /bi'naɣre/	The vinegar
El aceite /a'θɛjte/	The oil
La mostaza /mɔs'taθa/	The mustard
El salero /sa'lero/	The salt cellar
El azucarero /aθuka'rero/	The sugar bowl
La cafetera /kafe'tera/	The coffee urn
La tetera /te'tera/	The tea urn
La huevera /we'βera/	The egg cup
Echar /e't∫ar/	To pour out
Hágame el favor de servirme otra taza de té.	Please pour out another cup of tea for me.
Agua fresca	Fresh water
Sírvame un vaso de agua.	Pour me out a glass of water.
Agua fría /'fria/	Cold water
Agua caliente /ka'ljente/	Warm water
Agua tibia /'tiβja/	Lukewarm water
Agua muy caliente	Hot water
Agua hirviendo /ir'βjendo/	Boiling water
Agua mineral /mine'ral/	Mineral water
Agua con hielo /kɔn'dʒelo/	Ice water (water with ice)
Un jarro /'xarːɔ/	A pitcher

Los platos
/'platɔs/

The Dishes

Poner la mesa /'mesa/	To lay the table
El plato /'plato/	The plate
Limpio /'limpjo/	Clean

VOCABULARIO	VOCABULARY
Sírvase poner platos limpios.	Please serve clean plates.
El plato hondo /'ɔndo/	The soup plate
El plato La fuente /'fwente/ }	The dish, the platter
El cucharón /kutʃa'rɔn/	The ladle
La cuchara /ku'tʃara/	The spoon
La cuchara grande	The large spoon
La cucharita /kutʃa'rita/	The teaspoon
Una cucharada /kutʃa'raða/	A spoonful
El tenedor /tene'ðɔr/	The fork
El cuchillo /ku'tʃiʎo/	The knife
Déme un cuchillo limpio.	Give me a clean knife.
El mantel /man'tɛl/	The table cloth
La servilleta /sɛrβi'ʎeta/	The napkin
No me trajo V. servilleta. /'traxɔ/	You did not bring me a napkin.
El cubierto /ku'βjɛrto/	The cover—plate, fork, spoon, knife and napkin
Ponga V. otro cubierto. /'pɔŋga/	Put on another cover.
El vaso /'baso/	The glass

PART SIX

CONTENTS

El verbo "tener"

(*Continued from page* 120, *Part V*)

1. Con mucho gusto. El verbo "tener" se usa en el sentido de "to be" en inglés cuando expresa deseo o sentimiento. ˌsen'tiðo senti'mjento/

2. Siento decirle que no entiendo muy bien lo que quiere decir eso. Hágame el favor de ponerme unos ejemplos. /'aɣame po'nerme ɛ'xemplɔs/

3. Tiene V. razón. Con ejemplos se aprende prácticamente.

4. Así lo creo. El error de muchos gramáticos es el de preferir la teoría a la práctica. /gra'matikɔs prefe'rir teo'ria 'praktika/

5. Para hablar claro: "tener"[1] se usa en lugar del verbo inglés "to be," con las siguientes palabras: hambre, sed, frío, calor, sueño, vergüenza, razón y miedo. /si'ɣientes 'frio 'sweɲo bɛr'ɣwenθa r:a'θɔn 'mjeðo/

6. Ya entiendo esto, pero temo que se me va a hacer difícil recordar[2] tantas palabras sueltas. /r:ɛkɔr'ðar 'sweltas/

---

[1] **Tener** is used idiomatically with the following words:

Tengo hambre	*I am hungry*	(Literally: I have hunger)
tengo sed	*I am thirsty*	(" I have thirst)
tengo calor	*I am warm*	(" I have warmth)
tengo frío	*I am cold*	(" I have cold)
tengo sueño	*I am sleepy*	(" I have sleep)
tengo vergüenza	*I am ashamed*	(" I have shame)
tengo miedo de	*I am afraid to*	(" I have fear to)
tengo razón	*I am right*	(" I have right)
no tengo razón	*I am wrong*	(" I have *not* right)
tengo gana de	*I have a mind to, I feel inclined to*	
¿Qué tiene V.?	*What is the matter with you?*	
No tengo nada.	*Nothing is the matter with me.*	
Tengo algo.	*Something is the matter with me.*	
¿Tiene V. algo?	*Is anything the matter with you?*	

[2] This is a somewhat confusing construction, as the infinitive **recordar** is the subject of the sentence. The usual rule is that the preposition **de** is used before the infinitive after nouns and adjectives which govern the genitive:

The Verb "Tener"

(*Continued from page* 121, *Part V*)

1. With much pleasure. The verb "tener" is used in the sense [el sentido] of "to be" in English, when it expresses desire [deseo] or sentiment [sentimiento].

2. I regret to tell you that I can't quite understand what you mean by this. Kindly give me some illustrations [ponerme unos ejemplos].

3. You are quite right. We learn [se aprende] by practice [prácticamente] and through examples.

4. That is my opinion exactly. Grammarians [gramáticos] generally make the mistake of preferring theory [la teoría] to [a] practice [la práctica].

5. In plain words then, "tener"[1] is used in place of [en lugar del] our English verb "to be" in conjunction with the following [siguientes] words: hunger [hambre], thirst [sed], cold [frío], warmth [calor], sleep [sueño], shame [vergüenza], right [razón], and fear [miedo].

6. Ah, this I understand, but I am afraid [temo] it will be quite difficult for me [se me va a hacer difícil] to remember such a number [tantas] of isolated [sueltas] words.

Hágame V. el favor de venir conmigo.	*Do me the favor to come with me.*
No tengo el gusto de conocer a esa señora.	*I have not the pleasure of knowing that lady.*
Tiene vergüenza de pedirlo.	*He is ashamed to ask for it.*
Los verbos son difíciles de aprender.	*Verbs are difficult to learn.*
Es digno de hablar con ella.	*He is worthy to speak with her.*
Estoy deseoso de conseguirlo.	*I am desirous to attain it.*

All adjectives which express *worthiness, unworthiness, facility, difficulty, fulness, want, scarcity, anxiety, desire, exceptions, moral* or *physical qualities, distance, certainty* or *uncertainty,* or *danger* govern the preposition **de**:

Fácil de hacer	*Easy to do*
Penoso de hacer	*Difficult to do*
Lleno de soberbia	*Full of pride*
Deseoso de trabajar	*Desirous of working*
Codicioso de dinero	*Eager for money*
Gordo de talle	*Stout in body*
Blando de corazón	*Soft in heart*
Lejano de la ciudad	*Far from the city*
Seguro de peligro	*Safe from danger*

7. Las palabras sueltas, amigo mío, son muy difíciles de recordar. Las palabras sin conexión no componen un idioma. Puede uno aprenderse de memoria el diccionario entero, y no poder sostener una conversación. La naturaleza nos enseña con frases y éstas son las que tiene V. que aprender. /konɛk'sjɔn kɔm'ponen dikejo'narjoen'tero sɔste'nɛr natura'leθa en'seɲa/

8. Estoy enterado de eso y le agradecería que me formase V. unas frases con estas palabras. /ente'raðo aɣraðeθe'ria fɔr'mase/

9. Con mucho gusto, pero para aprovecharse de los ejemplos que voy a darle, debe V. hacer unos semejantes en casa y traérmelos para corregirlos. /aproβe't∫arse semɛ'xantes tra'ɛrmelɔs kɔr:ɛ'xirlɔs/

10. Lo haré. Usaré los verbos de sus frases en sus tiempos y personas diferentes. /pɛr'sonazðife'rentes/

11. Muy bien. Ahora empecemos. ¿Qué tiene V.? Tiene V. mal semblante. /a'ɔraempe'θemɔs sem'blante/

12. Ahora forme V. una frase semejante, pero póngala en el pasado. /semɛ'xante 'poŋgala pa'saðo/

13. Encontré ayer a su primo y tenía muy mal semblante. ¿Tiene algo? /a'jɛr 'primo te'nia/

14. ¡Bravo! Ahora forme V. una frase con "hambre" y "sed," pero que no sea[1] muy corta. /'kɔrta/

---

[1] The subjunctive is used in principal sentences to supply the **negative** form of the imperative.

It also supplies the **affirmative** form of the imperative in the *first* and *third* person:

7. Isolated words, my dear friend, are very difficult to remember. Disconnected words do not form [componen] a language. A person might learn [aprenderse] the whole dictionary [el diccionario entero] by heart and yet would not be able to carry on [sostener] a conversation. Nature [la naturaleza] teaches by sentences, and sentences you will have to [tiene V. que] learn.

8. I am aware [enterado] of that and should feel obliged [agradecería] to you if you would form [formase V.] some sentences with these words for me.

9. With much pleasure, but in order to derive full benefit [aprovecharse] from the examples which I am going to give you, you ought to form a number of similar [semejantes] phrases at home [en casa] and bring them to me for correction.

10. I will do so. I will put the verbs of your sentences into different [diferentes] tenses [tiempos] and persons.

11. Very well. Now let us begin. What is the matter with you? You do not look well [tiene V. mal semblante].

12. Now, form a similar [semejante] sentence, but put it into the past tense [el pasado].

13. I met your cousin [a su primo] yesterday and he looked very ill. Is anything [algo] the matter with him?

14. Very well! Now please form a phrase with **hambre** and **sed,** but don't make it too short [corta].

Que no escriba ella.	*Let her not write.*
Que haga él eso.	*Let him do that.*
No trabajemos hoy.	*Let us not work to-day.*
No se lo dé V.	*Don't you give it to him.*
No se vaya V.	*Don't you go away.*
¡Sea yo!	*Let me be!*
¡Sea él!	*Let him be!*
No me lo diga.	*Don't tell me.*

15. Desde el lunes[1] pasado que me resfrié he perdido el apetito (**or no tengo hambre**). Esta mañana sólo tomé una taza de café. /ˈlunes rːesfriˈe apeˈtito/

16. Bien, ¿no tiene V. hambre ahora? ¿No quisiera V. almorzar conmigo?

17. No gracias; no tengo hambre en absoluto y no podría comer un bocado. Pero ¿me hace V. el favor de un vaso de agua helada? Tengo mucha sed. /enaβsoˈluto boˈkaðo ˈaɣwaeˈlaða/

18. Ahora sírvase V. formar unas frases con "miedo," "vergüenza" y "ganas." Tengo deseos de ver[2] lo que hace V.[3] con estas palabras. /deˈseɔs/

19. Tengo ganas de ir este verano a las montañas, pero a decir verdad tengo miedo de estar en lugares altos.

---

[1] Days of the week:
Días de la semana:

lunes	Monday
martes	Tuesday
miércoles	Wednesday
jueves	Thursday
viernes	Friday
sábado	Saturday
domingo	Sunday

Months of the year:
Meses del año:

enero	January
febrero	February
marzo	March
abril	April
mayo	May
junio	June
julio	July
agosto	August
septiembre	September
octubre	October
noviembre	November
diciembre	December

The days are pronounced: /ˈlunes ˈmartes ˈmjɛrkoles ˈxweβes ˈbjɛrnes ˈsaβaðo doˈmiŋgo/

The article in Spanish takes the place of our preposition *on*, as el lunes, on Monday; los lunes, on Mondays; el martes, on Tuesday; los martes, on Tuesdays.

The months are pronounced: /eˈnero feˈβrero ˈmarɵo aˈβril ˈmajo ˈxunjo ˈxuljo aˈɣɔsto sɛpˈtjembre ɔkˈtuβre noˈβjembre diˈejembre/

The days of the week and months of the year are not written with capitals.

15. Since [desde] last Monday [el lunes[1]], when I caught a violent cold [me resfrié], I have lost all appetite [el apetito]. This morning I took [tomé] only a cup of coffee.

16. Well, do you not feel hungry now? Would you not like to eat lunch [almorzar] with me?

17. No, thank you. I am not at all [en absoluto] hungry and could not eat a mouthful [un bocado]. But may I trouble you for a glass [un vaso] of ice-water [agua helada]? I feel very thirsty.

18. Now please form some sentences with **miedo, vergüenza** and **ganas.** I am curious [tengo deseos] to see[2] how you will get along with these words.

19. I have a good mind to go to the mountains this summer, but to tell you the truth I am afraid to be in high places.

---

[2] The pupil should study the irregular verb **ver,** *to see.*

Modo indicativo

	Yo	Usted	Él	Nosotros	Ustedes	Ellos
Pres:	veo	ve	ve	vemos	ven	ven
Imp:	veía	veía	veía	veíamos	veían	veían
Pret:	vi	vió	vió	vimos	vieron	vieron
Fut:	veré	verá	verá	veremos	verán	verán
Cond:	vería	vería	vería	veríamos	verían	verían

Modo subjuntivo

	Yo	Usted	Él	Nosotros	Ustedes	Ellos
Pres:	vea	vea	vea	veamos	vean	vean
Imp:[1]	viera	viera	viera	viéramos	vieran	vieran
Imp:[2]	viese	viese	viese	viésemos	viesen	viesen
Fut:	viere	viere	viere	viéremos	vieren	vieren

Gerundio: viendo   *Participio:* visto

[3] The English Future is frequently replaced by the Present in Spanish, especially after the conjunction **si**:

Voy al instante.	*I'll go at once.*
¿Me hace V. el favor?	*Will you do me the favor?*
Si viene V. a mi casa saldremos a dar un paseo.	*If you will come to my house we will take a walk.*
¿Tiene V. la bondad?	*Will you have the kindness?*

On the other hand, the Future is often used in Spanish, especially in questions, when the speaker is convinced that his statement cannot be contradicted:

Veré muy pronto si V. sabe sus lecciones.	*I shall see very soon whether you know your lessons.*
¿Habrá felicidad semejante?	*Is there such happiness?*
No habrá desgracia como la mía.	*There is no misfortune like mine.*
¿Será cierto lo que he oído?	*Is it true what I have heard?*

20. ¡Cómo! ¿Tiene V. miedo de estar en lugares altos? ¿V. que ha estado trabajando en el piso cuarenta de un rascacielos por tantos años? Debería V. tener vergüenza.

21. Permítame decirle que V. no tiene razón[1] cuando dice tal cosa. Yo no estoy avergonzado en absoluto, ni tampoco me creo[2] un cobarde. Es fácil no tener miedo cuando uno está rodeado de paredes en una cómoda oficina, en lo alto de un edificio de cuarenta pisos. Pero no es fácil no tener miedo cuando uno está de pie al borde de una montaña, a cinco mil pies de altura. Especialmente, cuando hay peligro de que la tierra se desmorone. No deseo morir[3] todavía.

---

[1] We cannot say in Spanish: "*I am wrong,*" but must express it by: "*I have not right.*" As this mode of expression presents difficulties to students, other examples will make it clear.

V. no tiene razón.	*You are wrong.*
Ellos no tienen razón.	*They are wrong.*
Yo no tenía razón.	*I was wrong.*
¿No tengo yo razón?	*Am I wrong?*
Él no tenía razón.	*He was wrong.*
Él tenía razón.	*He was right.*

[2] Creer, *to believe,* is regular except that the diphthongs **ie** and **io** must always be consonantized. Thus:

INDICATIVE MOOD		SUBJUNCTIVE MOOD	
		Presente	
creo	*I believe*	crea	*I may believe*
crees	*thou believest*	creas	*thou mayst believe*
cree	*he believes*	crea	*he may believe*
creemos	*we believe*	creamos	*we may believe*
creéis	*you believe*	creáis	*you may believe*
creen	*they believe*	crean	*they may believe*
		Imperfecto	
creía	*I believed*	creyera	*I might believe*
creías	*thou believest*	creyeras	*thou mightst believe*
creía	*he believed*	creyera	*he might believe*
creíamos	*we believed*	creyéramos	*we might believe*
creíais	*you believed*	creyerais	*you might believe*
creían	*they believed*	creyeran	*they might believe*
		Pretérito	
creí	*I believed*	creyese	*I might believe*
creíste	*thou believedst*	creyeses	*thou mightst believe*
creyó	*he believed*	creyese	*he might believe*
creímos	*we believed*	creyésemos	*we might believe*

20. What! You are afraid of being in high places? You who have been working on the fortieth floor of a skyscraper for so many years? You should be ashamed of yourself!

21. Let me tell you you are wrong[1] when you say such a thing. I am not at all ashamed of myself, nor do I consider myself a coward. It is easy not to be afraid when one is surrounded by walls in a comfortable office at the top of [en lo alto de] a forty-story building. But it is not easy to have no fear when one is standing [está de pie] on the edge of a mountain five thousand feet high. Especially when there is the danger that the ground may slide from under you. I do not wish to die[3] yet.

---

creísteis	you believed	creyeseis	you might believe
creyeron	they believed	creyesen	they might believe

Futuro

creeré	I shall believe	creyere	I should believe
creerás	thou wilt believe	creyeres	thou wouldst believe
creerá	he will believe	creyere	he would believe
creeremos	we shall believe	creyéremos	we should believe
creeréis	you will believe	creyereis	you would believe
creerán	they will believe	creyeren	they would believe

Condicional — *Imperativo*

creería	I should believe	cree (tú)	believe
creerías	thou wouldst believe	crea (él.)	let him believe
creería	he would believe	crea V.	believe
creeríamos	we should believe	creamos	let us believe
creeríais	you would believe	creed	believe (you)
creerían	they would believe	crean (ellos)	let them believe

[3] Study the irregular verb **morir**, *to die*.

Modo indicativo

	Yo	Usted	Él	Nosotros	Ustedes	Ellos
Pres:	muero	muere	muere	morimos	mueren	mueren
Imp:	moría	moría	moría	moríamos	morían	morían
Pret:	morí	murió	murió	morimos	murieron	murieron
Fut:	moriré	morirá	morirá	moriremos	morirán	morirán
Cond:	morir-ía	—ía	—ía	—íamos	—ían	—ían

Modo subjuntivo

Pres:	muera	muera	muera	muramos	mueran	mueran
Imp:	mur-iera	—iera	—iera	—iéramos	—ieran	—ieran
Imp:	mur-iese	—iese	—iese	—iésemos	—iesen	—iesen
Fut:	mur-iere	—iere	—iere	—iéremos	—ieren	—ieren

Gerundio: muriendo
Participio pasado: muerto

22. Ya ve V. estos ejemplos del uso idiomático de "tener." Espero que lo vea V. claro.

23. Sí, perfectamente. Pero dígame V., ¿hay[1] otras expresiones en las que se usa el verbo "tener"?

24. Sí, lo empleamos por ejemplo cuando hablamos de la edad de las personas, verbigracia: ¿cuántos años tiene V.²? /'bɛrβi'ɣraɵja/ ¿Cuántos años puede tener su hermana? No sé exactamente cuántos años tiene, pero creo que tiene unos veintiuno o veintidós. No creía que tenía tantos.

25. Esta manera de expresarse es semejante a la de los franceses. /fran'ɵeses/

26. Así es. También usamos el verbo "tener" cuando hablamos del tamaño de los ríos o dimensiones en general; por ejemplo: Este río tiene ochenta pies de ancho y cincuenta pies de profundidad. /'rːio dimen'sjones profundi'ðað 'antʃo/

---

[1] The conjugation of "haber," when used impersonally, is perfectly regular. The present tense alone is irregular and forms hay, *there is, there are.*

MODO INDICATIVO	MODO SUBJUNTIVO
Hay, *there is* or *there are*	**Haya,** *there may be*
Había, *there was* or *there were*	**Hubiera,** *there might be*
Hubo, *there was* or *there were*	**Hubiese,** *there might be*
Habrá, *there will* or *shall be*	**Si hubiera,** or *si* **hubiese,** *if there*
Habría, *there should* or *would be*	*should be* or *if there were*

EXAMPLES

Hay un hombre en la calle,	*There is a man in the street.*
Hay dos mil personas el el teatro.	*There are two thousand persons in the theatre.*
Hubo una exposición universal en Chicago el año 1893.	*There was a universal exhibition in Chicago in the year 1893.*
Habría baile esta noche si **hubiera** (or **hubiese**) dinero para pagar la música.	*There would be a ball this evening, if there were money to pay for the music.*

Hay is a contraction of **ha** with the obsolete **y** *there.* **Ha-y** *there is, there are.* The compound tenses are formed regularly. The present is **ha** habido instead of **hay** habido, viz.:

22. Now, here you have some examples of the idiomatic use of "tener." I trust they are quite clear to you.

23. Yes, perfectly (clear). But tell me, are there any other expressions in which "tener" is used?

24. Yes, we employ it for instance in regard to the age [la edad] of persons. Thus we say [verbigracia]: How old are you? How old may his sister [su hermana] be? I don't know exactly how old she is, but I think she is twenty-one or twenty-two. I did not think she was as old as that.

25. This mode [manera] of expression is similar to the French way.

26. So it is. We also use "tener" in descriptions of the size [del tamaño] of rivers [los ríos] or dimensions [dimensiones] generally, as for example: This river is eighty feet [pies] broad [ancho] and fifty feet deep [profundidad]. (Literally: Thus [it] is. Also [we] use the verb "tener" when [we] speak of the size of the rivers or dimensions in general, for example: this river has eighty feet of breadth and fifty feet of depth.)

MODO INDICATIVO	MODO SUBJUNTIVO
Ha habido, *there has been*	**Hubiera habido,** *there might have been*
Había habido, *there had been*	**Hubiese habido,** *there might have been*
Hubo habido, *there had been*	
Habrá habido, *there shall* or *will have been*	
Habría habido, *there should* or *would have been*	
Haya habido, *there may have been*	(Si) **hubiera,** or (si) **hubiese habido,** (if) *there had* or *should have been*

EXAMPLES

Hoy **ha habido** un accidente en la calle.	*There has been an accident in the street to-day.*
Habrá habido muchos cambios.	*There will have been many changes.*
Habría habido más gente en el teatro si no hubiese llovido.	*There would have been more people in the theatre if it had not rained.*
[2] Instead of: ¿Cuántos años tiene V.? we can also say: ¿Qué edad tiene V.?	
Tengo treinta años.	*I am thirty years old.*
En mil ochocientos ochenta y ocho tenía ventiocho.	*In 1888 I was twenty-eight.*
Mi hermano tendrá mañana diez y siete años.	*My brother will be seventeen tomorrow.*

27. ¿Qué dimensiones tiene este cuarto?—Creo que tendrá unos veinticinco pies de largo por quince de ancho. /pjes ˈlarɣo/

28. Esta casa tiene sesenta pies de alto, ¿no es así?—Tiene[1] a lo menos ochenta pies. /aloˈmenɔs/

29. ¿Se encuentran todos estos modismos en la gramática?

30. Ciertamente, y debe V. estudiarlos con atención y practicarlos hasta que se familiarice V. con ellos. /ˈθjertaˈmente familjaˈriθe/

31. Otra peculiaridad del verbo "tener" hemos ya notado, y es el uso de "tengo que" por **"I must"** del inglés.

32. Permítame interrumpirle un momento. ¿Es ésta la única forma de expresión que tienen Vds. por nuestro **"must"**? /ˈunika/

33. Por supuesto que no. Usamos **tener que, haber de, hay que, es necesario, es preciso, es menester** o el verbo **deber**. Este se usa cuando se quiere expresar una obligación moral o un deber. En estos casos se puede cambiar el **"I must"** por **"I ought to."** ¿Me entiende V., no es verdad? /neθeˈsarjo preˈθiso menesˈter moˈral/

34. Sí, perfectamente, y por esta razón decimos en la frase primera: "Debo quedarme aquí," porque se expresa un deber y no una necesidad.[2] /neθesiˈðað/

35. Justamente. Ahora sírvase formar unos ejemplos con **tener que, haber de** y **hay que.**

36. Permítame preguntarle si hay alguna diferencia entre estas expresiones.

---

[1] Other peculiarities in the use of **tener** are given in Part X.

Tener algo malo means *to have a pain, a sore* or *an ache somewhere,* and is used with the definite article, as:

Tengo la mano mala.	*I have a sore hand.*
Tiene los pies malos.	*His feet are sore.*
Tengo la rodilla mala.	*I have a sore knee.*

27. What are the dimensions of this room?—I think it is about twenty-five feet long [largo] by [por] fifteen wide.

28. This house is about sixty feet high [alto], isn't it?—At least [a lo menos] eighty!

29. Do I find [se encuentran] all these idioms in the grammar [la gramática]?

30. Certainly [ciertamente], and you ought to study them carefully [con atención] and practise them [practicarlos] until [hasta que] they become quite familiar [se familiarice] to you.

31. Another peculiarity of "tener" we have noted before, and that is the use of "tengo que" for the English "I must."

32. Allow me to interrupt you for a moment. Is this the only mode of expression [la única forma de expresión] you have for our "must"?

33. By no means. We use either **tener que, haber de, hay que, es necesario, es preciso, es menester** or **deber**. The latter, however, can only be used when a moral obligation [una obligación moral] or duty [un deber] is expressed. In such cases **"I must"** can be changed to **"I ought to."** You understand me, don't you?

34. Yes, perfectly, and for this reason we say in our Main Sentence: "Debo quedarme aquí," because a duty is expressed and not a necessity [una necesidad].

35. Precisely so. Now please form some examples with **tener que, haber de** and **hay que**.

36. Allow me to ask you if there is any difference between these expressions.

The definite article is also used when moral or physical qualities are described:

Ella tiene los ojos azules.	*She has blue eyes.*
Tienen los pies grandes.	*They have large feet.*
Tiene la nariz grande.	*He has a big nose.*
Tengo las manos y los pies fríos.	*My hands and feet are cold.*
¿Tiene V. las manos frías?	*Are your hands cold?*

[2] Compare our Main Sentence on page 14. ¿Qué quiere V. hacer esta mañana? Quisiera salir para Buenos Aires en el primer avión, pero no me es posible, porque espero a un amigo de Nueva York y debo quedarme en Miami hasta que él llegue en vapor, autobús o tren.

No actual necessity is expressed here, but a moral obligation, consequently *deber* must be used.

37. No hay ninguna diferencia entre **haber de** y **tener que.** Las dos expresiones son tan sinónimas como: "I am obliged to go to my office" **and** "I must go to my office." "Tengo que ir al despacho" o "He de ir al despacho."

38. ¿Pero cómo se usa "hay que"?

39. "Hay que" significa **must** en un sentido general y corresponde exactamente al **il faut** del francés, cuando se usa sin pronombre personal. Por ejemplo: Hay que leer[1] estos libros pues son[2] de primer orden. /siɣni'fika 'il'fo 'ɔrðen/

40. Ahora déjeme ponerle unos ejemplos.

41. Dispense V. que le haga otra pregunta. ¿Cómo se usan **es menester, es necesario, es preciso?**

---

[1] Verbs ending in **eer** as **creer**, *to believe*, **leer**, *to read*, are irregular in so far as they change the diphthongs **ie** and **io** into **ye** and **yo.** In all other forms they are regular.

These irregularities appear in the *Gerundio*, *Pretérito*, and the *Imperfecto* (1st and 2nd form) of the Subjunctive.

	Pretérito	**1. Imperfecto subjuntivo**	
Yo leí	*I read*	Yo leyera	*I might read*
V. leyó	*you read*	V. leyera	*you might read*
él leyó	*he read*	él leyera	*he might read*
nos. leímos	*we read*	nos. leyéramos	*we might read*
Vds. leyeron	*you read*	Vds. leyeran	*you might read*
ellos leyeron	*they read*	ellos leyeran	*they might read*

	2. Imperfecto subjuntivo
Yo leyese	*I might read*
V. leyese	*you might read*
él leyese	*he might read*
nos. leyésemos	*we might read*
Vds. leyesen	*you might read*
ellos leyesen	*they might read*

Gerundio: leyendo, *reading*

Proveer, *to provide* (Participio **provisto**), **poseer,** *to possess*, and a few other verbs are conjugated in the same way.

[2] The pupil should master the conjugations of **ser** and **estar** now. Compare Part X.

37. There is no difference whatever between **haber de** and **tener que.** Both expressions are as synonymous as: "I am obliged to go to my office" and "I must go to my office."

38. But what about **hay que?** How is this expression used?

39. **Hay que** signifies **must** in a general sense and corresponds exactly to the French **il faut** when used without a personal pronoun. For instance: It will be necessary to read these books for they are standard works [de primer orden].

40. Now let me give you [ponerle] some examples.

41. Pardon me if I ask you still another question. How are <u>es menester, es necesario, es preciso</u> used?

Ser, To Be²
Modo indicativo

Pres:	soy	es	es	somos	son	son
Imp:	era	era	era	éramos	eran	eran
Pret:	fuí	fué	fué	fuímos	fueron	fueron
Fut:	seré	será	será	seremos	serán	serán
Cond:	sería	sería	sería	seríamos	serían	serían

Modo subjuntivo

Pres:	sea	sea	sea	seamos	sean	sean
*Imp:*¹	fuera	fuera	fuera	fuéramos	fueran	fueran
*Imp:*²	fuese	fuese	fuese	fuésemos	fuesen	fuesen
Fut:	fuere	fuere	fuere	fuéremos	fueren	fueren

Gerundio: siendo

Participio: sido

Estar, To be
Modo indicativo

Pres:	estoy	está	está	estamos	están	están
Imp:	estaba	estaba	estaba	estábamos	estaban	estaban
Pret:	estuve	estuvo	estuvo	estuvimos	estuvieron	estuvieron
Fut:	estaré	estará	estará	estaremos	estarán	estarán
Cond:	estaría	estaría	estaría	estaríamos	estarían	estarían

Modo subjuntivo

Pres:	esté esté estén	esté	estemos	estén
*Imp:*¹	estuviera estuviera estuvieran	estuviera	estuviéramos	eotuvieran
*Imp:*²	estuviese estuviese estuviesen	estuviese	estuviésemos	estuviesen
Fut:	estuviere estuviere estuvieren	estuviere	estuviéremos	estuvieren

Gerundio: estando

Participio: estado

VOCABULARIO

Los platos

El jarro para la leche /'xar:ɔparala'letʃe/	The milk pitcher
El vaso para el vino /'bino/	The wine-glass
Un vaso de vino	A glass of wine
La taza /'taɵa/	The cup
El platillo	The saucer
El sacacorchos /saka'kɔrtʃɔs/	The corkscrew
Sirva V. el café	Serve the coffee
Quite V. la mesa /'kite/	Clear the table

El viaje — The Journey; the Voyage

Hacer un viaje	To make a journey
¿Va V. a hacer un viaje?	Are you going to make a journey?
Estoy para[1] salir para Méjico /'mɛxiko/	I am on the point of leaving for Mexico.
Hacer un viaje; partir; salir; ir	To make a journey; to depart; to leave; to go
¿A dónde va V.?	Where are you going?
Parto para Méjico.	I am leaving for Mexico.
Salir de la ciudad /ɵju'ðað/	To go out of town
Salgo de la ciudad mañana.	I am going out of town tomorrow.
¿Está su esposo de V. fuera de la ciudad? /'fwera/	Is your husband out of town?

---

[1] **Estar para** means *to be on the point of.*

VOCABULARY

The Dishes

VOCABULARIO

¿Tuvo V. buen viaje?

¡Adiós; que tenga V. feliz viaje!
/fe'lie/

El ferrocarril
/fer:ɔka'r:il/

La estación /esta'ejɔn/

¿De cuál estación sale V.? /'sale/

Salgo de la estación Central.
/een'tral/

El billete

El despacho de billetes (boletos;
boletas; papeletas)

¿Me hace V. el favor de decirme
en dónde está el despacho de
billetes?

¿Dónde compro el billete?

La segunda puerta a la derecha (a
la izquierda)

De este lado

Al otro lado

Enfrente. Siga V. derecho. /'siɣa/

Sírvase darme un billete para
Veracruz.

Un billete de primera

Un billete de segunda

VOCABULARY

Did you have a good journey?

Good-bye. I hope you will have
a pleasant journey!

The Railroad

The station

From which station are you
going?

I leave from Central Station.

The Ticket

The ticket office

Could you please tell me where
the ticket office is?

Where do I buy my ticket?

Second door to the right (to the
left)

On this side

On the other side

Right opposite. Straight before
you (follow you straight).

Please give me a ticket to
Veracruz.

A first-class ticket

A second-class ticket

VOCABULARIO	VOCABULARY
Un billete de tercera	A third-class ticket
¿Desea V. un billete de primera o de segunda?	Do you want a first or second-class ticket?
El billete de vuelta	The return ticket
El billete de ida y vuelta /'iða/	The round-trip ticket
¿Para cuánto tiempo sirve el billete de vuelta?	For how long are return tickets good?
Los billetes de ida y vuelta sirven para un mes.	Return tickets are good for a month.
El billete directo /di'rɛkto/	The through ticket
¿Puede V. darme un billete directo hasta Chihuahua? /tʃi'wawa/	Can you give me a through ticket to Chihuahua?
¿Cuánto vale un billete de aquí a Orizaba? /ori'eaβa/	How much is a ticket from here to Orizaba?
El mozo /'moeo/	The porter
El camarero /kama'rero/	The waiter
Sírvase llamar al mozo. /ʎa'mar/	Call the porter please.
Mozo, sírvase facturar mi equipaje. /eki'paxɛ/	Porter, please check my baggage (my luggage).
¿Cuánto equipaje tiene V.?	How many pieces have you?
El baúl; los baúles	The trunk; the trunks
Sírvase V. facturar mi baúl para Méjico.	Please check my trunk for Mexico.
El mío es un baúl de cuero. /'kwero/	Mine is a leather trunk.
Un baúl con cubierta de lona /ku'βjɛrta/	A canvas covered trunk

VOCABULARIO	VOCABULARY
Un baúl con cubierta de metal /me'tal/	A metal covered trunk
Un baúl pequeño /pe'keɲo/	A small trunk
Un baúl grande	A large trunk
Un baúl cuadrado /kwa'ðraðo/	A square trunk
Este es mi baúl.	This is my trunk.
¿Dónde se puso mi baúl? /'puso/	Where was my trunk put?
La maleta /ma'leta/	The suitcase
La sombrerera /sombre'rera/	The hat-box
Tenga V. cuidado[1] con mi sombrerera. /kwi'ðaðo/	Be careful with my hat-box.
El talón /ta'lɔn/	The check
Deme su billete y le traeré su talón inmediatamente. /trae're/	Give me your ticket and I'll bring you your check at once.
El equipaje libre /'liβre/	The free baggage
Los ferrocarriles mejicanos permiten solamente cincuenta libras de equipaje libre. /peɾ'miten/	Mexican railroads allow only fifty pounds of baggage free.
El peso /'peso/	The weight
El exceso de peso /es'θeso/	The overweight
¿Tengo exceso de peso?	Have I any overweight?
Tiene V. doscientas libras de exceso.	You have two hundred pounds overweight.
No se debe viajar por Méjico con mucho equipaje. Es demasiado costoso. /dema'sjaðokɔs'toso/	You ought not to travel with much baggage in Mexico. It is too expensive.

[1] ¡Tenga V. cuidado! Take care! Look out!

VOCABULARIO	VOCABULARY
Mi equipaje fué facturado para Veracruz. He perdido mi talón. /perˈðiðo/	My baggage was checked for Veracruz. I have lost my check.

El salón de espera
/saˈlɔndesˈpera/

	The Waiting Room
Sírvase decirme dónde está el salón de espera.	Please tell me, where is the waiting room?
Se abren las puertas diez minutos antes de la salida del tren. /saˈliða/	The doors open ten minutes before the train leaves.
La cantina	The buffet

El tren; los trenes

	The Train; the Trains
El viajero /bjaˈxɛro/	The traveler
El pasajero /pasaˈxɛro/	The passenger
¡Pasajeros, al tren!	All aboard!
El tren expreso /esˈpreso/	The express train
El tren correo /kɔˈrːɛo/	The mail train
El tren mixto	The mixed train
El tren de mercancías /merkanˈθias/	The freight train
El revisor /rːɛβiˈsɔr/	The conductor
¿Es éste el tren para Veracruz?	Is this the Veracruz train?
Salir. Partir. Ir.	To leave; to start; to go.
El tren sale de aquí dentro de un minuto.	The train leaves in a minute.

VOCABULARIO	VOCABULARY
Sírvase entrar; el tren va a salir.	Please step aboard. The train is going to start.
¿Cuántos trenes hay al día para Veracruz?	How many trains a day are there for Veracruz?
¿Qué tren es el próximo para Méjico?	What is the next train for Mexico?
¿Dónde está el tren para Chihuahua?	Where is the train for Chihuahua?
El vagón de ferrocarril /ba'ɣɔn/	The railway carriage
El compartimento /kɔmparti'mento/	The compartment
¿Dónde está el compartimento de las señoras?	Where is the ladies' compartment?

Sentarse / To Take a Seat

Sentarse	To Take a Seat
El asiento /a'sjento/	The seat
Sentémonos en este compartimento.	Let us take a seat in this compartment.
Tomado; reservado	Taken; reserved
Libre; desocupado	Vacant, free; unoccupied
¿Está tomado este asiento? No, está desocupado.	Is this seat taken? No, it is unoccupied.
El rincón /r:in'kɔn/	The corner
El asiento de rincón	The corner-seat
Tome V. un asiento de rincón	Take a corner-seat

VOCABULARIO	VOCABULARY
Sentarse	To be seated
Cómodo	Comfortable
Incómodo	Uncomfortable
¿Está V. cómodo?	Are you comfortable?
Si no está V. cómodo tome V. este asiento.	If you are not comfortable take this seat.
No entre V. aquí. Este compartimento es para señoras.	Don't come in here. This compartment is for ladies.

PART SEVEN

CONTENTS

Tener que, hay que, etc.
(*Continuación*)

42. Vaya, me alegro que me haga V.[1] esa pregunta. Ya le expliqué a V. que a los verbos impersonales les sigue siempre el modo subjuntivo, a menos que se denote certeza. /'siɣe 'sjempre ɵɛr'teɵa/

43. Y ya que entiende V. todas las expresiones que se emplean por el must del inglés, quiero que forme V. algunas frases con ellas. Pero tenga la bondad de emplear diferentes tiempos y personas. /em'plean/

44. ¿Sobre qué deben ser?

45. Sobre cualquier cosa que V. guste,[2] con tal que sean frases prácticas. Hable V. de negocios. /kwal'kjɛr ne'ɣoɵjɔs/

46. ¿Quiere V., que forme frases sueltas, o sería mejor que fuese[3] una conversación? /'fwese/

47. En casos como éste en que se desea usar frases prácticas, una conversación no sería tan buena como frases sueltas; pues debe V. comprender que de frases sueltas puede pasarse fácilmente a una conversación corriente.

48. Trataré de hacer lo que pueda. Déjeme V. pensar[1] un momento y entonces empezaré.[4]

---

[1] The Present of the Subjunctive Mood is generally employed when the preceding verb stands in the *Present* or *Future Indicative,* or in the *Imperative.*

Me alegro que el tiempo favorezca la fiesta.	*I am glad the weather is favorable to the festival.*
Será preciso que se quede.	*It will be necessary for him to stay.*
Dígaselo cuando le vea.	*Tell him so when you see him.*

[2] **Cualquier** followed by que, requires the verb in the subjunctive mood:

Cualquier cosa que V. diga.	*Whatever you may say.*
Cualquiera que V. guste.	*Whatever you please.*

[3] The Imperfect of the Subjunctive in either form is employed after verbs in *any past tense in the Indicative* or in the *Conditional:*

Le suplicaron que fuera (o fuese) a su casa.	*They begged him to go to his house.*
Fué preciso que lo hiciera (o hiciese).	*It was necessary for him to do it.*
Desearía que V. me hiciera ese favor.	*I wish you would do me that favor.*

To Be Obliged, etc.
(Continuation from p. 139 Part VI)

42. Ah [vaya], I am glad [me alegro] you asked me this question. I explained to you before that impersonal verbs are followed by the Subjunctive Mood, unless [a menos que] certainty [certeza] is noted.

43. And now that you understand everything in regard to the various expressions which are employed for the English **must**, I want you to form a number of sentences with them. But employ different tenses and persons, if you please [tenga la bondad].

44. What shall they be about? (About [sobre] what ought they to be?)

45. About anything [cualquier cosa] you like, provided [con tal que] they are practical phrases. Talk about business [negocios].

46. Shall I form single phrases, or would it be better to work out a conversation?

47. In cases of this kind where it is desirable to employ practical sentences, a conversation would not be so well adapted as [como] disconnected phrases; for you will of course understand that from isolated phrases we can easily progress to an ordinary conversation.

48. I will try to [de] do the best I can. Let me think a moment and then I will begin.

---

[4] **Pensar,** *to think,* and **empezar,** *to commence,* belong to the class of slightly irregular verbs which change the stem-vowel **e** into **ie** throughout the singular and in the third person plural of the present indicative and subjunctive, and in the same persons in the imperative. **Pensar,** pensando, pensado, *to think.*

Pres. Ind:	pienso	piensa	piensa	pensamos	piensan	piensan
Pres. Sub:	piense	piense	piense	pensemos	piensen	piensen
Imperat:	pensemos	piensen	piensen	pensemos	piensen	piensen

Empezar, empezando, empezado, *To begin*

Pres. Ind:	empiezo	empieza	empieza	empezamos
	empiezan	empiezan		
Pres. Sub:	empiece	empiece	empiece	empecemos
	empiecen	empiecen		
Imperat:	empiecen	empecemos	empiecen	

The use of **c** has been explained before.

49. ¿A dónde va[1] V.? Parece que está V. de prisa. /'prisa/

50. Sí, estoy de prisa. He de ir al banco inmediatamente. Tengo que pagar un pagaré y no tengo sino diez minutos para llegar allí y hacer el negocio.

51. Ahora forme V. unas frases sobre la salud. Debe V. emplear nuestros modismos. Ponga la frase en el pasado.

52. Mi esposa cayó[2] enferma anoche. A las dos tuve que levantarme a buscar el médico. Ya está un poco mejor, pero tendrá que quedarse en cama por lo menos una semana.

53. Dice el médico que tiene que cambiar de clima. Él quiere que ella vaya a Méjico para pasar allí el invierno. /'klima/

54. Lo siento mucho. ¿Tendrá V. que ir con ella?

55. Sí. Me será muy difícil dejar mis negocios por mucho tiempo, pero la salud de mi señora es primero y por lo tanto debo arreglar las cosas para poder acompañarla.

56. Ahora forme V. unas cuantas frases sobre cualquier asunto que guste, pero emplee V. el verbo **haber de** y algunas veces otras expresiones en las que debe usarse el **must** que le he enseñado.

---

[1] Study now the whole conjugation of

Ir, *To go*

Modo indicativo

Pres:	voy	va	va	vamos	van	van
Imp:	iba	iba	iba	íbamos	iban	iban
Pret:	fuí	fué	fué	fuimos	fueron	fueron
Fut:	iré	irá	irá	iremos	irán	irán
Cond:	iría	iría	iría	iríamos	irían	irían

Modo subjuntivo

Pres:	vaya	vaya	vaya	vayamos	vayan	vayan
Imp:[1]	fuera	fuera	fuera	fuéramos	fueran	fueran
Imp:[2]	fuese	fuese	fuese	fuésemos	fuesen	fuesen
Fut:	fuere	fuere	fuere	fuéremos	fueren	fueren

Gerundio: yendo
Participio: ido

49. Where are you going? You seem to be in a hurry [de prisa].

50. Indeed I am in a hurry. I must go to the bank at once. I have to pay a note [un pagaré] and have but ten minutes left to go there and transact my business.

51. Now form a few phrases in regard to health. You must employ our idioms. Put the phrase into the past tense.

52. My wife was taken [cayó] ill last night [anoche]. I was obliged to get up [levantarme] at two o'clock [a las dos] and find [buscar] a physician. This morning she feels a little better, but she will have to stay [quedarse] in bed for at least [por lo menos] a week.

53. The doctor says she must have a change of climate [cambiar de clima]. He wants her to go to Mexico and spend the winter there.

54. I am very sorry. Will you have to go with her?

55. I must. It will be exceedingly difficult for me to leave my business for any length of time, but my wife's health is the first consideration [primero] and therefore [por lo tanto] I must make arrangements [arreglar las cosas] to accompany her.

56. Now form a few [unas cuantas] phrases in regard to any subject [cualquier asunto] you like, but work in sometimes [algunas veces] **haber de** and sometimes the other expressions for **must,** which I have taught you.

---

[2] Study the whole conjugation of the irregular verb.

Caer, *To fall*
Modo indicativo

Pres:	caigo	cae	cae	caemos	caen	caen
Imp:	caía	caía	caía	caíamos	caían	caían
Pret:	caí	cayó	cayó	caímos	cayeron	cayeron
Fut:	caeré	caerá	caerá	caeremos	caerán	caerán
Cond:	caería	caería	caería	caeríamos	caerían	caerían

Modo subjuntivo

Pres:	caiga	caiga	caiga	caigamos	caigan	caigan
Imp:[1]	cayera	cayera	cayera	cayéramos	cayeran	cayeran
Imp:[2]	cayese	cayese	cayese	cayésemos	cayesen	cayesen
Fut:	cayere	cayere	cayere	cayéremos	cayeren	cayeren

Gerundio: cayendo
Participio pasado: caído

Ya caigo en ello, *now I see; now I understand.*—Las ventanas caen a la plaza, *the windows look on (front) the square.*—Caérsele a uno la cara de vergüenza, *to blush with shame.*

57. ¿Hemos de ir al banco inmediatamente?—Sí señor, tenemos que ir en seguida porque los bancos cierran[1] a las tres.[2] Quiero hacer efectiva esta letra. Necesito dinero mejicano y no tengo sino de los Estados Unidos. /ense'γiδa 'θjɛr:an efɛk'tiβa neθe'sito/

58. ¿Cuándo he de enviar esos efectos?—Inmediatamente.

59. ¿No desea V. enviar antes un despacho a su agente?—Sí, he de enviarle un telegrama al momento, porque necesito salir esta noche.

60. Tengo que hacer algunas compras. ¿No puede V. venir[3] conmigo? —Lo siento, pero tengo mucho que hacer. Hoy estoy muy ocupado. Tengo tanto que hacer que no puedo perder[4] un instante.— ¿Qué es lo que tiene V. que comprar?

61. Quisiera comprar un vestido.—Mi hermana tendrá mucho gusto en acompañar a V., cuando desee hacer sus compras.

---

[1] **Cerrar**, *to shut, to close,* is regular except that **i** is inserted before the stem-vowel **e** = **ie** throughout the singular and in the third person plural of the present indicative and subjunctive, and in the same persons in the imperative:

Pres: Ind:	**cierro**	**cierra**	**cierra**	cerramos	**cierran**	**cierran**
Pres: Subj:	**cierre**	**cierre**	**cierre**	cerremos	**cierren**	**cierren**

[2] *At,* when relating to time, is expressed by **a.**

The word *o'clock* is not expressed in Spanish when the hour or time of day is indicated. The article **la** is used before **una** to express *one o'clock,* and **las** before the other hours. The word **hora** being understood, the feminine article must be used. Thus we say:

Es la una.	*It is one o'clock.*		Son las siete.	*It is seven o'clock.*	
Son las dos.	"	*two* "	" ocho.	"	*eight* "
" tres.	"	*three* "	" nueve.	"	*nine* "
" cuatro.	"	*four* "	" diez.	"	*ten* "
" cinco.	"	*five* "	" once.	"	*eleven* "
" seis.	"	*six* "	" doce.	"	*twelve* "

It is five minutes past one is expressed by **es la una y cinco** (minutos); *it is ten minutes past two,* **son las dos y diez;** *it is a quarter past two,* son las dos y cuarto; *it is half past two,* son las dos y media.—While thus far we add, we now begin to subtract: *it is twenty-five minutes to two,* son las dos menos veinte y cinco: *it is a quarter to two,* son las dos menos cuarto, etc.

Instead of **las doce** (12 *o'clock*), the Spaniards also say **es mediodía** (*it is midday*), **es medianoche** (*it is midnight*).

57. Must we go to the bank immediately? Yes, sir, we must go at once, as the banks close at three o'clock [a las tres²]. I want to cash [hacer efectiva] this draft [esta letra]. I need [necesito] some Mexican money. I have only [no tengo sino] United States currency with me.

58. When have I to send these goods?—At once.

59. Don't you want to send a dispatch to your agent first [antes]? —Yes, I have to send him a telegram at once as I must leave this evening (because I need to leave this evening).

60. I have some shopping to do. Can't you come³ with me?—I am sorry, but I have a great deal to do. I am very busy to-day. I have so much to do that I haven't a moment to spare (= to lose⁴). What is it that you have to buy?

61. I should like to buy a dress.—My sister will be delighted to accompany you on your shopping expedition.

---

³ Venir, *to come.*

Modo indicativo

Pres:	vengo	viene	viene	venimos	vienen	vienen
Imp:	venía	venía	venía	veníamos	venían	venían
Pret:	vine	vino	vino	vinimos	vinieron	vinieron
Fut:	vendré	vendrá	vendrá	vendremos	vendrán	vendrán
Cond:	vendría	vendría	vendría	vendríamos	vendrían	vendrían

Modo subjuntivo

Pres:	venga	venga	venga	vengamos	vengan	vengan
*Imp:*¹	vin-iera	—iera	—iera	—iéramos	—ieran	—ieran
Imp:	vin-iese	—iese	—iese	—iésemos	—iesen	—iesen
Fut:	vin-iere	—iere	—iere	—iéremos	—ieren	—ieren

Gerundio: viniendo
Participio pasado: venido

⁴ **Perder,** *to lose,* belongs to the same class of irregular verbs noted above. The conjugation is therefore regular with the following exceptions:

Pres. Ind:	pierdo	pierde	pierde	perdemos	pierden	pierden
Pres. Subj:	pierda	pierda	pierda	perdamos	pierdan	pierdan

62. Entremos aquí, es una buena tienda. Es mejor comprar siempre en las tiendas grandes donde se vende todo a precio fijo.

63. Enséñeme V. muestras de tela para hacer un vestido. Enséñeme la tela más fina que tenga V.—Aquí tiene V. muestras de telas finas.

64. ¿Es ésta la más fina que tiene V.?

65. Examine V. este tejido. Es imposible ver cosa mejor; es muy delicado. /teˈxiðo/

66. Este tejido es muy ligero.

67. Aquí hay otra pieza; éste es muy fuerte.

68. No me gusta el color; este color pasará pronto.

69. Perdóneme V. señor, durará mucho.

70. Me fío de V. ¿A cómo vende V. la vara?—A cinco pesos.

71. Me parece demasiado caro. Dígame V. el último precio, porque no me gusta regatear.

72. Caballero, yo nunca pido más de lo justo; no tengo más que un precio.

73. ¿Puede V. dármelo a cuatro pesos?—No señor, perdería dinero. Se lo daré a V. por cuarto pesos y medio. No lo puedo vender por menos.

74. ¡Muy bien! partamos la diferencia.—A la verdad, que lo lleva V. al precio de costo.

75. ¿Nada más necesita V.?—Por ahora no; envíeme V. el paquete con la factura; aquí tiene las señas de mi casa. /fakˈtura ˈseɲas/

62. Let us enter here; this is a good store. It is always advisable to buy in large establishments where all goods are sold at fixed prices.

63. Show me some cloth samples [muestras] for a dress. Show me the finest you have.—Here are some samples, sir.

64. Is this the finest you have?

65. Look at this cloth. It is impossible to find anything better; it is very soft [delicado].

66. This cloth is very thin.

67. Here is another piece; this is very strong.

68. I don't like this color; this color is not fast (= will pass soon [pasará pronto].)

69. Excuse me, sir, it will wear very well (= it will last [durará] well.)

70. I trust you [me fío de V.]. How much do you charge a yard?— Five dollars.

71. That seems too expensive to me. Tell me the lowest price, because I am not fond of bargaining [no me gusta regatear].

72. I never ask too much, sir; I have only one price.

73. Can you let me have it at four dollars?—No, I should lose money on it. I'll give it to you for four dollars and a half. I cannot sell it any cheaper.

74. Very well! Let us split the difference.—Upon my word you are getting it at cost.

75. Don't you need anything else?—Nothing just now. Send me the package C.O.D. [envíeme V. el paquete con la factura]. Here's my address [las señas de mi casa].

156

FRASE FUNDAMENTAL

(*Conclusión*)

Porque espero a un amigo de Nueva York y debo quedarme en Miami hasta que él llegue en vapor, autobús o tren.

Porque[1]	/'pɔrke/
espero	/es'pero/
a un amigo[2]	/awna'miɣo/
de	/de/
Nueva York	/nweβa'jɔr/ or /nweβa'jɔrk/
y debo	/i'ðeβo/
quedarme	/ke'ðarme/
en	/en/
Miami	/mi'ami/
hasta que[3]	/'astake/
él llegue	/'ɛl'ʎeɣe/
en vapor, autobús o tren.	/em'bapɔr, /awto'βuso'tren/

---

[1] Porque (written without accent) means *because;* por qué (two words, the second accentuated) *why?*

[2] The preposition a is used before personal objects after a transitive verb:

Conozco a este hombre.	*I know this man.*
Fueron a llamar a un médico.	*They went to call a physician.*
¿A quién busca V.?	*Whom are you looking for?*

But when the personal object is preceded by a cardinal number a is omitted:

He visto cuatro personas.   *I saw four persons.*

When the personal object is indeterminate or unknown a is left out also:

Busco una criada.   *I am looking for a servant-girl.*

MAIN SENTENCE

(Conclusion)

For I expect a friend from New York and must stay in Miami until he arrives by boat, bus or train.

For, because, as[1]

I expect

a friend[2]

from

New York

and must

stay

in

Miami

until[3]

he arrives

by boat, bus or train.

✳ After **querer**, we use **a** in the sense of *to love, to like:*

Quiero a esta muchacha.   *I like this girl. (I am fond of this girl.)*

Querer, without **a** means *to want, to wish:*

Quiero un hombre honrado que hable   *I want an honest man who speaks*
inglés.   *English.*

[3] **Hasta que** belongs to the conjunctions which govern the subjunctive mood. See Part X.

1. ¿Por qué permanece[1] V. todavía en la ciudad?

2. ¿Por qué me pregunta V. tal cosa? ¡Hay aquí tantos puntos de interés!

3. Aunque no esperase a nadie, sus muchas atracciones me retendrían en este hermoso lugar.

4. ¿Me permite V. que le pregunte a quién espera?

5. A una señorita que probablemente llegará mañana.

6. ¡A una señorita! ¡Qué sorprendente! Yo creía que V. era casado.

7. Ciertamente que soy casado. La joven es parienta mía;[2] es mi prima. /pa'rjenta 'prima/

8. ¿Hace[3] mucho tiempo que está V. aquí?
   ¿Llegó V. hace mucho?

9. Unos quince días. Desde el diez de mayo.[4] /'majo/

---

[3] All verbs ending in **cer** or **cir** preceded by a vowel insert before the stem-ending a **z** as often as the stem meets an **a** or **o**, as:

Conocer, *To know*

	Pres. Ind:	*Pres. Subj:*
Yo	conozco	conozca
Usted	conoce	conozca
Él	conoce	conozca
Nosotros	conocemos	conozcamos
Ustedes	conocen	conozcan
Ellos	conocen	conozcan

Imperativo: conozca   conozcamos   conozcan

Lucir, *To display, to shine*

	Pres. Ind:	*Pres. Subj:*
Yo	luzco	luzca
Usted	luce	luzca
Él	luce	luzca
Nosotros	lucimos	luzcamos
Ustedes	lucen	luzcan
Ellos	lucen	luzcan

Imperativo: luzca   luzcamos   luzcan

1. Why do you still remain in this city?

2. Why do you ask me such a thing? There are so many points of interest here.

3. Even if I did not expect someone, its many attractions would keep me [me retendrían] in this beautiful place.

4. May I ask you whom do you expect?

5. A young lady who will probably arrive to-morrow.

6. A young lady! How surprising! I thought that you were married.

7. Certainly I am married. The young lady is related to me [parienta mía]. She is my cousin [prima].

8. Have you been here long?

9. About two weeks. Since the tenth of May.

---

[2] El pariente, *the kinsman, the (male) relative;* la parienta, *the kinswoman, the (female) relative.* El primo, *the cousin (male);* la prima, *the cousin (female).*

[3] The present tense is used after hace, in expressions referring to time.

¿Cuánto tiempo hace que está V. aquí?	*How long have you been here?*
Hace mucho tiempo que no le veo.	*It is a long time since I saw him.*
Hace tres años que no nos hablamos.	*It is three years since we spoke to each other.*
Hace quince días que llueve.	*It has been raining for two weeks.*
Hace seis años que estoy aquí.	*I have been here six years.*

[4] With the exception of primero, *the first,* the Spaniards use the cardinal numbers for dates:

¿Qué día del mes tenemos hoy?	*What date is to-day?*
¿A cuántos del mes estamos hoy?	
Tenemos el doce de junio.	*Is it the 12th of June.*
Estamos a tres de febrero.	*It is the 3d of February.*

10. ¿En qué hotel se hospeda V.? /ɔs'peða/

11. Me hospedo en el Hotel Internacional.

12. ¿Le gusta a V.?

13. Sí, me gusta muchísimo. Las guías lo recomiendan[1] como unɔ ɑɛ los mejores de Méjico. /laz'ɣiazlɔr:ɛko'mjendan/

14. Su manejo es a la española,[2] o más bien a la mejicana, pues su dueño es un verdadero caballero mejicano. /ma'nɛxɔ 'dweɲo/

15. Todo es allí mejicano: la cocina extraordinaria y la numerosa y atenta servidumbre vestida con trajes típicos regionales.

16. Hoy, para variar, voy a comer un bistec tierno y jugoso con patatas fritas, pero a la mejicana.

17. ¿Le gusta a V. la cocina mejicana?

---

[1] **Recomendar,** *to recommend*, inserts **i** before the stem-vowel **e**—**ie** throughout the singular and in the third person plural of the Indicative and Subjunctive **present,** and in the same persons in the Imperative.

	Pres. Ind:	*Pres. Subj:*
Yo	recomiendo	recomiende
Usted	recomienda	recomiende
Él	recomienda	recomiende
Nosotros	recomendamos	recomendemos
Ustedes	recomiendan	recomienden
Ellos	recomiendan	recomienden

Imperativo: recomiende   recomendemos   recomienden

[2] An adverbial expression consisting of a feminine adjective in the **dative** singular, the noun **usanza,** *usage, fashion,* being understood:

a la francesa	*in the French fashion*
a la española	*in the Spanish style*
a la mejicana	*in the Mexican style*

The same idea may be expressed by **al estilo** or **al estilo de:**

al estilo francés	*in the French style*
al estilo de Méjico	*after the manner of Mexico*
al estilo de Castilla	*after the manner of Castile*

10. At what hotel do you stop [se hospeda V.]?

11. I stop at the Hotel International.

12. Do you like it?

13. Yes, I like it very much. The guide-books [las guías] recommend [recomiendan] it as one of the best in Mexico. (Literally: Yes, me it pleases very much. The guide-books [las guías] it recommend as one of the best of Mexico.)

14. It is conducted on the Spanish, or rather on the Mexican plan, because its owner is a real Mexican gentleman.

15. Everything is Mexican there: the extraordinary cooking, and the numerous and attentive servants dressed in typical regional costumes.

16. Today, for a change, I am going to eat a tender and juicy steak with fried potatoes, but Mexican style.

17. Do you like Mexican cooking?

Note: Oír *to hear*, is very irregular. The conjugation is:

Modo indicativo

	Yo	*Usted*	*Él*	*Nosotros*	*Ustedes*	*Ellos*
Pres:	oigo	oye	oye	oímos	oyen	oyen
Imp:	oía	oía	oía	oíamos	oían	oían
Pret:	oí	oyó	oyó	oímos	oyeron	oyeron
Fut:	oiré	oirá	oirá	oiremos	oirán	oirán
Cond:	oiría	oiría	oiría	oiríamos	oirían	oirían

Modo subjuntivo

	Yo	*Usted*	*Él*	*Nosotros*	*Ustedes*	*Ellos*
Pres:	oiga	oiga	oiga	oigamos	oigan	oigan
Imp:[1]	oyera	oyera	oyera	oyéramos	oyeran	oyeran
Imp:[2]	oyese	oyese	oyese	oyésemos	oyesen	oyesen
Fut:	oyere	oyere	oyere	oyéremos	oyeren	oyeren

Gerundio: oyendo
Participio: oído

18. Por supuesto. Es deliciosa.

19. ¿Practica V. su español en el hotel?

20. No tanto como desearía practicarlo; por este motivo es posible que vaya a vivir con una familia mejicana.

21. No valdrá[1] la pena, porque supongo que el vapor llegará pronto.

22. Se esperaba ayer, pero en esta estación del año cuando hay tantos huracanes en el Golfo de Méjico, uno no puede decir lo que va a suceder. El vapor puede llegar hoy o puede no llegar hasta la semana que viene.

23. ¿Qué dicen los consignatarios?
¿Cuál es el parecer de los consignatarios? /kɔnsiɣna'tarjɔs/

---

[1] **Valer,** *to be worth,* is slightly irregular.

Modo indicativo

	Pres:	*Imp:*	*Pret:*	*Fut:*	*Cond:*
Yo	valgo	valía	valí	valdré	valdría
Usted	vale	valía	valió	valdrá	valdría
Él	vale	valía	valió	valdrá	valdría
Nosotros	valemos	valíamos	valimos	valdremos	valdríamos
Ustedes	valen	valían	valieron	valdrán	valdrían
Ellos	valen	valían	valieron	valdrán	valdrían

18. Of course. It is delicious.

19. Do you practice your Spanish in the hotel?

20. Not so much as I should like to practice it. For this reason it is possible that I may go to live with a Mexican family.

21. It will not be worth while [no valdrá la pena], for I suppose [supongo] that the steamer will arrive soon [pronto].

22. It was due yesterday; but at this season of the year, when there are so many hurricanes in the Gulf of Mexico, one cannot say what is going to happen. The steamer may arrive to-day, or may not arrive until the coming week.

23. What do the agents [los consignatarios] say? **Or:** What is the opinion [el parecer] of the agents?

Modo subjuntivo

	Pres:	*1. Imp:*	*2. Imp:*	*Fut:*
Yo	valga	val -iera	val -iese	val -iere
Usted	valga	——iera	——iese	——iere
Él	valga	——iera	——iese	——iere
Nosotros	valgamos	——iéramos	——iésemos	——iéremos
Ustedes	valgan	——ieran	——iesen	——ieren
Ellos	valgan	——ieran	——iesen	——ieren

Gerundio: valiendo
Participio pasado: valido

VOCABULARIO

El ferrocarril

VOCABULARY

The Railroad

Vamos al vagón de fumar.	Let us go into the smoker.
Prohibir /prɔj'βir/	To forbid
No se permite fumar en este compartimento. /per'mite/	No smoking in this compartment. No smoking allowed in this compartment.
Este no es un vagón de fumar.	This is not a smoking car.
Fumar	To smoke
El humo /'umo/	The smoke
Abrir /a'βrir/	To open
Cerrar /θe'rːar/	To close
Sírvase abrir la ventana.	Please open the window.
Abra V. la puerta.	Open the door.
Sírvase cerrar la ventana.	Please shut the window.
La corriente de aire /'kɔ'rːjenteðe'ajre/	The draught (the current of air)
Hay aquí una corriente de aire.	There is a draught here.
¿Siente V. la corriente de aire cuando abro la ventana?	Do you feel the draught when I open the window?
No, señor, el compartimento está sofocante.	No, sir. It is close in this compartment.
El polvo	The dust
Hace mucho polvo.	It is very dusty.
Entra mucho polvo; sírvase cerrar la ventana.	It is very dusty here; please close the window.
¿Qué estación es ésa?	What station is that?
¿Cómo se llama[1] esta estación? /'ʎama/	What is the name of this station?

---

[1] ¿Cómo se llama V.? *What is your name?* Me llamo Fernández. *My name is Fernandez.*

VOCABULARIO	VOCABULARY
¿Cómo se llama la próxima estación?	What is the name of the next station?

Parar
/pa'rar/

¿Cuánto tiempo para aquí el tren?	How long does the train stop here?
Revisor, ¿cuándo paramos para almorzar?	When do we stop for breakfast, conductor?
¿Cuánto tiempo paramos aquí?	How long do we stop here?
¡Burgos! Cinco minutos de parada. /'burɣɔs/	Burgos! We stop here five minutes.

Cambiar de coches / To Change Cars

¿Tengo que cambiar de[2] coches?	Have I to change cars?
Déjeme ver su billete.	Let me see your ticket.
No, no tiene V. que cambiar; este tren va hasta Madrid.	No, you don't change; this train goes through to Madrid.
¿Mudamos de coches aquí? /mu'ðamɔs/	Do we change cars here?
¿Dónde mudamos de tren?	Where do we change trains?
Tiene V. que cambiar de vagón en Medina del Campo.	You'll have to change cars at Medina del Campo.
¿Empalma este tren en Alcázar? /al'kaθar/	Does this train connect in Alcázar?
¿A dónde va V.? A Valencia. /ba'lenθja/	Where are you going? To Valencia.
Tiene V. que hacer trasbordo en Alcázar para ir a Valencia.	You'll have to transfer in Alcázar to go to Valencia.
Este tren no enlaza.	This train does not connect.

---

[2] This de after cambiar or mudar is idiomatic.

VOCABULARIO

Debió V. haber tomado un tren directo en Madrid.

El coche-cama

¿Hay un coche-cama en el tren que va a Alcázar?

¿Cuánto cuesta el coche-cama?

Deseo encontrar el coche-cama.

La frontera
/lafrɔn'tera/

La aduana /a'ðwana/

¿Dónde está la aduana?

El oficial de aduana /ofi'ejal de a'ðwana/

¿Es V. oficial de la aduana?

Ya estamos en la frontera. Aquí viene el oficial de la aduana española.

¿Tiene V. algo que pague[1] derechos?

VOCABULARY

You ought to have taken a through train at Madrid.

The sleeping car

Is there a sleeping car on the train which goes to Alcázar?

What is the price on the sleeping car?

I wish to find the sleeping car.

The Frontier (The Border)

The custom-house

Where is the custom-house?

The custom-house officer

Are you a custom-house officer?

Here we are at the frontier. Here comes the Spanish customs officer.

Have you anything dutiable with you?

---

[1] The u is added to preserve the sound of **g** as γ before **e**. The verb is **pagar.**

PART EIGHT

CONTENTS

Teatro — Concierto

24. Creen que llegará aquí dentro de un día o dos, aunque a menudo hay retrasos inevitables. /r:ε'trasosineβi'taβles/

25. Pues bien; tenga paciencia.

26. Ya la tengo, aunque hay razones para perderla.

27. Permítame decirle algo sobre mis planes.

28. En seguida que mi prima llegue, iremos a la Ciudad de Méjico.

29. Allí espero ver muchas obras teatrales. Me muero por ir al teatro.

30. Naturalmente no podré entender todo al principio; pero, poco a poco, espero entender todo lo que en la escena se diga.

31. ¿Espera V. poder entender también los chistes?

32. Sí; y espero reírme mucho.

33. ¿Espera V. también asistir a los conciertos?

34. Tanto me place[1] la música que en Chicago no falto nunca a los conciertos que da la Sociedad Sinfónica.

Special Note: The verbs **hacer,** *to make, to do,* and **mandar,** *to send, to order,* followed by another verb in the Infinitive, have the meaning of the English verbs *to cause, to let* or *to have:*

Hago hacer un vestido.	*I am having a dress made.*
Mando lavar mi ropa.	*I have my clothes washed.*
Haga V. enviar este libro a la librería.	*Have this book sent to the bookstore.*
¿En dónde piensa él hacerse la ropa?	*Where does he intend to have his clothes made.*

[1] Some personal verbs are used impersonally, *i. e.* in the third person singular. The most important ones are:

Bastar, *To suffice, to be sufficient*

Basta que V. se empeñe.	*It is sufficient that you persist in it.*
Su palabra basta.	*Your word is enough.*
Basta que V. lo diga.	*It is sufficient that you say so.*

Convenir, *To agree, to suit*

Conviene hacer esto.	*It is expedient to do it.*
Me conviene.	*It suits me.*

Theatre — Concert

24. They think that it will be here in a day or two, although there are often unavoidable delays.

25. Well, then, have patience.

26. I have it, although there are reasons to lose it.

27. Permit me to tell you something about my plans.

28. Immediately after my cousin arrives, we shall go to the City of Mexico.

29. There I expect to see many plays. I am dying to go to the theatre.

30. Naturally I shall not be able to understand everything at the beginning; but, little by little, I expect to understand everything that may be said on the stage.

31. Do you also expect to understand the jokes?

32. Yes; and I expect to laugh a great deal.

33. Do you also expect to attend concerts?

34. I am so fond of music that in Chicago I never miss the concerts which the Symphonic Society gives.

Gustar, *To please*

Me gusta comer a la una.	*I like to dine at one.*
El estudio de idiomas me gusta.	*I like to study languages.*

Disgustar, *To displease*

Me disgusta oír tal cosa.	*I dislike to hear such a thing.*
Su conversación disgusta.	*His conversation is unpleasant.*

Fastidiar, *To annoy, to be tiresome*

Fastidia quedarse en casa.	*It is tiresome to stay at home.*
Me fastidia guardar cama.	*It is annoying that I have to stay abed.*
Tanta lluvia fastidia.	*So much rain is annoying.*

Importar, *To be of importance*

Importa decírselo.	*It is important to tell him so.*
No importa.	*Never mind.*
No me importa.	*I don't care.*

Placer, *To please*

Me place oírlo.	*It pleases me to hear it.*
¡Plegue a Dios!	*May it please God!*

Valer, *To be worth, to be better*

Más vale tarde que nunca.	*Better late than never.*
El trabajo vale más que la ociosidad.	*Work is better than idleness.*

35. Entonces acompáñeme V. esta noche. V. oirá las mejores melodías mejicanas por nuestra más famosa banda.

36. Los mejicanos son gente de talento para la música—¿no es así?

37. Sin duda alguna. Todos, pobres o ricos, son amantes de la música. Son músicos innatos. Muchos que no conocen ni aun las notas pueden tocar admirablemente cualquier composición musical después de oírla[1] algunas veces. Esto ocurre no sólo en Méjico, sino en toda Suramérica.

38. ¡Qué extraordinario! Había oído esto, pero jamás lo pude creer.

39. ¿Ejecutan bien? /ɛxɛ'kutan/

40. Algunas de nuestras orquestas son maravillosas. Tocan toda la música con gran fuego y expresión, y dan el color característico no sólo a nuestras melodías nacionales sino también a las grandes composiciones de todo el mundo.

41. Entonces, me decido a ir con V. esta noche. Ojalá tengan un programa muy bueno.

FRASE FUNDAMENTAL [2]

No debió V. haber salido sin sus chanclos haciendo un tiempo tan variable. A causa de su descuido V. ha pillado un resfriado terrible que le obligará a guardar cama por algún tiempo antes que V. pueda continuar su viaje.

Pronunciation

/'noðe'βjows'tea'βɛrsa'liðosinsus't∫aŋklɔs,
a'θjendown'tjempotamba'rjaβle. a'kawsaðesuðes'kwiðo,
us'teapi'ʎaðownr:esfri'aðote'r:iβle,
keleoβliɣa'raɣwar'ðar'kamaporal'ɣun'tjempo,
'anteskews'te'pweðakɔntinu'arsu'βjaxɛ/

---

[1] The Infinitive stands after all prepositions:

Despues de oír a ambas partes es como se puede juzgar.	*After hearing both parties one is able to judge.*
Para aprender algo es preciso estudiar.	*In order to learn anything one must study.*
Sin preguntar no se puede saber.	*Without asking, one cannot obtain knowledge.*
Para levantarse temprano es necesario acostarse temprano.	*In order to get up early one must retire early.*

35. Then accompany me this evening. You will hear the best Mexican melodies by our most famous band.

36. The Mexicans are talented people for music—are they not?

37. Without any doubt. All, poor or rich, are fond of music. They are innately musical. Many who do not even know one note from another are able to play any musical composition admirably after hearing it a few times. This happens not only in Mexico but in the whole of South America.

38. How extraordinary! I had heard this, but I could never believe it.

39. Do they perform well?

40. Some of our orchestras are marvelous. They play all music with great fire and expression and they give the characteristic color not only to our national melodies, but also to the great compositions of the whole world.

41. Then I decide to go with you this evening. I hope they will have a very good program.

MAIN SENTENCE

You ought not to have gone out without your overshoes in this changeable weather. Because of your carelessness you have caught a bad cold and you will be obliged to remain in bed for some time before you will be able to continue your journey.

---

[2] The study of this sentence will enable the student to master some difficult constructions in regard to the use of the Subjunctive Mood, the Infinitive, Prepositions, etc. The pupil will also observe that this phrase will lead to a new series of important conversational themes.

Note on gender of certain nouns: Nouns ending in **ción** or **tión** are of the feminine gender, as la cuestión, *the question:* la meditación, *the meditation.*

Compare Part X.

Nouns ending in Spanish in **tad** or **dad**—terminations which correspond to the English ty or the Latin **tas,**—are of the feminine gender, as humanidad, *humanity,* adversidad, *adversity,* vivacidad, *vivacity.*

No debió V. haber salido sin sus chanclos haciendo un tiempo tan variable.

/'noðe'βjows'tea'βɛrsa'liðosinsus't∫aŋklɔs,   a'ejendown'tjempotam ba'rjaβle/

No debió V. /'noðe'βjows'te/

haber salido[1] /a'βɛrsa'liðo/

sin /sin/

sus chanclos /sus't∫aŋklɔs/

haciendo[2] /a'ejendo/

un tiempo /un'tjempo/

tan /tan/

variable /ba'rjaβle/

---

[1] Study the whole conjugation of the irregular verb—

Salir, *To go out*

Modo indicativo

	Yo	*Usted*	*Él*	*Nosotros*	*Ustedes*	*Ellos*
Pres:	salgo	sale	sale	salimos	salen	salen
Imp:	salía	salía	salía	salíamos	salían	salían
Pret:	salí	salió	salió	salimos	salieron	salieron
Fut:	saldré	saldrá	saldrá	saldremos	saldrán	saldrán
Cond:	saldría	saldría	saldría	saldríamos	saldrían	saldrían

Modo subjuntivo

	Yo	*Usted*	*Él*	*Nosotros*	*Ustedes*	*Ellos*
Pres:	salga	salga	salga	salgamos	salgan	salgan
Imp:[1]	saliera	saliera	saliera	saliéramos	salieran	salieran
Imp:[2]	saliese	saliese	saliese	saliésemos	saliesen	saliesen
Fut:	saliere	saliere	saliere	saliéremos	salieren	salieren

Gerundio: saliendo
Participio: salido

[2] The Gerund is invariable in gender and number, and is used to denote a continuation of an action or state:

Andan entrando y saliendo.	*They continue coming and going.*
Canta bailando.	*He sings while dancing.*
Los dejé durmiendo.	*I left them sleeping.*
El lo dijo riendo.	*He said so laughing.*
Habla durmiendo.	*He talks in his sleep (while sleeping).*

You ought not to have gone out without your overshoes in this changeable weather.

The Gerund is, therefore, frequently used where we in English employ *while, whilst, as, since, although, if* or *by:*

Enseñando se aprende.	*One learns by teaching.*
La tos se cura sudando.	*A cough is cured by perspiring.*
Siendo así no quiero hacerlo.	*Since it is so, I don't want to do it.*
Dándole yo licencia, saldrá.	*If I give him permission, he will go out.*
Viendo que su hermano no venía, se fué.	*When he saw his brother was not coming, he went away.*
Teniendo malo el pie no puede levantarse.	*As he has a sore foot he cannot get up.*

The Gerund is used in connection with the verb **estar**, similar to the progressive conjugation in English, to express the action of the verb as unfinished and continuing.

¿De qué está V. hablando?	*Of what are you speaking?*
¿Qué está V. haciendo?	*What are you doing?*
Estoy escribiendo una carta.	*I am writing a letter.*
He estado leyendo todo el día.	*I have been reading all day long.*

The verb **estar** cannot be used with the Gerund of **ser**, *to be;* **ir**, *to go,* and **venir**, *to come.* Thus we must say:

Voy, *I am going.*   Viene, *He is coming, etc.*

EL TIEMPO

1. ¿Por qué salió V. sin sus chanclos con este tiempo tan variable? No debió V. haber hecho eso.

2. Seguramente que no lo habría hecho, si no hubiese creído que el tiempo aclararía.

3. ¿Cómo pudo V. haber supuesto semejante cosa? Hace algunos días que tenemos mal tiempo.

4. Sí; para la estación en que estamos ha sido bien malo, pero yo creí que despejaría.

5. Una suposición errónea, mi querido amigo. V. no conoce todavía nuestro clima.

Special Note: Many verbs are reflexive in Spanish which are not so in English, as:

Alegrarse	*to rejoice*	equivocarse	*to be mistaken*
figurarse	*to imagine*	engañarse	*to be deceived*
disgustarse	*to be displeased*	burlarse	*to laugh at*

It must also be observed that *permanently* reflexive verbs may be conjugated impersonally with se (the dative of the pronoun serving to distinguish the person) as:

Personal Inflection	**Impersonal Inflection**	
me figuro	se me figura	*I imagine*
(te figuras)	(se te figura)	(*thou imaginest*)
se figura	se le figura	*he imagines*
V. se figura	se le figura a V.	*you imagine*
nos figuramos	se nos figura	*we imagine*
(os figuráis)	(se os figura)	(*you imagine*)
se figuran	se les figura	*they imagine*
Vds. se figuran	se les figura a Vds.	*you imagine*

The pupil ought also to remember that almost all passive verbs in English and all verbs compounded with *to get* or *to become*, are reflexive in Spanish. The following examples will make this clear:

Llamarse, *To be called*

¿Cómo se llama V.?	*What is your name?*
Me llamo José.	*My name is Joseph.*

Equivocarse, *To be mistaken*

| V. se equivoca. | *You are mistaken.* |

THE WEATHER

1. Why did you go out in this so changeable weather without your overshoes? You ought not to have done that.

2. I surely would not have done so if I had not thought the weather would clear.

3. How could you have supposed such a thing? The weather has been bad for some days.

4. Yes, for this season [la estación] of the year it has been bad enough; nevertheless I thought it would clear [despejaría].

5. An erroneous supposition, my dear friend. You do not know our climate yet.

Sentarse, *To be seated*

Siéntese V., señor.	*Sit down, sir.*

Levantarse, *To get up, to arise*

¿A qué hora se levanta V.?	*At what time do you get up?*
Me levanto a las cinco.	*I rise at five o'clock.*

Acostarse, *To retire, to go to bed*

¿Está V. acostándose?	*Are you getting into bed?*
No estoy acostándome todavía, pero me acostaré pronto.	*I am not getting into bed yet, but I shall do so soon.*

Enfadarse, *To get angry*

No se enfade V.	*Don't get angry.*

Calentarse, *To get warm*

Caliéntese V.	*Get warm.*

Enfermarse, *To get sick*

Él se enfermó al salir del teatro.	*He became sick when leaving the theatre.*

Irse, *To go away*

Váyase V.	*Go away.*
Me voy.	*I am going away.*

Acordarse, *To remember*

Me acordaré siempre de eso.	*I shall always remember it.*

Pasearse, *To go for a walk (a promenade)*

¿Quiere V. pasearse conmigo?	*Will you take a walk with me?*
No tengo tiempo de pasearme.	*I have no time for promenades.*

6. Tenía entendido que[1] este clima era bueno, y según el pronóstico del tiempo supuse que seguramente iba a aclarar.

7. ¿Los pronósticos del tiempo? ¿Cree V. en ellos?

8. Por lo general no soy crédulo; pero ¿qué otra cosa podemos hacer? /pɔrlɔxene'ral 'kreðulo/

9. No podemos esperar siempre buen tiempo.

10. Lo probable será que tengamos que permanecer aquí toda la tarde. ¡Vea cómo llueve! /pɛrmane'θɛr/

11. Sí, la lluvia es torrencial. Es inútil pensar en salir con este tiempo tan espantoso. Es una gran lástima, ¿no es verdad?

12. Sí, pero ¿podríamos resolver el problema tomando un coche?

13. Siga V. mi consejo.[2] No se aventure a salir con este tiempo tan horroroso. Vea cómo relampaguea. /'siɣa kɔn'sexɔ ɔr:ɔ'roso r:ɛlampa'ɣea/

14. Ahora empieza a tronar. ¡Caramba! ¡Qué trueno tan formidable! La centella debe haber caído por aquí. /θen'teʎa/

15. Pero ¿qué es eso? ¿Se detiene aquí un taxi con esta tormenta?

16. Si no me equivoco[3] es su compatriota. /eki'βoko/

17. ¿Qué le puede traer aquí con este tiempo tan terrible?

18. Allí está.

19. Pero, mi querido Luis, ¿qué le trae aquí con este tiempo tan horrible? Está hecho una sopa.

---

[1] Idiomatic and frequently used.

[2] *To advise* is generally rendered by **aconsejar,** as:

¿Qué me aconseja V. hacer?	*What would you advise me to do?*
¿Qué lugares me aconseja V. visitar?	*What places would you advise me to visit?*
¿Quién le ha aconsejado a V. esto?	*Who has given you this advice?*
Si yo estuviera en su lugar, procedería según su consejo.	*If I were in your place, I should act upon his advice.*
Yo estoy seguro que lo sentirá V. si no sigue su consejo.	*I am sure you will be sorry if you don't follow his advice.*

6. I always understood that this climate was good, and according to the weather reports I supposed that it surely was going to clear.

7. The weather reports? Do you believe in them?

8. As a general thing [por lo general], I am not credulous [crédulo]; but what else can we do?

9. We cannot expect fair weather always.

10. Most likely we shall have to stay in all the afternoon. Just look how it rains!

11. Yes, it is really pouring. It is useless to think of going out in this fearful weather. A great pity, isn't it?

12. Yes, but we can solve the problem by taking a ride.

13. Follow my advice. Don't venture out in this horrid weather. See how it lightens!

14. And now it is beginning to thunder [tronar]. Goodness [Caramba]! what a clap of thunder; that must have struck [caído] near by [por aquí].

15. But what is that? A taxi in this storm at our door?

16. If I am not mistaken it is your compatriot [compatriota].

17. What can bring him here in this terrible weather?

18. There he is!

19. But, my dear Louis, what brings you here in this horrible weather? You are wet to the skin!

---

[3] A few sentences may give more clearness in regard to the use of this verb:

Si no me equivoco, creo que tengo el honor de dirigirme al señor Sirvent.	*If I am not mistaken, I think I have the honor of addressing Mr. Sirvent.*
Él se equivocó al hacer esta declaración.	*He was mistaken when he made this statement.*
¿No está V. equivocado?	*Are you not mistaken?*
Esta es una equivocación.	*This is a mistake.*
Hay una gran equivocación en esta cuenta.	*There is a great mistake in this bill.*
Dispénseme, V. ha cometido una equivocación. Permítame V. corregirla.	*Pardon me, you have made a mistake. Allow me to correct it.*

20. Pues sólo atravesé la calle para tomar el coche y me empapé.

21. Múdese la ropa, si no va a agarrar un terrible resfriado.

22. Acuéstese[1] en mi cama y cuelgue[1] su vestido. /a'kwestese
'kwɛlɣe/

23. Vine a traerle una invitación. El amigo envía saludos[2] y . . .
/imbita'θjɔn/

24. Dispense que le interrumpa, pero su salud es primero que nada.

25. Como V. guste. Pero verdaderamente yo no me resfrío tan
fácilmente como V. se imagina.

26. Aquí está todo lo que le hace falta. Gracias a que somos de igual
estatura todo le sentará espléndidamente. /i'ɣwalesta'tura/

27. Quítese su ropa mojada y póngase inmediatamente la mía.

28. En seguida que V. se vista llamaré al criado. Él hará que se
seque[3] su ropa.

A causa de su descuido V. ha pillado un resfriado terrible.
/a'kawsaðesuðes'kwiðo us'teapi'ʎaðownrːesfri'aðotɛ'rːiβle/
A causa de /a'kawsaðe/
su descuido /suðes'kwiðo/
V. ha pillado /us'teapi'ʎaðo/
un resfriado terrible /unrːesfri'aðotɛ'rːiβle/

---

[1] The conjugation of **acostar** has been given before. Always remember that
when a verb has **ue** in the stem-syllable the Infinitive must have an **o** in place of
it. **Colgar** has the same irregularities; the euphonic changes of **g** have been
explained before. Compare Part X.

[2] There are numerous ways of expressing this phrase:

Muchos recados en su casa de V.   *My regards at home.*
Dígale mil cosas de mi parte.   *Give my regards to her.*
Póngame a los pies de su señora de V.   *Please give my kindest regards to your*
                                        wife.

20. I only went across [atravesé] the street to take a cab and got wet to the skin [empapé].

21. Change [múdese] your clothes [la ropa] or you will catch a terrible cold.

22. Lie down on my bed and hang up your clothes.

23. I came to bring you an invitation. Our friend sends his regards to you and . . .

24. Pardon me for interrupting you, but your health is very important.

25. Just as you like. But I really do not catch cold as easily as you imagine.

26. Here is everything you need [todo lo que le hace falta]. Fortunately we are of the same size [igual estatura] and everything will fit [sentará] you splendidly.

27. Take off [quítese] your damp clothes [ropa mojada] and put on [póngase] mine at once.

28. As soon as you are dressed I will ring for the servant. He will see that your clothes are dried.

Because of your carelessness you have caught a bad cold

Because of
your carelessness
you have seized
a terrible cold.

Presente V. mis respetos a su madre.	*Present my respects to your mother.*
Muchas memorias de mi parte a su hermana.	*Give my regards to your sister.*
Memorias a todos en casa.	*Remember me to all at home.*
Muchas expresiones al Sr. Gómez.	*My regards to Mr. Gomez.*
Gracias, las apreciará mucho.	*Thanks, she will appreciate them greatly.*
Gracias, las estimará mucho.	*Thanks, she will esteem them greatly.*

[3] From **secar**, *to dry*. The euphonic changes have been explained before.

La salud y la enfermedad

1. ¿De qué trata la lección de hoy? /lɛk'ejɔn/

2. Nos ocuparemos de las enfermedades y de la salud, asunto importantísimo.

3. Y el estudio de ese tema nos conducirá probablemente al de muchas expresiones nuevas.

4. Sin duda alguna. Pues empecemos. ¿Qué tal está V. hoy? Parece estar un poco fatigado y enfermo.

5. No me siento bien. Creo que me resfrié anoche a la salida del teatro.

6. Lo siento muchísimo. ¿No llevaba V. los chanclos?

7. Al ir al teatro no se me ocurrió la idea del paraguas ni de los chanclos.

8. V. tiene una tos muy mala. Verdaderamente parece[1] que V. ha agarrado un tremendo resfriado.

---

[1] **Parecer** has many idiomatic meanings. The following phrases will help to explain them:

Él parece un perfecto caballero, y más que eso, lo es.	*He seems a perfect gentleman, and what is more, he is one.*
Él pareció muy incomodado a su demanda.	*He seemed greatly annoyed at your request.*
No me parece que iré a verle esta mañana.	*I don't think I shall call on him this morning.*
¿Qué le parece a V. esta actriz?	*What do you think of this actress?*

Health and Illness

1. What is the subject of [de qué trata] to-day's lesson?

2. We will talk [nos ocuparemos] about illness [las enfermedades], and health a most important subject [asunto importantísimo].

3. And the consideration of this theme will probably lead to many new expressions?

4. Without any doubt. Now let us begin. How are you to-day? You look somewhat tired and ill.

5. I do not feel [me siento] well. I think I caught cold last night on leaving [a la salida] the theatre.

6. I am exceedingly sorry to hear that. Did you not wear your overshoes?

7. In going [al ir] to the theatre the idea of umbrella or overshoes never occurred to me.

8. You have a very bad cough. You really seem to have a wretched cold.

¿No le parece a V. muy linda esa dama?	*Don't you think that lady is very pretty?*
Este retrato no se parece a Vd.	*This picture does not resemble you (does not look like you).*
¿No cree Vd. que esta fotografía se parece mucho a ella?	*Don't you think this photograph is very much like her?*
Parece un alemán (un mejicano).	*He looks like a German (a Mexican).*
¡Se parece a él!	*That's just like him!*
¡Se parece a ella!	*That's just like her!*
¡Qué mal parecía su madre anoche!	*How ill your mother looked last night!*
¡Qué bien parecía el señor Barbozo cuando llegó de Buenos Aires!	*How well Mr. Barbozo was looking when he arrived from Buenos Aires!*

VOCABULARIO	VOCABULARY

¿Sobre qué artículos hay que pagar derechos?

On which articles do you have to pay duty?

Solamente sobre los cigarros. /θi'ɣarːɔs/

On cigars only.

No traigo ni cigarros ni cigarrillos.

I carry neither cigars nor cigarettes.

Sírvase abrir el baúl.

Please open your trunk.

¿Qué hay en este baúl?

What does this trunk contain?

No hay sino ropa de uso.

Nothing but used wearing apparel.

Llegar / To Arrive

La llegada /ʎe'ɣaða/

The arrival

¿Cuándo llega este tren a Méjico?

When is this train due in Mexico?

Este tren viene atrasado hora y media. /atra'saðo'ɔraj'meðja/

The train is an hour and thirty minutes late.

¿A qué hora llegaremos?

At what time shall we arrive?

¿Encontraremos taxímetros en la estación?

Shall we find taxicabs at the station?

Por supuesto. El policía le dará a V. un billete con el número de su taxi. /poli'θia/

Most certainly. The policeman will hand you a check with the number of your taxi.

¿Cuál es el precio del taxi hasta el Hotel Internacional?

What is the taxi fare to the Hotel International?

¿En dónde recojo mi equipaje?

Where do I get my baggage?

No tiene V. necesidad de molestarse. /neθesi'ðað/

You don't need to trouble yourself.

Déle V. la contraseña al portero.

Just give your check to the porter.

Él traerá el equipaje al taxi.

He will bring the baggage to your taxi.

VOCABULARIO	VOCABULARY
Chófer, al Hotel Internacional.	Chauffeur, to the Hotel International.
Vaya de prisa; tengo hambre y estoy cansado.	Drive quickly; I am hungry and tired.

El hotel; La posada; cuartos; muebles

The Hotel; The Inn; Rooms; Furniture

Un hotel de primera clase.	A first class hotel
Un hotel de segunda clase.	A second class hotel
¿Puede V. dirigirme a un buen hotel? /diri′xirme/	Can you direct me to a good hotel?
¿Puede V. dirigirme a un hotel donde se hable inglés?	Can you direct me to a hotel where English is spoken?
Le recomiendo a V. este hotel.	I can recommend this hotel.
La casa de huéspedes /′wespeðes/	The boarding-house (= the house of guests)
¿Recibe V. huéspedes?	Do you take boarders?
El casero /ka′sero/	The landlord
La casera	The landlady
El portero	The porter
El mozo	The waiter
La criada /kri′aða/	The chamber-maid
El criado	The man-servant
El portero	The porter
Limpiar /lim′pjar/	To clean
Sírvase limpiar mi cuarto inmediatamente.	Please clean my room at once.
Sírvase hacer la cama.	Please make the bed.
Sírvase cepillar mi ropa. /θepi′ʎar/	Please brush my clothes.
Límpieme las botas /′limpjeme/	Shine (polish) my boots.

VOCABULARIO	VOCABULARY
Cepillar	To brush off
Sírvase cepillarme.	Please brush me off.
¿Ha cepillado V. mi ropa?	Have you brushed my clothes?
El ascensor /asɵen'sɔr/	The elevator

El cuarto	The Room
Este cuarto es demasiado grande.	This room is too large.
Este cuarto es demasiado pequeño. /pe'keɲo/	This room is too small.
Este cuarto es caliente (frío).	This room is hot (cold).
Este cuarto es oscuro (húmedo). /'umeðo/	This room is dark (damp).
Este cuarto es demasiado alto.	This room is too high up.

PART NINE

CONTENTS

La salud y la enfermedad
(*Continuación*)

9. Sí. He agarrado un fuerte resfriado.

10. Ojalá no sea nada más que un resfriado. Tenga cuidado de arroparse debidamente, porque aquí fácilmente se agrava un resfriado.

11. Es verdad. En lo futuro me cuidaré más. Me duele[1] la garganta. /me′ðwelelaɣar′ɣanta/

12. Si estuviese en su lugar[2] consultaría con un médico. V. está muy ronco.

13. El estar ronco no me molesta mucho, porque fácilmente me pongo en esa condición. Lo que me inquieta es el dolor de garganta.

14. Temo haberle puesto nervioso; pero ésa no era mi intención. Mi único objeto era advertirle que no descuidara su resfriado.

15. Oh, no; yo no me pongo nervioso tan fácilmente. Sin embargo, haré lo que V. dice y consultaré con un médico.

Con un médico

16. Doctor, ¿cuándo cree V. que podré seguir[3] mi viaje?

17. Es imposible decir. En primer lugar hay que quitar la fiebre. De cualquier manera prepárese V. a pasar aquí una semana.

Special Note on **soler**, a defective verb: In general, only the following tenses and persons are used:

Suelo, *I am accustomed to;* **sueles, suele,** *solemos, soléis,* **suelen.**

Solía, *I was accustomed to;* solías, solía, solíamos, solíais, solían.

[1] **Doler** belongs to that numerous class of slightly irregular verbs which change the stem-vowel o into ue throughout the singular and in the third person plural of the Present Indicative and Subjunctive, and in the same persons in the Imperative.

Doler, doliendo, dolido, *to pain.*

Pres. Ind:	**duelo**	**dueles**	**duele**	dolemos	doléis	**duelen**
Pres. Subj:	**duela**	**duelas**	**duela**	dolamos	doláis	**duelan**
Imperat:	——	**duele**	**duela**	dolamos	doled	**duelan**

Regular: dolía, dolí, doliera, doliese, doliere, doleré, dolería.

Health and Illness

(*Continuation*)

9. Yes, I caught a miserable cold.

10. I trust [ojalá] it is nothing more than a cold. Be careful and dress warmly, for a cold becomes easily serious here.

11. Quite true and I will take better care of myself in the future. My throat hurts.

12. If I were in your place, I would see a doctor. You are very hoarse.

13. Being hoarse does not trouble me much, for I easily get in that condition. What worries me is the pain in my throat.

14. I am afraid I have made you nervous, but that was not my intention. My only object was to warn you not to neglect your cold.

15. Oh, no, I do not get nervous as easily as that. Nevertheless I shall do as you say and see a doctor.

With a Physician

16. Doctor, when do you think I can continue [seguir] my journey?

17. It is impossible to say. In the first place we must get rid of your fever. At any rate you must be prepared to spend a week here.

---

[2] A few sentences showing uses of **lugar.**

¿Qué haría V. si se encontrase en mi lugar? ¿Lo haría V. o no?
What would you do if you were in my place? Would you do it or not?

Si me encontrase en su lugar no lo haría.
If I were in your place I would not do it.

Si yo estuviera en su lugar, procedería de acuerdo con su consejo.
If I were in your place I should act upon his advice.

[3] Seguir, siguiendo, seguido, *to follow.*

Pres. Ind:	sigo	sigues	sigue	seguimos	seguís	siguen
Pres. Sub:	siga	sigas	siga	sigamos	sigáis	sigan
Imperat:	——	sigue	siga	sigamos	seguid	sigan
Imperf:	segu-ía	—ías	—ía	—íamos	—íais	—ían
Past:	segu-í	—iste	siguió	segu-imos	—isteis	siguieron
Imp. Sub:[1]	sigu-iera	—ieras	—iera	—iéramos	—ierais	—ieran
Imp. Sub:[2]	sigu-iese	—ieses	—iese	—iésemos	—ieseis	—iesen
Fut. Sub:	sigu-iere	—ieres	—iere	—iéremos	—iereis	—ieren
Future:	seguir-é	—ás	—á	—emos	—éis	—án
Cond:	seguir-ía	—ías	—ía	—íamos	—íais	—ían

Verbs of this class ending in **guir,** lose the **u** before **a** and **o.**

18. ¿Cuándo volverá² V. a verme?

19. Son las doce menos cuarto. Mis horas de consulta duran hasta las dos. Después tengo que visitar a tres enfermos de gravedad.

20. ¿Está V. muy ocupado?—Por desgracia; hay muchas enfermedades en la ciudad. /pɔrðes'ɣraɵja/

21. ¿Y cuándo desea V. que le espere?

22. Lo visitaré sin falta entre cuatro y cinco. Entretanto siga con la medicina recetada; una cucharadita cada dos horas.

23. Conserve la misma temperatura en su habitación. Mejor es que tenga fuego.

24. Abríguese y evite el frío. Estaré con V. entre cuatro y cinco. ¡Adiós! Hago votos por que V. se restablezca pronto.

Méjico

1. ¿Es cierto que, durante la época colonial española, Méjico fué el país más importante de Hispano-América?

2. Indudablemente. En la época colonial española Méjico tenía bellas ciudades con edificios de gran valor artístico. La riqueza económica de ese hermoso país, que ahora tiene unos veintinueve millones de habitantes, era extraordinaria. El nivel cultural de Méjico, en aquella época, era en verdad muy alto. La famosa Universidad Nacional de Méjico fué fundada en mil quinientos cincuenta y tres.

3. ¿Sería V. tan amable que me dijera algo sobre el Méjico de hoy?

4. Con mucho gusto. La capital de la nación vecina es, en todos los respectos, digna de admiración. Esta metrópoli tiene cerca de dos millones y medio de habitantes. Pocas ciudades del mundo son tan bellas como la capital mejicana.

5. ¿Es Méjico muy rico?

---

² **Volver,** volviendo, **vuelto,** *to return.*

Pres. Ind:	vuelvo	vuelves	vuelve	volvemos	volvéis	**vuelven**
Pres. Sub:	vuelva	vuelvas	vuelva	volvamos	volváis	**vuelvan**
Imperat:	——	vuelve	vuelva	volvamos	volved	**vuelvan**

Reg: volvía, volví, volviera, volviese, volviere, volveré, volvería

18. When will you call on me?

19. It is now a quarter to twelve. My office hours last [duran] till two. After that I have three patients to visit, who are dangerously ill.

20. You seem to be very busy?—Unfortunately so [por desgracia]; there is much sickness in town.

21. And when may I expect you?

22. I will visit you between four and five without fail. In the meanwhile take the medicine I prescribed for you; a teaspoonful every [cada] two hours.

23. Keep the proper temperature in your room. You had better have a fire.

24. Keep yourself warm and avoid catching cold. I will be with you between four and five. Good-bye! I trust you soon will be better.

Mexico

1. Is it true that during the Spanish colonial period Mexico was the most important country in Spanish America?

2. Undoubtedly. In the Spanish colonial period Mexico had beautiful cities with buildings of great artistic value. The economic wealth of that beautiful country, which now has some twenty-nine million inhabitants, was extraordinary. The cultural level of Mexico at that time was very high indeed. The famous National University of Mexico was founded in 1553.

3. Would you be so kind as to tell me something about the Mexico of today?

4. With great pleasure. The capital of the neighboring nation is in every respect worthy of admiration. This metropolis has nearly two and a half million inhabitants. Few cities in the world are as lovely as the Mexican capital.

5. Is Mexico very rich?

6. Sí. Méjico es riquísimo. Sus principales fuentes de riqueza son sus minas de plata, el petróleo y la agricultura. Los productos más importantes de su suelo son, entre otros, el maíz, el arroz, el azúcar, el trigo, el cacao, el henequén, las piñas y los plátanos.

7. ¿Sabe V. lo que Méjico exporta?

8. Sí. Méjico exporta principalmente los minerales enterrados en sus valles y montañas y el petróleo de sus regiones petrolíferas. También exporta algunas frutas y hortalizas y la planta llamada henequén. La fuerte fibra blanca de esta planta sirve para hacer sogas, cuerda, etc.

9. ¿Puede V. decirme lo que Méjico importa?

10. Sí. Méjico importa maquinaria, tejidos, automóviles y camiones. También importa artículos de tocador y medicinas; radios, fonógrafos y discos fonográficos; carbón y artículos de ferretería, etc., etc.

11. ¿Tiene Méjico buenas comunicaciones con los Estados Unidos?

12. Sí. Méjico tiene excelentes comunicaciones marítimas, ferroviarias y aéreas con este país. La nación vecina, unida ahora a los Estados Unidos por la Carretera Panamericana, también tiene buenas comunicaciones con nosotros por teléfono, telégrafo, cable y radio.

13. Muy pronto haremos un viaje en nuestro automóvil hasta Méjico. Iremos por la Carretera Panamericana desde Laredo hasta la capital mejicana.

14. ¿Quiere V. venir con nosotros? ¿Acepta V. nuestra invitación?

15. Con el mayor placer. Tendré la satisfacción de acompañarles a ustedes por lo menos hasta Monterrey.

Cuba

1. ¿Le gustaría a V. ir este invierno a la Habana a pasar allí unas semanas bajo su hermoso cielo?

2. Por supuesto. Espero que me sea posible realizar este deseo dentro de unos días. Francamente le digo que no espero morirme sin haber vuelto a ver esa ciudad tropical.

3. ¿Cómo es el clima de la Habana?

4. Ideal durante el invierno.

6. Yes, Mexico is very, very rich. Its principal sources of wealth are its silver mines, oil and agriculture. The most important products of its soil are, among others, corn, rice, sugar, wheat, cocoa, sisal, pineapples and bananas.

7. Do you know what Mexico exports?

8. Yes. Mexico mainly exports the minerals buried in its valleys and mountains and the oil of its oil-bearing regions. It also exports some fruits and vegetables, and the plant called sisal. The strong white fibre of this plant serves to make ropes, twine, etc.

9. Are you able to tell me what Mexico imports?

10. Yes. Mexico imports machinery, textiles, automobiles and trucks. It also imports toilet articles and medicines; radios, phonographs, and phonograph records; coal and hardware articles, etc., etc.

11. Has Mexico good communications with the United States?

12. Yes. Mexico has excellent sea, railroad, and air communications with this country. The neighboring nation, now joined to the United States by the Pan-American Highway, also has good telephone, telegraph, cable, and radio communications with us.

13. Very soon we shall take a trip in our car to Mexico. We shall go by the Pan-American Highway from Laredo as far as the Mexican capital.

14. Do you want to come with us? Do you accept our invitation?

15. With the greatest pleasure. I shall have the satisfaction of accompanying you at least as far as Monterrey.

Cuba

1. Would you like to go to Havana this winter to spend a few weeks there under its beautiful sky?

2. Of course. I hope that it will be possible for me to fulfil this desire in a few days. I frankly tell you that I do not expect to die without having seen again that tropical city.

3. How is the climate of Havana?

4. Ideal during the winter.

5. ¿Recuerda V. el número de habitantes que la capital cubana tiene?

6. Un millón doscientos mil, en números redondos, son los habitantes de esta soberbia ciudad, cuya bahía es una de las más hermosas del mundo.

7. ¿Es verdad que en la Habana florece la cultura?

8. Sí. En esta modernísima ciudad hay muchísimos centros docentes.

9. ¿Cual es la principal riqueza de Cuba?

10. La principal riqueza de esta hermosa isla es el azúcar y el tabaco. La fertilidad del suelo cubano es enorme.

11. Después de haber pasado tres o cuatro semanas en la Habana, tengo la intención de visitar uno de los ingenios de azúcar más importantes de la isla. También visitaré algunas de las vegas donde se cultiva el tabaco más preciado del mundo.

12. ¿Hay buenas carreteras en Cuba?

13. Sí, excelentes. Por la mejor carretera de la isla iré en automóvil hasta Santiago, es decir, hasta el otro extremo del país.

14. En esta ciudad cubana tomaré un vapor para hacer una visita a la cercana isla de Santo Domingo. En su romántica capital veré todo lo que me interesa desde los puntos de vista histórico y cultural. Naturalmente allí veré la Universidad que Carlos Quinto fundó en el siglo dieciséis, y la primera catedral del Nuevo Mundo donde los restos de Colón fueron enterrados.

15. Después visitaré la bella isla de Puerto Rico. En San Juan, su capital, y en otras partes de esta encantadora tierra tropical, espero pasar unos quince días muy felices.

La América Central

1. ¿Espera V. ir pronto a la América Central?

2. Sí. Muy pronto espero hacer un viaje a esa parte del mundo.

3. ¿Qué países de la América Central tiene V. la intención de visitar?

4. Todos. En primer lugar visitaré Guatemala; y después El Salvador, Honduras, Nicaragua, Costa Rica y Panamá.

5. Do you remember the number of inhabitants that the Cuban capital has?

6. 1,200,000, in round numbers, are the inhabitants of this superb city whose bay is one of the most beautiful in the world.

7. Is it true that culture flourishes in Havana?

8. Yes. In this most modern city there are very many centers of learning.

9. What is the principal wealth of Cuba?

10. The principal wealth of this beautiful island is sugar and tobacco. The fertility of the Cuban soil is enormous.

11. After having spent three or four weeks in Havana, I have the intention of visiting one of the most important sugar plantations in the island. I shall also visit some of the flat lands where the most valuable tobacco in the world is cultivated.

12. Are there good highways in Cuba?

13. Yes, excellent. By the best highway of the island I shall go by automobile to Santiago, that is to say, as far as the other end of the country.

14. In this Cuban city I shall take a boat to pay a visit to the nearby island of Santo Domingo. In its romantic capital I shall see everything which interests me from the historical and cultural points of view. Naturally I shall see there the University which Charles V founded in the sixteenth century, and the first cathedral of the New World where the remains of Columbus were buried.

15. Afterwards I shall visit the beautiful island of Puerto Rico. In San Juan, its capital, and in other parts of this enchanting tropical land I expect to spend a couple of very happy weeks.

Central America

1. Do you expect to go to Central America soon?

2. Yes. Very soon I expect to take a trip to that part of the world.

3. What countries of Central America do you intend to visit?

4. All. In the first place I shall visit Guatemala and afterwards El Salvador, Honduras, Nicaragua, Costa Rica and Panama.

5. ¿Verá V. en Guatemala los sagrados centros ceremoniales que los indios construyeron hace muchos siglos?

6. Esa es mi intención. Aunque esos maravillosos monumentos de la civilización maya están hoy en ruinas, son los más grandiosos que el hombre ha concebido y edificado en los dos continentes americanos.

7. ¿No exagera V. un poquito, amigo mío?

8. Creo que no. En ninguna parte de los dos continentes hay iglesias o monumentos que puedan compararse, en magnitud o magnificencia, a los modelos extraordinarios de belleza arquitectónica que todavía pueden verse en la pintoresca Guatemala.

9. ¿Visitará V. también algunos mercados, ya en Guatemala o en alguna otra república centro-americana?

10. Naturalmente; especialmente los mercados al aire libre. Estos pintorescos centros comerciales muestran al viajero aspectos muy interesantes de la vida del país.

11. ¿Es verdad que los indios van a estos lugares a pie desde distancias muy respetables?

12. Sí; y también es verdad que generalmente llevan a estos mercados, sobre los hombros, los productos de sus huertas y árboles frutales; pollos y otros animales domésticos, etc.

13. ¿Cuando irá V. a Panamá?

14. Visitaré Panamá, tierra de sol, flores y alegría, después de haber visto Costa Rica, Honduras, El Salvador y Nicaragua. Nicaragua, entre paréntesis, es la patria del gran poeta Rubén Darío.

15. ¿Visitará V. entonces el Canal de Panamá?

16. Por supuesto. Anhelo ver esa asombrosa obra de ingeniería que une el Atlántico con el Pacífico.

17. Después de haber visto en las naciones centro-americanas sus mejores ciudades, sus más hermosos lagos y sus más altas montañas, iré hacia el sur.

5. Will you see in Guatemala the sacred ceremonial centers that the Indians built many centuries ago?

6. That is my intention. Although those wonderful monuments of the Mayan civilization are today in ruins, they are the most grandiose that man has conceived and built in the two American continents.

7. Do you not exaggerate a little bit, my friend?

8. I do not think so. In no part of the two continents are there churches or monuments which can be compared, in size or magnificence, with the extraordinary models of architectural beauty which still can be seen in picturesque Guatemala.

9. Will you also visit some markets, either in Guatemala or in some other Central American republic?

10. Naturally, especially the open-air markets. These picturesque commercial centers show the traveler some very interesting aspects of the life of the country.

11. Is it true that the Indians go to these places on foot, from very long distances?

12. Yes; and it is also true that they generally carry to these markets, on their backs, the products of their truck gardens and fruit trees; chickens, and other domestic animals, etc.

13. When will you go to Panama?

14. I shall visit Panama, land of sun, flowers and joy, after having seen Costa Rica, Honduras, El Salvador and Nicaragua. Nicaragua, by the way, is the native land of the great poet, Rubén Darío.

15. Will you then visit the Panama Canal?

16. Of course. I am anxious to see that astonishing engineering work which unites the Atlantic with the Pacific.

17. After having seen in the Central American nations their best cities, their most beautiful lakes and their highest mountains, I shall go towards the south.

18. ¿Visitará V., en su viaje hacia el sur, las prósperas repúblicas de Venezuela y Colombia?

19. Ese es el plan que tengo, pues quiero ver los países en que el gran Simón Bolívar, Libertador de Sudamérica, nació y murió.

20. Después iré al Brasil, Ecuador, Perú, Bolivia, Paraguay, Chile, Argentina y Uruguay.

18. Will you visit, in your trip toward the south, the prosperous republics of Venezuela and Colombia?

19. That is the plan I have, for I want to see the countries where the great Simon Bolivar, the Liberator of South America, was born and died.

20. Afterwards I shall go to Brazil, Ecuador, Peru, Bolivia, Paraguay, Chile, Argentina and Uruguay.

TRANSLATION EXERCISES IN PROSE AND POETRY

Anécdotas

I

Continuando las disputas entre Francisco primero, rey de Francia, y Enrique octavo, rey de Inglaterra,[1] resolvió éste[2] enviar al primero un embajador[3] portador de palabras fieras y amenazas;[4] para lo cual hizo elección del obispo[5] Bonner en quien tenía gran confianza. Este obispo le dijo que ponía su vida en gran peligro,[6] si llevaba tales recados[7] a un rey tan altivo[8] como Francisco primero. "No temas,"[9] le dijo el rey. "Si el rey de Francia hiciese[10] tal, yo haría caer muchas cabezas de franceses que están aquí." " ¿Pero cuál de esas cabezas me vendría[11] tan bien sobre los hombros[12] como ésta?" le replicó el obispo poniendo el dedo en la suya.

II

Luis doce, rey de Francia, cuando no era sino duque[13] de Orleáns, había padecido[14] muchos agravios[15] de dos personas que habían sido favoritos en el reinado[16] precedente. Uno de sus allegados[17] procuraba[18] inducirlo a que les mostrase resentimiento. "No," respondió Su Majestad, "que indigno es de un rey de Francia tomar parte en la venganza del duque de Orleáns."

III

La reina Isabel observando el donaire de un español en un torneo,[19] le suplicó un día que le dijese[20] el nombre de su dama. El español se resistió algún tiempo. En fin, cediendo a la curiosidad de Su Majestad, prometió enviarle el retrato[21] de la dama. Al día siguiente hizo presentar a Su Majestad un paquetillo,[22] donde la reina, no[23] hallando sino[23] un espejito,[24] quedo sonrojada al punto.

---

[1] England. [2] The latter. [3] Ambassador. [4] Threats. [5] Bishop. [6] Danger. [7] Messages. [8] Haughty. [9] Imperative of *temer*, to fear. [10] From *hacer*. [11] *Me vendría*, would become me. [12] Shoulders. [13] Duke. [14] *Padecer*, to suffer. [15] Injuries. [16] Reign. [17] Followers. [18] *Procurar*, to try. [19] Tournament. [20] From *decir*. [21] Picture. [22] Little package. [23] *No . . . sino*, only. [24] Little mirror.

IV

El caballero[1] Tomás Moro,[2] famoso canciller de Inglaterra, puesto[3] en prisión por Enrique[4] octavo, se dejó crecer los cabellos[5] y la barba, y viniendo[6] un barbero para cortarlos[7] y afeitarle,[8] "Amigo," le dijo, "el rey y yo discutimos sobre mi cabeza; y yo no quiero hacer el menor gasto en este pleito,[9] sin saber antes quién de los dos ha[10] de disponer de ella."

V

Los cortesanos del rey Felipe[11] le aconsejaban que se vengase de un hombre que había hablado mal de él. "Antes es menester saber si yo no le he dado razón," dijo Felipe, y, habiéndose averiguado que el tal hombre jamás había recibido cosa alguna, le envió ricos presentes. Supo el rey poco después que el mismo le llenaba de alabanzas. "Mirad pues," dijo a los cortesanos,[12] "que yo sé mejor que vosotros apaciguar[13] una lengua mala."

---

[1] Knight (Sir) [2] *Thomas More.* [3] From *poner.* [4] Henry. [5] Hair. [6] From *venir.* [7] Cut them. [8] Shave him. [9] Pleito, lawsuit, dispute. [10] Is to. [11] Philip. [12] Courtiers. [13] Silence.

REFRANES

Más[1] vale tarde que nunca.

El que calla,[2] otorga.[3]

El que tarde llega, caldo bebe[4].

La necesidad carece[5] de ley.

Lo que no se puede remediar se ha de aguantar.[6]

Más vale pájaro en mano que ciento volando.

Al hierro caliente, batir[7] de repente.[8]

Amor con amor se paga.[9]

Cada oveja[10] con su pareja.[11]

Donde fuego se hace, humo sale.

Donde hay gana[12] hay maña.[13]

De la mano a la[14] boca desaparece la sopa.

Piedra movediza no coge musgo.[15]

Salir de llamas[16] y caer en brasas.[17]

No es oro todo lo que reluce.

A quien madruga[18] Dios ayuda.

Donde[19] fueres, haz[20] como vieres.

La caridad bien ordenada empieza[21] por uno mismo

Más vale buen callar que mal hablar.

Obra de común,[22] obra de ningún.

A lo hecho, pecho.[23]

---

[1] Más valer—to be worth more, to be better than. [2] Callar—to be silent. [3] Consents. [4] "First come, first served." [5] Carecer de—lack. "Necessity knows no law." [6] Aguantar—endure. [7] *Batir*, Infinitive instead of Imperative. [8] At once. [9] Is paid. "One good turn deserves another." [10] Oveja—ewe. [11] Mate. [12] Desire or will. [13] Dexterity, "way." [14] From hand to mouth. "There's many a slip, etc." [15] Moss. [16] Flames. [17] Live coals. [18] *Madrugar*—to get up early. [19] *Donde fueres*—wherever you may be. [20] Imp. of *hacer*, to do. "When at Rome, do as the Romans do." [21] Empieza por—begins with. [22] Everybody. [23] "What cannot be cured must be endured."

FÁBULA

Las dos zorras[1]

Una noche entraron dos zorras furtivamente en un gallinero,[2] mataron el gallo,[3] las gallinas,[4] y los pollos.[5] Después de esta matanza,[6] empezaron[7] a devorar su presa.[8] Una que era joven y sin reflexión, propuso[9] comerlos todos de una vez. La otra, vieja y codiciosa[10], quería ahorrar[11] para otro día. "Hija," dijo la vieja, "la experiencia me hizo[12] sabia; en mi tiempo he visto mucho mundo. No consumamos a la vez pródigamente todo nuestro caudal;[13] tuvimos buen éxito, y debemos cuidar[14] de no malgastarlo."[15]

Replicó la joven "Estoy resuelta a recrearme mientras lo tengo por delante, y saciar mi apetito por toda una semana; por lo que toca a venir[16] aquí mañana, es cuento:[17] eso es exponernos. Mañana vendrá aquí el amo,[18] y por vengar la muerte de sus pollos, nos dará[19] con una tranca[20] en la cabeza."

Después de esta réplica, cada una de ellas obra[21] como le parece más propio. La joven come hasta que revienta,[22] sin poder apenas arrastrarse[23] a su cueva[24] antes de morir. La vieja que le pareció mucho más prudente gobernar su apetito, y ser frugal, fué el día siguiente al gallinero, y la mató el labrador.

Así cada edad tiene su vicio favorito: los jóvenes son fogosos[25] e insaciables en sus placeres; y los viejos incorregibles en su avaricia.

---

[1] Foxes. [2] Hen-coop. [3] Cock. [4] Hen. [5] Chicken. [6] Slaughter. [7] Began. [8] Prey. [9] From *proponer*. [10] Miserly. [11] Save. [12] From *hacer*. [13] Stock. [14] Take care to. [15] To waste it. [16] *Por lo que toca a venir,* as for coming. [17] Nonsense. [18] Master. [19] *Nos dará con,* he will hit us. [20] Bar, stick. [21] Acts. [22] *Reventar,* to burst. [23] To drag. [24] Den. [25] Impetuous.

RIMA LXIX

Al brillar un relámpago[1] nacemos
y aun dura su fulgor[2] cuando morimos:
¡tan corto es el vivir!
La gloria y el amor tras que corremos
sombras de un sueño son que perseguimos:[3]
¡despertar es morir!

—GUSTAVO A. BÉCQUER.

LETRILLA QUE LLEVABA POR REGISTRO[4] EN SU BREVIARIO

Nada te turbe;[5]
Nada te espante;
Todo se pasa;
Dios no se muda,[6]
La paciencia todo lo alcanza.[7]
Quien a Dios tiene
Nada le falta.
Sólo Dios basta.[8]

—SANTA TERESA DE JESÚS.

---

[1] In a flash of lightning. [2] brilliance. [3] we pursue. [4] Book-mark. [5] *Turbar*, to disturb. [6] *Mudarse*, to change. [7] *Alcanzar*, to attain. [8] *Bastar*, to suffice.

COLLOQUIAL EXPRESSIONS

Estoy muy de prisa.	I am in a terrible hurry.
Deseo guardar esto como recuerdo.	I want this for a souvenir.
¿Está ocupado este asiento?	Is this seat taken?
¿Cómo puedo llegar al otro lado sin pasar el puente?	How can I get across without using (crossing) the bridge?
He estado otra vez esta mañana en el centro de la ciudad.	I have been downtown again this morning.
Todavía me corresponden 20 centavos. Di a V. medio dólar y V. sólo me ha devuelto diez centavos.	There are twenty cents coming to me yet. I gave you a half-dollar and you have given me only ten cents back.
¿Hombre, de dónde viene?	Say, where have you been?
¿Hombre, puede V. decirme qué es esto?	Say, can you tell me what this is?

204

VOCABULARIO
Comiendo y bebiendo

Tráigame la carta (lista).

Quiero huevos frescos, una taza de café, mantequilla y tostadas.

Alcánceme la pimienta y la mostaza.

Tráiganos dos cigarros habanos.

¿Qué tiene V. para cenar?

Eso basta; pero dénos V. buen vino y frutas.

Déme V. un poco de pan.

Déme cerveza fuerte.

Muchacho, danos pan caliente.

Muchacho, da de beber al señor.

Veamos, ahora, ¿qué nos dará V. de cenar?

He comido muy bien.

Y yo también.

Probemos el vino.

Destape esa botella.

No tengo sacacorchos.

¿Que quiere Vd. más, una ala o un muslo?

A mí me da igual.

El hambre es la mejor salsa.

Vamos, señor, por la salud del Presidente.

Le corresponderé con mucho gusto.

VOCABULARY
Eating and Drinking

Bring me the bill of fare.

I want fresh eggs, a cup of coffee, butter and toast.

Reach me the pepper and the mustard.

Bring us two Havana cigars.

What have you for supper?

That is enough; but give us some good wine and some fruit.

Give me a little bread.

Give me some strong beer.

Boy, give us hot bread.

Boy, give the gentleman some drink.

Now let us see, what will you give us for supper?

I have dined very well.

So have I.

Let us taste the wine.

Uncork that bottle.

I have no corkscrew.

Which do you like best, a wing or a leg?

It is all one to me.

Hunger is the best sauce.

Come, sir, to the health of the President.

I will pledge you with a great deal of pleasure.

VOCABULARIO	VOCABULARY
El vino es exquisito.	The wine is exquisite.
¿Sabe V. trinchar?	Can you carve?

Del Comer y Beber	**Of Eating and Drinking**
La comida	Dinner
La cena	Supper
El convidado	Guest
El convite	Feast
El pastel	Pie, pastry
La bebida	Drink
El aguardiente	Brandy
La cerveza	Beer
La sidra	Cider
La limonada	Lemonade

El cuarto	**The Room**
¿Tiene V. un cuarto para alquilar? /alki'lar/	Have you a room to let?
¿Cuál es el precio de este cuarto?	What is the price of this room?
No quiero un cuarto oscuro ni húmedo.	I don't want a dark or a damp room.
El cuarto del frente /'frente/	The front-room
El cuarto del fondo /'fɔndo/	The rear-room
¿Da este cuarto al frente o al fondo?	Does this room face the front or the rear?
Este cuarto da al fondo, pero puedo darle uno del frente si V. lo desea.	This room is in the rear, but I can give you a front room if you wish.
Prefiero uno con vista al patio. /'bista 'patjo/	I prefer one that looks on the court.
Quiero un cuarto que dé a la calle. /'kaʎe/	I want a room that looks on the street.

VOCABULARIO	VOCABULARY
El piso /ˈpiso/	The floor; the story
¿En qué piso está esta habitación?	On which floor is this room located?
Déme dos cuartos que se comuniquen.	Give me two adjoining rooms.
Por favor déjeme V. ver el cuarto.	Please let me see the room.
Enséñeme sus mejores habitaciones. /meˈxɔres/	Show me your best rooms.
Tomaré este cuarto.	I will take this room.

La puerta / The Door

Esta puerta no cierra.	This door will not shut.
¿A dónde da esta puerta?	Where does this door lead to?
Esta puerta comunica con la sala.	This door communicates with the sitting room.

La ventana / The Window

Con una ventana; con dos ventanas.	With one window; with two windows
Déme V. un cuarto con dos ventanas; los cuartos con una ventana son muy oscuros.	Give me a room with two windows; the rooms with one window are too dark.
El piso (de un cuarto)	The floor (of a room)
La alfombra	The carpet
Un tapete } Una estera }	A bed-carpet; a mat
Nosotros no tenemos más que esteras junto a las camas.	We have only mats before the beds.
Es raro encontrar alfombras que cubran todo el suelo en Méjico.	One rarely finds carpets covering the whole floor in Mexico.

La cama / The Bed

Limpio	Clean
Fresco	Fresh

VOCABULARIO

La manta

La almohada

Un colchón

Un colchón de muelles

Una sábana

Haga poner sábanas limpias.

Las sábanas no están bien limpias.

Esta manta no me abriga, déme V. otra.

Me gusta que la cabeza esté alta; déme otra almohada.

Dormir

¿Descansó V. bien?
¿Durmió V. bien?

Generalmente duermo muy bien, pero anoche dormí mal.

Hacer la cama.

Sírvase hacer mi cama.

Estoy muy cansado y deseo irme a la cama ahora mismo.

¿A qué hora se acostó?

Él se acostó a las diez.

Yo no he cerrado los ojos en toda la noche.

Llamar

Llámeme temprano, quiero salir por el primer tren.

Quiero descansar toda la noche. No permita a ninguno que me moleste.

VOCABULARY

The blanket

The pillow

A mattress

A spring-mattress

A sheet

Have clean sheets put on.

The sheets are not quite clean.

This blanket does not keep me warm; give me another.

I like my head to be high; give me another pillow.

To Sleep

Did you rest well?

Generally I sleep very well, but last night I slept badly.

To make the bed.

Please make my bed.

I am very tired and wish to go to bed at once.

At what time did he go to bed?

He went to bed at ten.

I have not slept a wink (not closed eyes) the whole night.

To Call; To Awaken

Call me early. I want to leave by the first train.

I want to have a long night's rest. Don't allow anyone to disturb me.

VOCABULARIO
La mesa

VOCABULARY
The Table

El mantel	The table-cloth
La silla	The chair
El armario	The wardrobe
La cómoda	The chest of drawers
El espejo	The mirror
El sofá	The sofa
La lámpara	The lamp
Una pantalla (de lámpara)	A shade (of a lamp)
La chimenea	The chimney
El candelero	The chandelier
El candelabro	The candlestick
La vela	The candle
El gas	The gas
La luz (eléctrica)	The (electric) light
Encender	To light
Apagar	To put out
Encienda el gas.	Light the gas.
Apague el gas.	Turn off the gas.
Un fósforo	A match
Fósforos	Matches
Tráigame agua fresca para beber.	Bring me fresh water to drink.
Tráigame agua fresca para lavarme.	Bring me fresh water to wash with.
Llene la jarra.	Fill the pitcher.
¿Dónde está el timbre?	Where is the bell?
Cepille esta ropa, mozo.	Brush these clothes, young man.
Mi vestido y botas están mojados; sírvase secarlos.	My clothes and boots are wet please dry them.

VOCABULARIO

Encienda fuego.

Tráigame un recadero, si es posible, uno que hable inglés.

¿No hay cartas para mí?

¿Preguntó alguien por mí?

Si alguien pregunta por mí, dígale que espero volver a las seis.

Si alguien pregunta por mí, dígale que he ido a casa del señor Martínez, donde estaré hasta las cuatro.

Si el sastre me trajera mi chaqueta, dígale que vuelva mañana por la mañana.

Si algunos paquetes viniesen para mí, sírvase hacer que se pongan en mi cuarto.

¿Podría yo escribir algunas líneas en la oficina?

Sírvase darme recado de escribir.

Yo salgo mañana en el tren de las seis, estación del Este. ¿Irá el ómnibus allá?

¡Que se me llame a tiempo!

Tráigame un taxi a tiempo y haga bajar mi equipaje.

Haz que me hagan la cuenta.

Sírvase darme la cuenta.

Yo no he tenido esto.

Eso ha sido ya pagado.

VOCABULARY

Light a fire.

Get me a messenger-boy, if possible, one who speaks English.

Are there any letters for me?

Did anyone inquire for me?

If anyone asks for me, tell him that I expect to be back at six.

If anyone inquires for me, tell him that I have gone to Mr. Martinez's where I can be found till four o'clock.

If the tailor should bring me my coat, tell him to call again to-morrow morning.

If any packages should come for me, have them put into my room, please.

Could I write a few lines in the office?

Please give me some writing materials.

I start to-morrow by the six o'clock train, Eastern Station. Will the omnibus go there?

Let me be called in time!

Get me a taxi in good time and have my baggage brought down.

Have my bill made out.

Please give me my bill.

I have not had this.

That has already been paid.

Encuentro este precio muy alto.

I find this charge too high.

Llámeme a las cinco mañana; toque fuerte a la puerta. Yo sentiría mucho perder el tren.

Call me at five to-morrow; knock loudly at my door. I should be sorry to lose the train.

Vestirse

To Dress

El vestido	The dress
Un traje	A suit of clothes
El abrigo o gabán	The overcoat
Un abrigo de verano	A summer overcoat
Un abrigo de invierno	A winter overcoat
La chaqueta	The jacket
El frac	The dress-coat
Un chaleco	A waist-coat—a vest
Un pantalón	Trousers
Los tirantes	Suspenders
El bolsillo	The pocket
Un pañuelo	A handkerchief
El botón	The button
Un botón se ha caído de aquí.	A button is off here.
Haga que se ponga un botón, pero bien cosido.	Please have a button put on, but strongly (well sewed on).
Abróchese el abrigo.	Button your overcoat.
Desabróchese la chaqueta.	Unbutton your coat.
El ojal	The buttonhole
El ojal está descosido; tenga la bondad de remendarlo.	The buttonhole is torn; please mend it.
La camisa	The shirt
El pijama	The pyjama
Ponerse una camisa limpia	To put on a clean shirt

VOCABULARIO

VOCABULARY

El cuello (de camisa)	The collar-band (of a shirt)
Abotonar	To button on
Los puños	The cuffs
La corbata	The necktie
Anudar	To tie
Hacer un nudo	To tie a knot
Ropa interior	Underwear
Los calzoncillos /kaleɔn'eiʎɔs/	The drawers
Las medias	The stockings
Los calcetines /kalee'tines/	The socks
Las botas	The boots
Un par de botas	A pair of boots
Los zapatos	The shoes
Un par de zapatos	A pair of shoes
Tómeme la medida para un par de botas.	Measure me for a pair of boots.
Las zapatillas /eapa'tiʎas/	The slippers
Un vestido	A dress
La bata	The wrapper; the robe
Unas enaguas	The petticoat
El corsé	The corset
La camiseta	The undershirt
Los guantes	The gloves
Un par de guantes	A pair of gloves
Guantes de cabritilla /kaβri'tiʎa/	Kid gloves
La capa	The cloak
Una capa de piel	A fur cloak
El manguito	The muff

212

VOCABULARIO

En casa del sastre

¿Puede V. recomendarme un buen sastre?

¿Es su trabajo bueno?

Enséñeme V. sus muestras.

Quiero un abrigo.

Tómeme V. la medida para un traje completo.

A la última moda

No muy ajustado

No muy ancho

Un poco más largo

No tan largo

Quiero una chaqueta de una hilera de botones.

El forro

¿Cuándo puedo tener este abrigo?

¿No antes?

No puedo esperar tanto tiempo; debo tenerlo para el martes.

Mándemelo con el recibo.

¿Puede V. recomendarme un fabricante de paños?

Enséñeme un paño claro (oscuro)

¿Cómo me cae? }
¿Cómo me sienta? }

Está muy ajustado en la cintura.

Está muy ajustado en los sobacos.

VOCABULARY

At the Tailor's

Can you recommend a good tailor to me?

Is his workmanship good?

Show me your patterns

I want an overcoat.

Measure me for a complete suit.

In the latest fashion

Not too tight

Not too wide (loose)

A little longer

Not quite so long

I want a single-breasted coat.

The lining

When can I have this overcoat?

Not before?

I cannot wait so long; I must have it by Tuesday.

Send it to me C. O. D. (with the bill).

Can you recommend a clothier to me?

Show me light (dark) goods (cloth).

How does it fit me?

It is too tight in the waist.

It is too tight under the arms (in the arm-pits).

VOCABULARIO

¿No están las mangas muy largas?

Me gusta el pantalón ajustado.

¿Toma V. vestidos para reparar?

El doblez del pantalón está gastado; remételo un poco.

Póngale botones a mi chaleco.

Quítele esas manchas.

Una modista

Yo quiero que me haga un vestido.

Enséñeme algunos modelos.

Déjeme ver unos figurines.

Hágame el vestido por este estilo.

Tome mi medida.

El frente

La espalda

La falda

Yo pondré mis proprios materiales.

¿Cuántas varas (cuántos metros) se necesitan?

¿Cuánto costará este vestido completo?

¿Está este figurín todavía de moda?

Yo deseo una falda corta (una falda larga).

VOCABULARY

Are not the sleeves too long?

I like my trousers to be close fitting.

Do you take clothes to make repairs?

The cuff of the trousers is worn at the bottom; turn it in a little.

Put buttons on my waistcoat (vest).

Remove those stains.

A Dressmaker

I wish to have a dress made.

Show me some patterns.

Let me see some fashion-plates.

Make the dress in this style.

Take my measure.

The front

The back

The skirt

I shall supply my own materials.

How many yards (meters) will it take?

What would this dress cost complete?

Is this pattern still fashionable?

I wish to have a short skirt (a long skirt).

VOCABULARIO	VOCABULARY
No debe entrar muy apretada; me gusta sentirme cómoda.	It must not fit too tightly; I like to feel comfórtable.
La guarnición de vestido	The trimming
Ponga botones de marfil en este vestido.	Put ivory buttons on this dress.
Desearía tener el vestido el sábado temprano.	I should like to have this dress early on Saturday.
¿Cuándo puedo venir para probármelo?	When can I call to try it on?
La cintura	The waist
La blusa	The blouse
Póngase la blusa.	Try on the blouse.
Le viene bien en la cintura.	It fits you well in the waist.
La blusa le queda muy bien.	The blouse fits you well.
Alterar; cambiar	To alter; to change
Cambie el cuerpo, no me queda bien.	Alter the waist; it does not fit.
El hombro	The shoulder
El vestido me queda mal en los hombros; sírvase cambiarlo.	The dress fits badly in the shoulders; please alter it.
Las mangas están muy estrechas (muy anchas, muy largas; muy cortas).	The sleeves are too narrow (too wide; too long; too short).
Arrugar	To wrinkle
La manga se arruga allí; sírvase cambiarla.	The sleeve wrinkles right there; change it, please.
El cuello está muy bajo. /ˈkweʎo/	The collar is too low.
El cuello no está bastante alto.	The collar is not high enough.
¿Cuándo estará hecho mi vestido?	When will my dress be done?
Estará hecho mañana sin falta.	It will be done to-morrow without fail.

VOCABULARIO	VOCABULARY
El tocador	**The Toilet**

Vestirse	To dress
Él se está vistiendo.	He is dressing.
¿Qué, no se ha vestido V. todavía?	Aren't you dressed yet?
¿Qué, no está V. listo todavía?	Aren't you ready yet?
Ella se está cambiando el vestido.	She is changing her dress.
Él se está desnudando.	He is undressing.
El gusto	The taste
Ella se viste con grandísimo gusto.	She dresses with a great deal of taste.
¿Cree Vd. que este sombrero me viene bien?	Do you think this hat is becoming to me?
Este sombrero le queda a Vd. muy bien.	This hat is very becoming to you.
El color	The color
Este color no me está a mí bien.	This color is not becoming to me.
La cara	The face
La tez; el cutis	The complexion; the skin.
Delicado	Delicate
Sonrosado	Rosy
Claro	Clear; light
Pálido	Pale
Ella tiene un delicado color sonrosado; no puede usar un color tan subido.	She has a delicate, rosy complexion; she can not wear such a deep tinge of color.
Este color está muy subido; este es el proprio.	This color is too deep; this is the right one.

Lavar	**To Wash**
Quisiera lavarme las manos.	I should like to wash my hands.
Quisiera lavarme y cepillarme.	I should like to wash and brush up.

216

VOCABULARIO

Tráigame agua, jabón y toallas.
/to'aʎas/

¿Hay agua en mi cuarto?

Primero que todo debo lavarme.

La palangana

La jarra /'xarːa/

Una pastilla de jabón.

Una esponja /es'pɔnxa/

Una toalla

Secar

Me estoy secando las manos.

Séquese Vd. las manos con esta toalla.

Limpiarse la boca

Me estoy limpiando la boca.

El diente; los dientes

Un cepillo de dientes

Me estoy limpiando los dientes.

Un cepillo de cabeza.

Un cepillo para las uñas /'uɲas/

Él está peinándose.

Un peine

Me estoy peinando el pelo (or los cabellos).

La raya

La raya está derecha.

La raya está torcida.

El aceite

La pomada

VOCABULARY

Bring me some water, soap and towels.

Is there any water in my room?

First of all I must have a wash.

The wash-basin

The pitcher

A cake of soap

A sponge

A towel

To dry

I am drying my hands.

Dry your hands with this towel.

To clean one's mouth

I am cleaning my mouth.

The tooth; the teeth

A tooth-brush

I am brushing my teeth.

A hair-brush

A nail-brush

He is combing his hair.

A comb

I am combing my hair.

The part

The part is straight.

The part is crooked.

The oil

The pomatum

VOCABULARIO	VOCABULARY
La lima /'lima/	The file
Me estoy limando las uñas.	I am filing my nails.
El polvo	The powder
El polvo de tocador	Toilet-powder
Los polvos de dientes	Tooth-powder
La caja de polvo	The powder-box
La borla para empolvarse	The powder-puff
Ella se empolvó la cara.	She powdered her face.
Bañarse; tomar un baño	To bathe; to take a bath
Él está bañándose; él toma un baño.	He is bathing; he is taking a bath.
Afeitarse	To shave
Siempre me afeito yo mismo.	I always shave myself.

El barbero / The Barber

Sírvase afeitarme.	Please shave me.
Las patillas	The sideburns
La barba	The beard
La barba entera	The full-beard
El bigote	The moustache
Mi barba es muy recia.	My beard is very stubborn.
Su navaja no está bastante afilada /na'βaxa/	Your razor is not sharp enough.

El peluquero / The Hairdresser

Quiero que me corte el pelo.	I wish to have my hair cut.
Corto detrás, algo más largo delante.	Short behind, a little longer in front.
Quíteme solamente un poco; se me está cayendo el pelo.	Take off only a little; I am losing my hair.
Hágame el favor de arreglarme el pelo.	Dress my hair, please.

VOCABULARIO	VOCABULARY
Hágame la raya en medio.	Part my hair in the middle.
Hágame la raya a un lado.	Part my hair on the side.
Cepílleme el pelo.	Brush my hair.
Sírvase rizarme el pelo.	Curl my hair, please.
Las tijeras /ti'xeras/	The scissors

La ropa limpia	**Clean Linen**
Sucio, sucia	Soiled
Mande esta ropa a la lavandera.	Send these clothes to the laundress.
La lista está ahí.	The laundry list is there.
¿Cuándo puede Vd. mandarla a casa?	When can you send it home?
Debo tener la ropa para el jueves.	I must have the laundry by Thursday.
No se olvide de remendar las camisas.	Do not forget to mend the shirts.
El almidón	The starch
Almidonar	To starch
Planchar	To iron
No planche tanto mis cuellos.	Do not iron my collars so stiff.

Artículos de tocador	**Articles of Dress**
Joyas /'xɔjas/	Jewels
Diamantes /ðja'mantes/	Diamonds
La perla; las perlas	The pearl; the pearls
El anillo; la sortija	The ring
El anillo de diamantes	The diamond ring
Los pendientes; los zarcillos	The ear-rings
Un brazalete; una pulsera	A bracelet
Un collar	A necklace

VOCABULARIO	VOCABULARY
Un broche	A brooch
El reloj /rːɛ'lo/	The watch
Una cadena	A chain
La llave	The key
Los botones de camisa	The studs
Los anteojos	The spectacles
Los lentes ⎫ Las gafas ⎭	The eye-glasses
Los gemelos	The opera-glasses
El bastón	The cane
Una sombrilla; un parasol	A parasol
Un paraguas	An umbrella
El abanico	The fan

El tiempo — The Time

La hora	The time; the hour
El compás	The time (in music)
Seguir el compás	To keep time
Perder el compás	To get out of time
Tres veces	Three times
Otra vez	Another time; again
En ese tiempo	At that time
Al presente	At the present time
Al mismo tiempo	At the same time
Por largo tiempo; por mucho tiempo	For a long time
No le he visto a Vd. por mucho tiempo.	I have not seen you for a long time.
En buen tiempo	In good time
En mis tiempos	In my time

VOCABULARIO

Por algún tiempo	For some time
De tiempo en tiempo	From time to time
Venir a tiempo	To come in time
Eso viene a buen tiempo.	That comes just at the right time.
¿Llegaremos a tiempo? ¿Estaremos a tiempo?	Shall we be in time?
¿A qué hora sale el tren para Querétaro?	At what time does the train start for Queretaro?
¿Estamos a tiempo para el tren?	Are we in time for the train?
¿Dónde tendré tiempo de comer algo?	Where shall I have time to eat something?
¿Tenemos tiempo para ello?	Have we time for it?
¿Tiene Vd. tiempo de acompañarme?	Have you time to accompany me?

La hora

¿Qué hora es?	What o'clock is it? (What time is it)?
¿Puede V. decirme qué hora es?	Can you tell me what time it is?
No puedo decírselo exactamente.	I cannot tell you precisely.
¿Sabe V. qué hora es?—No lo sé.	Do you know what time it is?—No, I don't.
Es la una.	It is one o'clock.
Es la una y cuarto.	It is a quarter past one.
Es la una y media.	It is half past one.
Son las dos menos cuarto.	It is a quarter to two.
Son las dos menos veinte y cinco minutos.	It is twenty-five minutes to two.

VOCABULARIO	VOCABULARY
Son las dos en punto.	It is precisely two o'clock.
Son cerca de las cinco.	It is about five.
Van a dar las tres. Pronto darán las tres.	It is just going to strike three.
Han dado las ocho.	It has struck eight.
¿Qué hora está dando?—Las once.	What time is it striking?—Eleven.
¿Qué hora podrá ser?—Acaban de dar las siete.	What o'clock may it be?—It just struck seven.
Hágame el favor de decirme qué hora es. Creo que mi reloj está atrasado (adelantado).	Have the kindness to tell me what time it is. I think my watch is slow (fast).

División del tiempo	Division of Time
Hoy	To-day
Mañana	To-morrow
Pasado mañana	The day after to-morrow
Ayer	Yesterday
Anteayer	The day before yesterday
Mañana por la mañana	To-morrow morning
Mañana por la tarde	To-morrow afternoon
Anoche	Last night
Esta semana	This week
La semana pasada	Last week
La semana que viene	Next week
Por una semana	For a week
En una semana	In a week
De mañana en ocho días	A week from to-morrow

VOCABULARIO	VOCABULARY
Quince días Una quincena	A fortnight
Un mes	A month
Un año	A year
Un siglo	A century
El año pasado	Last year
El año que viene	Next year
El principio	The beginning
El medio	The middle
El fin	The end

PART TEN

THE SPANISH GRAMMAR

CONTENTS

THE SPANISH ALPHABET

a	a	n	ene
b	be	ñ	eñe
c	ce	o	o
ch	che	p	pe
d	de	q	cu
e	e	r	ere
f	efe	rr	erre
g	ge	s	ese
h	hache	t	te
i	i	u	u
j	jota	v	uve
k	ka	x	equis
l	ele	y	i griega
ll	elle	z	zeta
m	eme		

THE ARTICLES

There are two articles: the definite **el**, the, for the masculine, **la**, the, for the feminine form, and the indefinite **un**, a, an (masculine), **una**, a, an (feminine).

Declension of the Articles

	Masculine		Feminine		
	Singular	*Plural*	*Singular*	*Plural*	
Nom.	el	los	la	las	the
Gen.	del	de los	de la	de las	of the, *or* from the
Dat.	al	a los	a la	a las	to the, *or* at the
Acc.	el	los	la	las	the

	Masculine	Feminine	
Nom.	un	una	a
Gen.	de un	de una	of a, *or* from a
Dat.	a un	a una	to, *or* at a
Acc.	un	una	a

Remarks on the Article

1. There are three genders in the Spanish language: masculine, feminine, and neuter. The definite article has in the singular a distinct form for each gender: masculine, **el**; feminine, **la**; neuter, **lo**.

El padre, *the father*   La madre, *the mother*   Lo bueno, *the good*

REMARKS—1. The neuter gender is applicable only to adjectives taken in an unlimited or indefinite sense, as: lo bueno, *the good or that which is good;* lo peor, *the worst or what is worst, etc.*

This neuter gender, which has no plural, is therefore never applied to persons or things, but only to adjectives used as nouns, and to nouns taken adjectively: Todo era grande en San Luis, lo rey, lo santo, lo capitán, *everything was great in St. Luis (Louis IX), the king, the saint, the captain.*

2. The neuter article is not placed indifferently before all adjectives used as nouns. Thus, in the following sentences: El malo será castigado, *the wicked shall be punished;* el azul de este paño es demasiado oscuro, *the blue of this cloth is too dark;*—the neuter article, **lo,** would not be used, because these adjectives are used as nouns and are sufficiently determinate. It is evident that in the first sentence, the word **hombre,** *man,* is understood, before **malo,** *wicked;* and in the second sentence, the word **color,** *color,* before **azul,** *blue.*

2. Although the article **el** belongs only to the masculine gender, it may be placed, for the sake of euphony, before feminine nouns beginning with a stressed **a** : el agua, **the water;** el alma, **the soul**, el ala, **the wing;** el águila, **the eagle;** el ave, **the bird.** This change of article is, however, only allowed in the singular, and the plural is las aguas, las almas, las alas, etc.

Adjectives accompanying the singular of such nouns must be placed in the feminine: el agua está fría, **the water is cold.**

The same rules apply to words beginning with an **h** followed by a stressed **a,** as: el hacha es pesada, **the axe is heavy;** las hachas, **the axes,** etc.

Nouns like América, **America;** alegría, **joy;** habitación, **habitation,** etc., take the feminine article **la,** because the first a is not stressed: La América, la habitación, etc.

3. The indefinite article **a, an,** or the numeral **one,** is rendered by **un** before a masculine noun and by **una** before a feminine noun.

Un hermano, *a brother*   Una hermana, *a sister*
Un libro, *a book*   Una mesa, *a table*

4. The definite article should always be repeated before the nouns it defines:

El padre y la madre	*The father and mother*
La casa y el jardín	*The house and garden*
El buen lápiz y la buena pluma	*The good pencil and pen*

5. The definite article is used in Spanish in place of the possessive pronoun in English whenever the sense of the sentence indicates who the possessor is. This is especially the case when parts of the body are mentioned.

Tengo algo en el ojo.	*I have something in my eye.*
¿Qué tiene V. en la mano?	*What have you in your hand?*
Déme V. la mano.	*Give me your hand.*
El tiene el sombrero en la mano.	*He has his hat in his hand.*
Este soldado ha perdido el brazo.	*This soldier has lost his arm.*

Peculiarities in the Use of the Definite Article

The definite article is used in Spanish:

1. Before the names of **some cities** and **countries** and, generally, before the names of **rivers** and **mountains**:

La Habana es más grande que Veracruz.	*Havana is larger than Vera-Cruz.*
La India tiene altas montañas.	*India has lofty mountains.*
El Canadá está al norte de los Estados Unidos de América.	*Canada is north of the United States of America.*
La Guaira es una ciudad.	*Guaira is a city.*
Los Alpes y los Pirineos son muy altos.	*The Alps and the Pyrenees are very high.*
El Vesuvio es un volcán.	*Vesuvius is a volcano.*
El Danubio es un río grande.	*The Danube is a large river.*

2. Before names of **days** and **seasons**:

El domingo es un día de descanso.	*Sunday is a day of rest.*
El sábado es el último día de la semana.	*Saturday is the last day of the week.*
El invierno es muy frío en este país.	*Winter is very cold in this country.*

3. Before **abstract nouns**:

La juventud es imprudente.	*Youth is imprudent.*
La virtud es amable.	*Virtue is amiable.*
La esperanza sostiene al hombre.	*Hope sustains man.*

4. Before names of **metals, colors, substances, elements, dignities, systems of doctrine, arts,** and **sciences:**

El oro y el plomo son metales.	*Gold and lead are metals.*
El blanco y el negro son colores.	*White and black are colors.*
El fuego y el agua son elementos.	*Fire and water are elements.*
La geografía es la descripción de la tierra.	*Geography is the description of the earth.*
El azúcar es dulce.	*Sugar is sweet.*
La música y la danza son hermanas.	*Music and dancing are sisters.*
El catolicismo y el protestantismo	*Catholicism and Protestantism*

5. Before **adjectives,** or other parts of speech, used **as nouns:**

Los ricos y los pobres	*The rich and the poor*
El comer y el beber	*Eating and drinking*
El sí y el no	*Yes and no*
El pro y el contra	*Pro and con*
El bien y el mal	*Good and evil*

6. Before **nouns** representing a whole species of **objects,** and before every noun taken in a general sense:

El hombre es mortal.	*Man is mortal.*
La vida es corta.	*Life is short.*
El tiempo es precioso.	*Time is precious.*
Los perros son fieles.	*Dogs are faithful.*
Los sombreros redondos están de moda.	*Round hats are in fashion.*
Las flores son el adorno de la naturaleza.	*Flowers are the ornament of nature.*

7. Before **titles** prefixed to names:

El emperador don Pedro	*Emperor Don Pedro*
El rey Luis Catorce	*King Louis the Fourteenth*
El presidente Lincoln	*President Lincoln*
El general Wáshington	*General Washington*
El señor Fernández	*Mr. Fernandez*

8. Before **proper names** preceded by adjectives:

El pequeño Juan	*Little John*
La vieja María	*Old Mary*

9. Before nouns specifying **quantity** or **measure:**

Tres pesos la libra	*Three dollars a pound*
Un peso la vara	*One dollar a yard*

10. Before the four **cardinal points** of the compass:

El norte	*North*
El sur, *or* mediodía	*South*
El este, *or* oriente	*East*
El oeste, poniente *or* occidente	*West*

11. The definite article may also be used before a whole sentence, when the latter serves as the subject of another sentence:

Mucho me alegra el que venga V.	*I am very glad that you are coming.*

12. When several nouns follow each other, the article is placed before each of them:

Cuando la justicia, la fidelidad, el honor, la compasión, la vergüenza, y todos los sentimientos que pueden mover un corazón generoso, etc.	*When justice, fidelity, honor, compassion, modesty, and all feelings which can move a generous heart, etc.*

13. It may happen that the article is separated from its noun by several other words, as in the following sentences:

La nunca bastante ponderada virtud	*The never sufficiently praised virtue*
El sobrado paseo	*Excessive walking*

14. The definite article is placed before **titles** or other designations preceding proper names:

El Exmo. (excelentísimo) señor duque de . . .	*His Excellency the Duke of . . .*

If the word **su** precedes the honorific designation, the article is placed before the title:

Su Majestad el Rey	*His Majesty the King*

15. In describing the characteristic features of persons or things, the definite article is also used:

Carlos tiene los ojos negros.	*Charles has black eyes.*
Luis tiene la nariz grande.	*Louis has a large nose.*

Exceptions

The definite article is omitted:

1. When the name of the country figures as the place of origin, or is preceded by a preposition:

He recibido una carta de Francia.	*I have received a letter from France.*
Mi hermano está en Alemania.	*My brother is in Germany.*
Este vino es de España.	*This wine is from Spain.*

2. Before the **names of most countries:**

Méjico, *Mexico*	España, *Spain*	Inglaterra, *England*

3. Before a few nouns preceded by verbs of **motion** or **rest:**

Voy a casa—a misa—a palacio, etc.	*I am going home—to mass—to the palace, etc.*
Vengo de casa de mi amigo.	*I come from my friend's house.*

4. Before a noun in apposition:

Juan, hermano de Enrique	*John, the brother of Henry*
París, capital de Francia	*Paris, the capital of France*
Hablamos de Pedro, hombre de gran talento.	*We speak of Peter, a man of great talent.*

5. Before **titles of books, headings of chapters,** etc.

Vida de Cervantes	*The Life of Cervantes*
Historia de Roma	*A History of Rome*
Capítulo tercero	*Third Chapter*

6. For the use of the article with the relative pronoun and the infinitive compare the respective chapters.

NOUNS

Spanish nouns have two genders,—masculine and feminine.

The gender of a noun may be determined partly by its meaning, and partly by its ending.

Nouns ending in **o** are generally masculine, and those ending in **a,** feminine (except those which designate males). Compare the examples given.

Plural of Nouns

1. Nouns ending in an unstressed vowel or diphthong form their plural by adding **s,** as:

El padre, *the father*	los padres, *the fathers*
el niño, *the child*	los niños, *the children*
la tía, *the aunt*	las tías, *the aunts*
la iglesia, *the church*	las iglesias, *the churches*

2. Nouns ending in a consonant, in a stressed vowel (except e) or in a stressed diphthong the last letter of which is **y** form their plural by adding **es**, as:

el general, *the general*	los generales, *the generals*
la mujer, *the woman*	las mujeres, *the women*
el pan, *the bread*	los panes, *the loaves of bread*
la flor, *the flower*	las flores, *the flowers*
el tisú, *the tissue*	los tisúes, *the tissues*
el rubí, *the ruby*	los rubíes, *the rubies*
la ley, *the law*	las leyes, *the laws*

3. Nouns ending in **s** remain unchanged if their last syllable is unstressed. If the last syllable is stressed they add **es**.

la crisis, *the crisis*	las crisis, *the crises*
el jueves, *Thursday*	los jueves, *on Thursdays*
el martes, *Tuesday*	los martes, *on Tuesdays*
el francés, *the Frenchman*	los franceses, *the Frenchman*
el inglés, *the Englishman*	los ingleses, *the Englishmen*

4. Nouns ending in **z** change the same into **c** and add **es** in the plural, as:

el juez, *the judge*	los jueces, *the judges*
la voz, *the voice*	las voces, *the voices*
la paz, *the peace*	las paces, *the conditions of peace*
la luz, *the light*	las luces, *the lights*

5. Forms of salutation are used in the plural only:

buenos días, *good day*
buenas tardes, *good evening*
buenas noches, *good night*

The Gender of Nouns

1. Designations of male beings are masculine regardless of ending: el papa, **the pope**; el caballo, **the horse**; el rey, **the king**.

2. Designations of female beings are feminine regardless of ending: la madre, **the mother**; la actriz, **the actress**; la muchacha, **the girl**.
The gender of nouns is, however, generally determined by their endings.

3. Nouns ending in **o** are masculine. Except: la mano, **hand**; and la nao, **vessel**.

4. Nouns ending in **a** are generally feminine. Except: el día, **the day,** and a number of words ending in **ma** derived from the Greek,

as el clima, **climate**; el idioma, **idiom**; el poema, **poem**; el dilema, **dilemma**; el diploma, **diploma**; el dogma, **dogma**, etc.

5. Nouns ending in **ión, dad, tad, tud, ie** are feminine: la cuestión, **the question**; la verdad, **the truth**; la libertad, **the liberty**; la virtud, **the virtue**; la serie, **the series**.

6. Compound nouns take the gender of the second word if it is in the singular: el guardapolvo, **the duster**; el portafusil, **the gun belt**.

7. Compound words of which the second word is in the plural are always masculine, as: el cortaplumas, **the pen-knife**; el mondadientes, **the tooth-pick**; el limpiabotas, **the bootblack**.

OBSERVATIONS ON OTHER ENDINGS.—Nouns having other endings are subject to so many exceptions that it is impossible to establish satisfactory rules in regard to them. Their gender should, therefore, be committed to memory.

Augmentative and Diminutive Nouns and Adjectives

1. Spanish has many diminutives and augmentatives.

2. The diminutives serve to decrease or soften the meaning of the word from which they are derived.

Those most in use end in **ico, illo, cillo, ito, cito, uelo,** and **zuelo,** for the masculine, as: hombrecico, hombrecillo, hombrecito, hombrezuelo, **little man**; and in **ica, illa, cilla, ita, cita, uela, zuela,** for the feminine, as: mujercilla, mujercita, mujercica, mujerzuela, **little woman**.

a. Diminutives ending in **zuelo** always denote contempt or irony.

b. Diminutives ending in **illo** and **cillo** often express contempt, pity, or ugliness; while those in **ito** and **cito** generally express affection, gentleness, or beauty.

> Librillo, *contemptible little book*
> Pobrecillo, *poor little fellow*
> Hijito mío, *my dear little son*
> Pobrecito, *poor good little fellow*

c. The diminutives **ito, ita,** may be used with different parts of speech to give a special expression to the words:

> Vengo solito, *I come quite alone.*

3. The augmentatives serve to increase the meaning of the words from which they are derived. They end in: **ón, achón, azo,** or **ote** for the masculine; and in: **ona, aza, onaza,** or **ota** for the feminine, as:

Hombrón, hombrachón, hombrote (from hombre, *man*), *big, strong man.*
Grandón, grandote, grandazo (from grande, *large*), *very large.*
Mujerona, mujeraza, mujerota (from mujer, *woman*), *large, strong woman.*

a. There are many words, however, ending in **azo,** which express an action, motion, or result, and are, therefore, not augmentatives:

Fusil, *rifle, gun*   fusilazo, *a shot from a rifle*
Pistola, *pistol*   pistoletazo, *a shot from a pistol*
Cañón, *gun*   cañonazo, *a shot from a gun*

4. FORMATION OF DIMINUTIVES AND AUGMENTATIVES.—Words ending in **o** or **a** drop the last letter and add **ito, ita; ico, ica; illo, illa;** according to their gender:

Herman-ito, herman-ico, herman-illo, *little brother;* from hermano, *brother.*
Cas-ita, cas-ica, cas-illa, *little house;* from casa, *house.*

NOTE.—Words ending in **go,** besides dropping the **o,** insert **u** after the g to preserve the sound /γ/ of this letter:

Un amigo, *a friend*   un amiguito, *a little friend*

Those ending in **co** change **c** into **qu** to preserve the sound /**k**/ of the **c**:

Un barco, *a ship*   un barquito, *a little ship*

A few words ending in **o** and **a,** after dropping the last letter, add, however, the termination **ecito, ecillo,** etc.

Un huevo, *an egg*   un huevecillo, *a small egg*
Una mano, *a hand*   una manecita, *a small hand*

5. Monosyllables ending in a consonant form their diminutive by adding **ecito, ecico, ecillo,** or **ezuelo**:

Una flor, *a flower*   una florecita, *a little flower*
Una cruz, *a cross*   una crucecita, *a little cross*
Un pez, *a fish*   un pececito, *a little fish*
Un rey, *a king*   un reyezuelo, *a king (with a small kingdom)*

NOTE.—Cruz and **pez** change the final **z** into **c.**

6. Words of two or more syllables ending in a consonant form their diminutive by adding **ito, ico, illo**:

Un papel, *a paper*   un papelito, *a small paper*
Un reloj, *a watch*   un relojito, *a small watch*

7. Words of two syllables ending in **e,** and those of several syllables ending in **n** or **z,** add **cito, cico, cillo,** or **zuelo.**

Un sastre, *a tailor*	un sastrecillo, *a little tailor*
Una nube, *a cloud*	una nubecilla, *a little cloud*
Un capitán, *a captain*	un capitancillo, *a little captain*
Un autor, *an author*	un autorzuelo, *an insignificant author*
Una mujer, *a woman*	una mujercita, *a little woman*

EXCEPTIONS.—Juanito, from Juan, **John;** and all words ending in **in,** form an exception to this rule, the latter adding **ito,** etc. Thus:

Jardín, *garden*	jardinito, *a small garden*
Rocín, *jade*	rocinito, *a little jade*
Serafín, *seraph*	serafinito, *a little seraph*

Jardincito is, however, often used.

GENERAL OBSERVATIONS.—The words pequeño, **small,** and grande, **large,** may be used at all times with the noun, but in many cases they would go against the genius of the language. This is especially the case with diminutives.

Diminutives or augmentatives generally involve a shift in the stress of the word from which they are derived, as:

Árbol, *tree*	arbolito, *small tree*
Pájaro, *bird*	pajarito, *small bird, etc.*

The Auxiliary Verb Haber, To Have
SIMPLE TENSES

Indicative Mood	Subjunctive Mood
PRESENT	PRESENT
he, *I have*	haya, *I may have*
has, *thou hast*	hayas, *thou mayest have*
ha, *he has*	haya, *he may have*
hemos, *we have*	hayamos, *we may have*
habéis, *you have*	hayáis, *you may have*
han, *they have*	hayan, *they may have*
IMPERFECT	IMPERFECT (*first form*)
había, *I had*	hubiera, *I might have*
habías, *thou hadst*	hubieras, *thou mightest have*
había, *he had*	hubiera, *he might have*
habíamos, *we had*	hubiéramos, *we might have*
habíais, *you had*	hubierais, *you might have*
habían, *they had*	hubieran, *they might have*

Indicative Mood	**Subjunctive Mood**
### Past	### Imperfect (*second form*)

Indicative Mood

Past

hube, *I had*
hubiste, *thou hadst*
hubo, *he had*
hubimos, *we had*
hubisteis, *you had*
hubieron, *they had*

Subjunctive Mood

Imperfect (*second form*)

hubiese, *I might have*
hubieses, *thou mightest have*
hubiese, *he might have*
hubiésemos, *we might have*
hubieseis, *you might have*
hubiesen, *they might have*

Future

habré, *I shall have*
habrás, *thou wilt have*
habrá, *he will have*
habremos, *we shall have*
habréis, *you will have*
habrán, *they will have*

Future

hubiere, *I should have*
hubieres, *thou shouldst have*
hubiere, *he should have*
hubiéremos, *we should have*
hubiereis, *you should have*
hubieren, *they should have*

Conditional

habría, *I should have*
habrías, *thou wouldst have*
habría, *he would have*
habríamos, *we should have*
habríais, *you would have*
habrían, *they would have*

Infinitive	**Gerund**	**Past Participle**
haber, *to have*	habiendo, *having*	habido, *had*

COMPOUND TENSES

Indicative Mood

Present Perfect

he habido, *I have had*
has habido, *thou hast had*
ha habido, *he has had*
hemos habido, *we have had*
habéis habido, *you have had*
han habido, *they have had*

Subjunctive Mood

Present Perfect

haya habido, *I may have had*
hayas habido, *thou mayst have had*
haya habido, *he may have had*
hayamos habido, *we may have had*
hayáis habido, *you may have had*
hayan habido, *they may have had*

Past Perfect

había habido, *I had had*
habías habido, *thou hadst had,*
    etc.   *etc.*

Past Perfect (*first form*)

hubiera habido, *I might have had*
hubieras habido, *thou mightest have*
    etc.   *had, etc.*

Indicative Mood	**Subjunctive Mood**
PAST ANTERIOR	PAST PERFECT (*second form*)
hube habido, *I had had*	hubiese habido, *I might have had*
hubiste habido, *thou hadst had,*	hubieses habido, *thou mightest have*
etc. *etc.*	etc. *had, etc.*
FUTURE PERFECT	FUTURE PERFECT
habré habido, *I shall have had*	habiere habido, *I shall have had*
habrás habido, *thou wilt have*	hubieres habido, *thou wilt have had,*
etc. *had, etc.*	etc. *etc.*

PAST CONDITIONAL

habría habido, *I should have had*
habrías habido, etc., *thou wouldst have had, etc.*

Remarks on Haber

1. **Haber** can only be used as an auxiliary verb preceding the past participle, as:

He recibido una carta.	*I have received a letter.*
Hemos venido de París.	*We have come from Paris.*
¿Han llegado Vds. solos?	*Have you (pl.) arrived alone?*

2. In interrogative sentences **haber** must always stand next to the principal verb, as:

¿Ha venido su hermano?	*Has your brother come?*
¿Ha pagado V.?	*Have you paid?*

3. **Haber de** with the infinitive of another verb signifies—like **tener que**—duty or obligation, and must be translated by to have to, must, to be to, etc., as:

He de hacer la correspondencia.	*I have to attend to the correspondence.*
Había de escribir una carta.	*I had to write a letter.*
¿Qué había de hacer yo?	*What was I to do?*

4. **Haber** can be used impersonally, *i. e.*, in the third person singular. When followed by **que** and the infinitive of some other verb it expresses necessity or obligation, and is rendered by **to be necessary**, as:

¿Qué hay que hacer?	*What is to be done?*
Ha habido que salir.	*It was necessary to go out.*

5. When used impersonally, **haber** has many idiomatic meanings and corresponds:

a. to the English **there is, there are,** as:

Presente: Hay hombres en el jardín.   *There are some men in the garden.*

Imperfecto: Había fiestas en la ciudad.   *There were some festivities in town.*

Pretérito: Hubo baile en palacio.   *There was a ball at the palace.*

Futuro: ¿Habrá un baile mañana?   *Will there be a ball to-morrow?*

Condicional: Habría paz en el mundo, si ...   *There would be peace in the world, if ...*

NOTE.—The present perfect is **ha habido.**

b. **Hay** expresses **distance,** as:

¿Qué distancia hay de aquí a Chihuahua?   *How far is it from here to Chihuahua?*

Hay treinta millas.   *It is thirty miles.*

Conjugation of the Impersonal Verb

Haber que, *To be necessary*

MODO INDICATIVO	MODO SUBJUNTIVO
Hay que, *it is necessary*	Haya que, *it may be necessary*
Había que, *it was or it used to be necessary*	Hubiera que, *it might be necessary*
Hubo que, *it was necessary*	Hubiese que, *it might be necessary*
Habrá que, *it will be necessary*	
Habría que, *it should or would be necessary*	

Examples

Hay que ir al correo.   *It is necessary to go to the post-office.*

Habrá que leer los libros.   *It will be necessary to read the books.*

Si hubiese cartas habría que contestarlas.   *If there were any letters it would be necessary to answer them.*

The compound tenses are formed in the same way as their corresponding forms with **haber** adding **que,** thus:

MODO INDICATIVO		MODO SUBJUNTIVO	
Ha habido que	*It has been*	Haya habido que	*It may have*
Había habido que	*necessary*	Hubiera habido que	*been neces-*
Hubo habido que	*to, etc.*	Hubiese habido que	*sary to, etc.*
Habrá habido que			
Habría habido que			

Example

Ha habido que ir a la aduana.   *It has been necessary to go to the Custom House.*

The Auxiliary Verb Tener, To Have
SIMPLE TENSES

INFINITIVE	GERUND	PAST PARTICIPLE
tener, *to have*	teniendo, *having*	tenido, *had*

Indicative Mood

PRESENT

tengo, *I have*
tienes, *thou hast*
tiene, *he has*
tenemos, *we have*
tenéis, *you have*
tienen, *they have*

IMPERFECT

tenía, *I had*
tenías, *thou hadst*
tenía, *he had*
teníamos, *we had*
teníais, *you had*
tenían, *they had*

PAST

tuve, *I had*
tuviste, *thou hadst*
tuvo, *he had*
tuvimos, *we had*
tuvisteis, *you had*
tuvieron, *they had*

FUTURE

tendré, *I shall have*
tendrás, *thou wilt have*
tendrá, *he will have*
tendremos, *we shall have*
tendréis, *you will have*
tendrán, *they will have*

Subjunctive Mood

PRESENT

tenga, *I may have*
tengas, *thou mayst have*
tenga, *he may have*
tengamos, *we may have*
tengáis, *you may have*
tengan, *they may have*

IMPERFECT (*first form*)

tuviera, *I should have*
tuvieras, *thou shouldst have*
tuviera, *he should have*
tuviéramos, *we should have*
tuvierais, *you should have*
tuvieran, *they should have*

IMPERFECT (*second form*)

tuviese, *I might or should have*
tuvieses, *thou mightest have*
tuviese, *he might have*
tuviésemos, *we might have*
tuvieseis, *you might have*
tuviesen, *they might have*

FUTURE

tuviere, *I shall have*
tuvieres, *thou wilt have*
tuviere, *he will have*
tuviéremos, *we shall have*
tuviereis, *you will have*
tuvieren, *they will have*

CONDITIONAL

tendría, *I should have*
tendrías, *thou wouldst have*
tendría, *he would have*
tendríamos, *we should have*
tendríais, *you would have*
tendrían, *they would have*

Imperative Mood

ten (tú), *have thou*	tengamos, *let us have*
tenga (él), *let him have*	tened, *have (you)*
tenga V., *have (you)*	tengan, *let them have*

COMPOUND TENSES

Indicative Mood	Subjunctive Mood
PRESENT PERFECT	PRESENT PERFECT
he tenido, *I have had*	haya tenido, *I may have had*
PAST PERFECT	PAST PERFECT (*first form*)
había tenido, *I had had*	hubiera tenido, *I might have had*
PAST ANTERIOR	PAST PERFECT (*second form*)
hube tenido, *I had had*	hubiese tenido, *I shall have had*
FUTURE PERFECT	FUTURE PERFECT
habré tenido, *I shall have had*	hubiere tenido, *I shall have had*

PAST CONDITIONAL

habría tenido, *I should have had*

Remarks on Tener, To Have

1. There are two verbs in Spanish corresponding to our **to have**—**haber** and **tener**.

2. **Haber** is used exclusively in the formation of compound tenses, while **tener** is used as an active verb indicating possession (in which case **to have** may generally be replaced by **to possess** or **to hold**, without affecting the meaning of the sentence).

Thus:

He comprado un sombrero.	*I have bought a hat (compound tense)*
Tengo un sombrero.	*I have a hat (i.e., I possess a hat)*
Tuvo amigos.	*He had (i.e., he possessed) friends.*

3. **Tener** is used idiomatically with the following words:

Tengo hambre, *I am hungry.*	(*Literally, I have hunger.*)
tengo sed, *I am thirsty.*	(" *I have thirst.*)
tengo calor, *I am warm.*	(" *I have warmth.*)
tengo frío, *I am cold.*	(" *I have cold.*)
tengo sueño, *I am sleepy.*	(" *I have sleep.*)
tengo vergüenza, *I am ashamed.*	(" *I have shame.*)
tengo miedo de.., *I am afraid to*	(" *I have fear to ..*)
tengo razón, *I am right.*	(" *I have right.*)
no tengo razón, *I am wrong.*	(" *I have not right.*)
tengo gana de.., *I have a mind to*	

¿Qué tiene V.? *What is the matter with you?* (*What have you?*)

No tengo nada, *Nothing is the matter with me* (*I have nothing.*)

Tengo algo, *Something is the matter with me* (*I have something*).

¿Tiene V. algo? *Is anything the matter with you?* (*Have you something?*)

4. Tener is used in statements or inquiries about the age of persons:

¿Qué edad *or* ⎱
¿Cuántos años ⎰ tiene V?

How old are you? (*What age* [or, *how many years*] *have you*)?

Tengo cuarenta y cinco años.　　　*I am forty-five years old.*

5. Tener is used in speaking of the size or dimensions of objects, as:

Este río tiene ochenta pies de ancho.

This river is 80 feet broad (*has 80 feet of breadth*).

Este árbol tiene cien pies de alto.　*This tree is a hundred feet high.*

La calle tiene cincuenta pies de ancho.

The street is fifty feet wide.

6. Tener que with the infinitive of another verb expresses necessity or obligation, as:

Tengo que escribir una carta.　　　*I must write a letter.*

Tenía que hacer una visita.　　　　*I was obliged to make a call.*

Tenemos que salir.　　　　　　　*We have to start.* / leave

OBSERVATION.—Tener más edad, **or** ser de más edad is used for **older,** when comparing the age of persons.

7. Tener algo malo means **to have a pain, a sore,** or **ache somewhere;** the definite article is used before the affected part of the body:

Tengo el ojo malo.　　　　　　　*I have a sore eye.*

Tenemos los pies malos.　　　　　*We have sore feet.*

Él tiene la rodilla mala.　　　　　*He has a sore knee.*

8. The definite article is also used before nouns denoting mental or physical properties:

Tiene los ojos azules.　　　　　　*He has blue eyes.*

Tiene la memoria buena.　　　　　*He has a good memory.*

OBSERVATION.—The same article is used in the singular, when speaking of several persons, if the property spoken of is single:

Él tiene la nariz larga.　　　　　*He has a long nose.*

Ellos tienen la nariz larga.　　　　*They have long noses.*

TRANSLATION EXERCISE

¿Qué tiene V.? — Tengo dolor de cabeza. — Tuve la satisfacción de verla ayer. — Tenemos el honor de anunciarlo a V. — Tengo que

1240

hablar con V. cuando V. tenga tiempo. — ¿Qué ha estudiado V.
hoy? — He estado muy ocupado escribiendo la correspondencia. —
¿Ha escrito V. las cartas en español? — No señor, yo he hecho la
correspondencia francesa, y el corresponsal español escribió la
española. — ¿Hay mucha correspondencia española en su casa de
V.? — Sí, tenemos relaciones comerciales con la América del Sur. —
¿Quiere V. hacerme efectiva esta letra? Necesito dinero mejicano y
no tengo sino americano. — Con mucho gusto, señor. ¿Cuánto desea
V.? — ¿Hemos de ir al banco inmediatamente? — Sí, señor, hemos
de ir en seguida, porque los bancos cierran a las tres. — Tengo que
ir al correo ahora, pues espero algunas cartas. — ¿Espera V. unas de
Boston? — Sí; necesito tener un poder[1] de nuestra casa. — El poder
tiene que ser firmado y atestiguado[2] por un notario público;[3] de
otra manera[4] no es válido. — ¿Quiere V. venir conmigo a la ciudad?
— Con mucho gusto. ¿Qué tiene V. que hacer? — Tengo que ir a la
mercería. Tengo que hacer algunas compras. — ¿Qué es lo que tiene
V. que comprar? — Deseo comprar unas bagatelas.[5] — ¿Cuándo
habrá vapor correo[6] para Barcelona? — Hay correo para España los
días cinco, quince y veinticinco de cada mes.

The Auxiliary Verb Ser, To Be
SIMPLE TENSES

INFINITIVE	GERUND	PAST PARTICIPLE
ser, *to be*	siendo, *being*	sido, *been*

Indicative Mood	Subjunctive Mood
PRESENT	PRESENT
soy, *I am*	sea, *I may be*
eres, *thou art*	seas, *thou mayst be*
es, *he is*	sea, *he may be*
somos, *we are*	seamos, *we may be*
sois, *you are*	seáis, *you may be*
son, *they are*	sean, *they may be*
IMPERFECT	IMPERFECT (*first form*)
era, *I was*	fuera, *I might be*
eras, *thou wast*	fueras, *thou mightest be*
era, *he was*	fuera, *he might be*
éramos, *we were*	fuéramos, *we might be*
erais, *you were*	fuerais, *you might be*
eran, *they were*	fueran, *they might be*

---

[1] A power of attorney. [2] Must be signed and witnessed. [3] A Notary Public.
[4] Otherwise. [5] Trifles. [6] Mail-steamer.

PAST	IMPERFECT (*second form*)
fuí, *I was*	fuese, *I might be*
fuiste, *thou wast*	fueses, *thou mightest be*
fué, *he was*	fuese, *he might be*
fuimos, *we were*	fuésemos, *we might be*
fuisteis, *you were*	fueseis, *you might be*
fueron, *they were*	fuesen, *they might be*

FUTURE	FUTURE
seré, *I shall be*	fuere, *I should be*
serás, *thou wilt be*	fueres, *thou shouldst be*
será, *he will be*	fuere, *he should be*
seremos, *we shall be*	fuéremos, *we should be*
seréis, *you will be*	fuereis, *you should be*
serán, *they will be*	fueren, *they should be*

Indicative Mood

CONDITIONAL

sería, *I should be*
serías, *thou wouldst be*
sería, *he would be*
seríamos, *we should be*
seríais, *you would be*
serían, *they would be*

Imperative Mood

sé, *be (thou)*	seamos, *let us be*
sea, *let him be*	sed, *be (you)*
sea V., *be (you)*	sean, *let them be*

COMPOUND TENSES

Indicative Mood	**Subjunctive Mood**
PRESENT PERFECT	PRESENT PERFECT
he sido, *I have been*	haya sido, *I may have been*
PAST PERFECT	PAST PERFECT (*first form*)
había sido, *I had been*	hubiera sido, *I might have been*
PAST ANTERIOR	PAST PERFECT (*second form*)
hube sido, *I had been*	hubiese sido, *I might have been*
FUTURE PERFECT	FUTURE PERFECT
habré sido, *I shall have been*	hubiere sido, *I shall have been*

PAST CONDITIONAL
habría sido, *I should have been*

The Auxiliary Verb Estar, To Be

SIMPLE TENSES

INFINITIVE	GERUND	PAST PARTICIPLE
estar, *to be*	estando, *being*	estado, *been*

Indicative Mood · **Subjunctive Mood**

PRESENT

estoy, *I am*
estás, *thou art*
está, *he is*
estamos, *we are*
estáis, *you are*
están, *they are*

PRESENT

esté, *I may be*
estés, *thou mayst be*
esté, *he may be*
estemos, *we may be*
estéis, *you may be*
estén, *they may be*

IMPERFECT

estaba, *I was*
estabas, *thou wast*
estaba, *he was*
estábamos, *we were*
estabais, *you were*
estaban, *they were*

IMPERFECT (*first form*)

estuviera, *I might be*
estuvieras, *thou mightest be*
estuviera, *he might be*
estuviéramos, *we might be*
estuvierais, *you might be*
estuvieran, *they might be*

PAST

estuve, *I was*
estuviste, *thou wast*
estuvo, *he was*
estuvimos, *we were*
estuvisteis, *you were*
estuvieron, *they were*

IMPERFECT (*first form*)

estuviese, *I might be*
estuvieses, *thou mightest be*
estuviese, *he might be*
estuviésemos, *we might be*
estuvieseis, *you might be*
estuviesen, *they might be*

FUTURE

estaré, *I shall be*
estarás, *thou wilt be*
estará, *he will be*
estaremos, *we shall be*
estaréis, *you will be*
estarán, *they will be*

FUTURE

estuviere, *I should be*
estuvieres, *thou shouldst be*
estuviere, *he should be*
estuviéremos, *we should be*
estuviereis, *you should be*
estuvieren, *they should be*

CONDITIONAL

estaría, *I should be*
estarías, *thou wouldst be*
estaría, *he would be*
estaríamos, *we should be*
estaríais, *you would be*
estarían, *they would be*

Imperative Mood

está, *be (thou)*
esté, *let him be*
esté V., *be (you)*

estemos, *let us be*
estad, *be (you)*
estén, *let them be*

COMPOUND TENSES

Indicative Mood

PRESENT PERFECT

he estado, *I have been*

PAST PERFECT

había estado, *I had been*

PAST ANTERIOR

hube estado, *I had been*

FUTURE PERFECT

habré estado, *I shall have been*

Subjunctive Mood

PRESENT PERFECT

haya estado, *I may have been*

PAST PERFECT (*first form*)

hubiera estado, *I might have been*

PAST PERFECT (*second form*)

hubiese estado, *I might have been*

FUTURE PERFECT

hubiere estado, *I should have been*

PAST CONDITIONAL

habría estado, *I should have been*

Remarks on Ser and Estar

There are two verbs in Spanish corresponding to our verb **to be**—
ser and **estar**. Their proper use presents great difficulty to English-
speaking persons, which—to a certain extent—may be removed if
the following rules are mastered:

1. **Ser** is used when the attribute is **natural, inherent,** or **essential,**
that is to say, when the person or thing spoken of is likely to remain
where it is, what it is, or as it is. It therefore must always be employed
when the nationality, rank, profession, employment, dignity, inherent
mental or bodily quality is described, as:

Este señor es juez.	*This gentleman is a judge.*
Este señor es francés.	*This gentlemen is a Frenchman.*
Este señor es librero.	*This gentleman is a bookseller.*
Este señor es alto.	*This gentleman is tall.*
Este señor es pequeño.	*This gentleman is small.*
El hierro es duro.	*Iron is hard.*
Esta planta es venenosa.	*This plant is poisonous.*
Esta niña es bonita.	*This girl is pretty.*

a. **Ser** is used to indicate **possession, origin,** or **material,** as:

Aquella casa es mía, y ésta es de don Pedro.	*That house is mine and this is Don Pedro's (or, this belongs to Don Pedro).*
Esas plumas son de Juan, y esta carta es para V.	*These pens belong to John, and this letter is for you.*
El sombrero es de aquel caballero.	*The hat belongs to that gentleman.*
La casa es de mármol.	*The house is marble (of marble).*
El reloj es de oro.	*The watch is gold.*

b. **Ser** is used when speaking of the time of day or night or to express the number of things or persons, as:

¿Qué hora es?	*What time is it?*
Es la una.	*It is one o'clock.*
Son las diez y cuarto.	*It is a quarter past ten (= ten and a quarter).*
Es de día.	*It is day.*
Es de noche.	*It is night.*
Es tarde.	*It is late.*
Es temprano.	*It is early.*
Eran noventa discípulos.	*There were ninety pupils.*

2. **Estar** must always be employed when the attribute is only **temporary** or **accidental,** that is to say, when a change may take place or may, at least, be reasonably expected. Thus we say: Yo estoy aquí, **I am here,** that is to say: **I am here just now, but at any moment I may go somewhere else.**

a. **Estar** is used therefore to express the state of health, as:

¿Cómo está V.?	*How do you do?*
Estoy bueno.	*I am well.*
¿Desde cuándo está V. malo?	*Since when have you been ill?*

b. **Estar** is used in connection with certain adjectives to express emotions, feelings, or a state of being, as:

Estoy contento.	*I am satisfied.*
Estoy triste.	*I am sad.*
Esta sopa está caliente.	*This soup is hot.*
Este pan está frío.	*This bread is cold.*
El vino está agrio.	*The wine is sour.*

c. **Estar** is used to express temporary existence in a certain locality, as:

Está er. el café.	*He is at the café.*
Yo estoy aquí.	*I am here.*
Los soldados estarán aquí mañana.	*The soldiers will be here tomorrow.*
Él estaba a la puerta.	*He was at the door.*

d. **Estar** is used to express intention or willingness to do a thing, as:

Estoy para salir.	*I intend to go out.*

e. **Estar** is used before adverbs or adverbial expressions denoting condition, as:

Mi sombrero está de moda.	*My hat is the fashion (in the fashion).*
¿Está V. de prisa?	*Are you in a hurry?*

f. **Estar** is used as an auxiliary with the Gerund to form the progressive tenses:

Estoy leyendo un libro.	*I am reading a book.*
Juan está escribiendo una carta.	*John is writing a letter.*
Los discípulos estaban estudiando su le ;ción.	*The pupils were studying their lesson.*
Los marineros estarán cargando sus barcos.	*The bargemen will be loading their vessels.*

Comparison of Ser and Estar

To make the difference between **ser** and **estar** clearer we give the following examples:

Esta puerta es alta.	*This door is high.*
Esta puerta está cerrada.	*This door is locked.*

We must say **es alta,** because its height is an inherent attribute of the door in question. But we must use **está cerrada,** because its being shut is only a temporary condition.

For this reason many adjectives have an entirely different meaning when used with **ser** or **estar.**

INHERENT QUALITY	TEMPORARY STATE
Ser bueno, *to be good; to be kind-hearted*	Estar bueno, *to be well; to be in good health*
Ser malo, *to be bad*	Estar malo, *to be ill*
Ser vivo, *to be lively*	Estar vivo, *to be alive*
Ser listo, *to be clever*	Estar listo, *to be ready*
Esto es muy alto, *this is very high.*	Esto está muy alto, *this happens to be placed very high.*

TRANSLATION EXERCISE

¿Cómo está V., señor? — Muy bien, gracias. — ¿Es V. el maestro de idiomas? — Sí, señor. — Quiero aprender el idioma español. Mi hermano me dijo que V. enseña este idioma y yo deseo hablar y comprenderlo muy pronto, porque voy a Méjico. Mi hermana está en España con mi padre y yo, que soy el hijo menor, he quedado aquí solo. ¿Qué está V. haciendo tan tarde? — Estoy escribiendo una carta a mi agente. — Y su hermano de V. ¿qué hace? — Está estudiando el castellano y al mismo tiempo hace la correspondencia para nuestra casa en francés. — ¿Quién es ese hombre? — Es el tenedor de libros de mi casa. — ¿Y qué vende V.? — Soy fabricante de mesas para comedor. — ¿No está la casa del general López en la calle de Madrid? — El general no tiene casa aquí.

¿Qué edificio es éste? — Es un hotel. — Entremos. Dénos un cuarto con dos camas. Estoy muy cansado y deseo descansar.[1] — ¿Qué es la gramática? — Es el arte[2] de expresarnos correctamente por medio[3] de palabras. — ¿Qué son palabras? — Son los sonidos articulados[4] con que nos expresamos. — ¿De qué se componen las palabras? — De sílabas. — ¿Y las sílabas? — De letras. — ¿En qué se dividen éstas? — En vocales y consonantes. — ¿Cuáles son las partes de la oración? — Nombre, adjetivo, artículo, pronombre, verbo, adverbio, participio, preposición, conjunción e[5] interjección. — ¿Qué quiere V. comprar esta mañana? — Lléveme a casa de un sastre. — Vamos a casa del sastre parisiense.[6] — ¿A qué distancia de aquí está esa sastrería? — Como a una milla. Vamos a tomar el tranvía; aquí viene. ¡Conductor, pare V.![7] — Sentémonos; aquí hay lugar para los dos. — Esta es la sastrería. Aquí encontrará V. el surtido[8] más completo de ropa hecha[9] que hay en la ciudad.

Conjugation of the Regular Verbs

1. All verbs in Spanish end in **ar, er,** or **ir.**

2. Verbs of the first conjugation end in **ar.**
   Verbs of the second conjugation end in **er.**
   Verbs of the third conjugation end in **ir.**

---

[1] To rest. [2] The art. [3] By means of. [4] Articulated sounds. [5] Before words commencing with i or hi the conjunction y is changed into e, as verano e invierno, *summer and winter;* padre e hijo, *father and son.* [6] Parisian. [7] Stop. [8] The stock. [9] Ready made clothing.

3. By striking off these endings we get the **stem of the verb,** as: am-ar, to love (stem am-); com-er, to eat (stem com-); recib-ir, to receive (stem recib-).

4. To the stem we add the verb endings of the different tenses, persons, and moods.

Table of Verb Endings

	INFINITIVE	GERUND	PARTICIPLE
1.	—ar	—ando	—ado
2.	—er	—iendo	—ido
3.	—ir	—iendo	—ido

Indicative Mood			Subjunctive Mood		

PRESENT

PRESENT

1.	**2.**	**3.**	**1.**	**2.**	**3.**
—o	—o	—o	—e	—a	—a
—as	—es	—es	—es	—as	—as
—a	—e	—e	—e	—a	—a
—amos	—emos	—imos	—emos	—amos	—amos
—áis	—éis	—ís	—éis	—áis	—áis
—an	—en	—en	—en	—an	—an

IMPERFECT

IMPERFECT (*first form*)

1.	**2.**	**3.**	**1.**	**2.**	**3.**
—aba	—ía	—ía	—ara	—iera	—iera
—abas	—ías	—ías	—aras	—ieras	—ieras
—aba	—ía	—ía	—ara	—iera	—iera
—ábamos	—íamos	—íamos	—áramos	—iéramos	—iéramos
—abais	—íais	—íais	—arais	—ierais	—ierais
—aban	—ían	—ían	—aran	—ieran	—ieran

PAST

IMPERFECT (*second form*)

1.	**2.**	**3.**	**1.**	**2.**	**3.**
—é	—í	—í	—ase	—iese	—iese
—aste	—iste	—iste	—ases	—ieses	—ieses
—ó	—ió	—ió	—ase	—iese	—iese
—amos	—imos	—imos	—ásemos	—iésemos	—iésemos
—asteis	—isteis	—isteis	—aseis	—ieseis	—ieseis
—aron	—ieron	—ieron	—asen	—iesen	—iesen

	FUTURE			FUTURE	
1.	**2.**	**3.**	**1.**	**2.**	**3.**
—aré	—eré	—iré	—are	—iere	—iere
—arás	—erás	—irás	—ares	—ieres	—ieres
—ará	—erá	—irá	—are	—iere	—iere
—aremos	—eremos	—iremos	—áremos	—iéremos	—iéremos
—aréis	—eréis	—iréis	—areis	—iereis	—iereis
—arán	—erán	—irán	—aren	—ieren	—ieren

	CONDITIONAL			Imperative Mood	
1.	**2.**	**3.**	**1.**	**2.**	**3.**
—aría	—ería	—iría	—a	—e	—e
—arías	—erías	—irías	—e (V.)	—a (V.)	—a (V.)
—aría	—ería	—iría	—emos	—amos	—amos
—aríamos	—eríamos	—iríamos	—ad	—ed	—id
—aríais	—eríais	—iríais	—en (Vds.)	—an (Vds.)	—an (Vds.)
—arían	—erían	—irían			

First Conjugation

Model Verb — Hablar, To Speak

SIMPLE TENSES

INFINITIVE	GERUND	PAST PARTICIPLE
habl-ar, *to speak*	habl-ando, *speaking*	habl-ado, *spoken*

Indicative Mood	Subjunctive Mood
PRESENT	PRESENT
habl-o, *I speak*	habl-e, *I may speak*
habl-as, *thou speakest*	habl-es, *thou mayst speak*
habl-a, *he speaks*	habl-e, *he may speak*
habl-amos, *we speak*	habl-emos, *we may speak*
habl-áis, *you speak*	habl-éis, *you may speak*
habl-an, *they speak*	habl-en, *they may speak*
IMPERFECT	IMPERFECT (*first form*)
habl-aba, *I was speaking*	habl-ara, *I might speak*
habl-abas, *thou wast speaking*	habl-aras, *thou mightest speak*
habl-aba, *he was speaking*	habl-ara, *he might speak*
habl-ábamos, *we were speaking*	habl-áramos, *we might speak*
habl-abais, *you were speaking*	habl-arais, *you might speak*
habl-aban, *they were speaking*	habl-aran, *they might speak*

Indicative Mood	Subjunctive Mood
PAST	IMPERFECT (*second form*)

habl-é, *I spoke*	habl-ase, *I might speak*
habl-aste, *thou spokest*	habl-ases, *thou mighest speak*
habl-ó, *he spoke*	habl-ase, *he might speak*
habl-amos, *we spoke*	habl-ásemos, *we might speak*
habl-asteis, *you spoke*	habl-aseis, *you might speak*
habl-aron, *they spoke*	habl-asen, *they might speak*

FUTURE	FUTURE
habl-aré, *I shall speak*	habl-are, *I should speak*
habl-arás, *thou wilt speak*	habl-ares, *thou shouldst speak*
habl-ará, *he will speak*	habl-are, *he should speak*
habl-aremos, *we shall speak*	habl-áremos, *we should speak*
habl-aréis, *you will speak*	habl-areis, *you should speak*
habl-arán, *they will speak*	habl-aren, *they should speak*

CONDITIONAL

habl-aría, *I should speak*
habl-arías, *thou wouldst speak*
habl-aría, *he would speak*
habl-aríamos, *we should speak*
habl-aríais, *you would speak*
habl-arían, *they would speak*

Imperative

habl-a, *speak (thou)*	habl-emos, *let us speak*
habl-e, *let him speak*	habl-ad, *speak (you)*
habl-e V., *speak (you)*	habl-en, *let them speak; speak (you)*

COMPOUND TENSES

Indicative Mood	Subjunctive Mood
PRESENT PERFECT	PRESENT PERFECT
he hablado, *I have spoken*	haya hablado, *I may have spoken*
PAST PERFECT	PAST PERFECT (*first form*)
había hablado, *I had spoken*	hubiera hablado, *I might have spoken*
PAST ANTERIOR	PAST PERFECT (*second form*)
hube hablado, *I had spoken*	hubiese hablado, *I might have spoken*
FUTURE PERFECT	FUTURE PERFECT
habré hablado, *I shall have spoken*	hubiere hablado, *I shall have spoken*

PAST CONDITIONAL
habría hablado, *I should have spoken*

Second Conjugation

Model Verb — Vender, To Sell

INFINITIVE	GERUND	PAST PARTICIPLE
vend-er, *to sell*	vend-iendo, *selling*	vend-ido, *sold*

Indicative Mood	Subjunctive Mood

PRESENT	PRESENT
vend-o, *I sell*	vend-a, *I may sell*
vend-es, *thou sellest*	vend-as, *thou mayst sell*
vend-e, *he sells*	vend-a, *he may sell*
vend-emos, *we sell*	vend-amos, *we may sell*
vend-éis, *you sell*	vend-áis, *you may sell*
vend-en, *they sell*	vend-an, *they may sell*

IMPERFECT	IMPERFECT (*first form*)
vend-ía, *I was selling*	vend-iera, *I might sell*
vend-ías, *thou wast selling*	vend-ieras, *thou mightest sell*
vend-ía, *he was selling*	vend-iera, *he might sell*
vend-íamos, *we were selling*	vend-iéramos, *we might sell*
vend-íais, *you were selling*	vend-ierais, *you might sell*
vend-ían, *they were selling*	vend-ieran, *they might sell*

PAST	IMPERFECT (*second form*)
vend-í, *I sold*	vend-iese, *I might sell*
vend-iste, *thou soldest*	vend-ieses, *thou mightest sell*
vend-ió, *he sold*	vend-iese, *he might sell*
vend-imos, *we sold*	vend-iésemos, *we might sell*
vend-isteis, *you sold*	vend-ieseis, *you might sell*
vend-ieron, *they sold*	vend-iesen, *they might sell*

FUTURE	FUTURE
vend-eré, *I shall sell*	vend-iere, *I should sell*
vend-erás, *thou wilt sell*	vend-ieres, *thou shouldst sell*
vend-erá, *he will sell*	vend-iere, *he should sell*
vend-eremos, *we shall sell*	vend-iéremos, *we should sell*
vend-eréis, *you will sell*	vend-iereis, *you should sell*
vend-erán, *they will sell*	vend-ieren, *they should sell*

CONDITIONAL

vend-ería, *I should sell*
vend-erías, *thou wouldst sell*
vend-ería, *he would sell*
vend-eríamos, *we should sell*
vend-eríais, *you would sell*
vend-erían, *they would sell*

Imperative Mood

vend-e, *sell (thou)*

vend-amos, *let us sell*

vend-a, *let him sell*

vend-ed, *sell (you)*

vend-a V., *sell (you)*

vend-an, *let them sell; sell (you)*

COMPOUND TENSES

Indicative Mood

Subjunctive Mood

PRESENT PERFECT

he vendido, *I have sold*

PRESENT PERFECT

haya vendido, *I may have sold*

PAST PERFECT

había vendido, *I had sold*

PAST PERFECT (*first form*)

hubiera vendido, *I might have sold*

PAST ANTERIOR

hube vendido, *I had sold*

PAST PERFECT (*second form*)

hubiese vendido, *I might have sold*

FUTURE PERFECT

habré vendido, *I shall have sold*

FUTURE PERFECT

hubiere vendido, *I should have sold*

PAST CONDITIONAL

habría vendido, *I should have sold*

Third Conjugation

Model Verb — Vivir, To Live

SIMPLE TENSES

INFINITIVE

GERUND

PAST PARTICIPLE

viv-ir, *to live*

viv-iendo, *living*

viv-ido, *lived*

Indicative Mood

Subjunctive Mood

PRESENT

viv-o, *I live*
viv-es, *thou livest*
viv-e, *he lives*
viv-imos, *we live*
viv-ís, *you live*
viv-en, *they live*

PRESENT

viv-a, *I may live*
viv-as, *thou mayst live*
viv-a, *he may live*
viv-amos, *we may live*
viv-áis, *you may live*
viv-an, *they may live*

Indicative Mood	Subjunctive Mood
PERFECT	IMPERFECT (*first form*)

viv-ía, *I was living*	viv-iera, *I might live*
viv-ías, *thou wast living*	viv-ieras, *thou mightest live*
viv-ía, *he was living*	viv-iera, *he might live*
viv-íamos, *we were living*	viv-iéramos, *we might live*
viv-íais, *you were living*	viv-ierais, *you might live*
viv-ían, *they were living*	viv-ieran, *they might live*

PAST	IMPERFECT (*second form*)
viv-í, *I lived*	viv-iese, *I might live*
viv-iste, *thou livedst*	viv-ieses, *thou mightest live*
viv-ió, *he lived*	viv-iese, *he might live*
viv-imos, *we lived*	viv-iésemos, *we might live*
viv-isteis, *you lived*	viv-ieseis, *you might live*
viv-ieron, *they lived*	viv-iesen, *they might live*

FUTURE	FUTURE
viv-iré, *I shall live*	viv-iere, *I should live*
viv-irás, *thou wilt live*	viv-ieres, *thou wouldst live*
viv-irá, *he will live*	viv-iere, *he would live*
viv-iremos, *we shall live*	viv-iéremos, *we should live*
viv-iréis, *you will live*	viv-iereis, *you would live*
viv-irán, *they will live*	viv-ieren, *they would live*

CONDITIONAL

viv-iría, *I should live*
viv-irías, *thou wouldst live*
viv-iría, *he would live*
viv-iríamos, *we should live*
viv-iríais, *you would live*
viv-irían, *they would live*

Imperative Mood

viv-e, *live (thou)*	viv-amos, *let us live*
viv-a, *let him live*	viv-id, *live (you)*
viv-a V., *live (you)*	viv-an, *let them live, live (you)*

COMPOUND TENSES

Indicative Mood	Subjunctive Mood
PRESENT PERFECT	PRESENT PERFECT
he vivido, *I have lived*	haya vivido, *I may have lived*
PAST PERFECT	PAST PERFECT (*first form*)
había vivido, *I had lived*	hubiera vivido, *I might have lived*
PAST ANTERIOR	PAST PERFECT (*second form*)
hube vivido, *I had lived*	hubiese vivido, *I might have lived*
FUTURE PERFECT	FUTURE PERFECT
habré vivido, *I shall have lived*	hubiere vivido, *I should have lived*

PAST CONDITIONAL

habría vivido, *I should have lived*

Observations on Certain Regular Verbs

Certain orthographical changes take place in the following regular verbs:

1. Verbs ending in **gar** insert **u** before **e,** as:

INFINITIVE	SUBJUNCTIVE PRES.	PAST
pagar, *to pay*	pague, pagues, pague, etc.	pagué

2. Verbs ending in **car** change **c** into **qu** before **e,** as:

INFINITIVE	SUBJUNCTIVE PRES.	PAST.
tocar, *to play*	toque, toques, toque, etc.	toqué

3. Verbs ending in **zar** change **z** into **c** before **e,** as:

INFINITIVE	SUBJUNCTIVE PRES.	PAST.
rezar, *to pray*	rece, reces, rece, etc.	recé

4. Verbs ending in **cer** or **cir** change **c** into **z** before **o** or **a,** to preserve the /θ/ sound, as:

INFINITIVE	PRESENT INDICAT.	SUBJUNCTIVE PRES.
vencer, *to vanquish*	venzo, etc.	venza, etc.
resarcir, *to compensate*	resarzo	resarza, etc.

5. Verbs ending in **ger** or **gir** change **g** into **j** before **o** or **a**, as:

INFINITIVE	IND. PRESENT	SUBJ. PRESENT
coger, *to take*	cojo, etc.	coja, etc.
erigir, *to erect*	erijo, etc.	erija, etc.

6. Verbs ending in **guir** change **gu** into **g**, and verbs ending in **quir** change **qu** into **c** before **o** or **a**, as:

INFINITIVE	IND. PRESENT	SUBJ. PRESENT
distinguir, *to distinguish*	distingo, etc.	distinga, etc.
delinquir, *to offend*	delinco, etc.	delinca, etc.

7. Verbs ending in **cer** or **cir** preceded by a vowel insert before the stem-ending a **z** as often as the stem meets an **a** or an **o**, as:

conocer, *to know*

INDICAT. PRES.   conozco (*but:* conoces, conoce, conocemos, etc.)
SUBJUNCT. PRES.   conozca, conozcas, conozca, conozcamos, conozcáis, conozcan
IMPERATIVE.   conozca, conozcamos, conozcan

lucir, *to shine, to display*

INDICAT. PRES.   luzco (*but:* luces, luce, lucimos, etc.)
SUBJUNCT. PRES.   luzca, luzcas, luzca, luzcamos, luzcáis, luzcan
IMPERATIVE.   luzca, luzcamos, luzcan

8. The following six regular verbs have an irregular past participle:

INFINITIVE	PAST PARTICIPLE
abrir, *to open*	abierto, *opened*
cubrir, *to cover*	cubierto, *covered*
descubrir, *to discover*	descubierto, *discovered*
escribir, *to write*	escrito, *written*
imprimir, *to print*	impreso, *printed*
romper, *to break*	roto, *broken*

Conjugation of the Passive Verb

Model Verb — Ser llamado, To be called

SIMPLE TENSES

INFINITIVE

ser $\begin{Bmatrix} \text{llamado, a} \\ \text{llamados, as} \end{Bmatrix}$ *to be called*

GERUND

siendo $\begin{Bmatrix} \text{llamado, a} \\ \text{llamados, as} \end{Bmatrix}$ *being called*

PARTICIPLE

llamado, llamada; llamados, llamadas, *having been called*

Indicative Mood	**Subjunctive Mood**
### PRESENT	### PRESENT
I am called, etc.	*I may be called, etc.*
soy llamado, a	sea llamado, a
eres llamado, a	seas llamado, a
es llamado, a	sea llamado, a
somos llamados, as	seamos llamados, as
sois llamados, as	seáis llamados, as
son llamados, as	sean llamados, as
### IMPERFECT	### IMPERFECT (*first form*)
I was called, etc.	*I might be called, etc.*
era llamado, a	fuera llamado, a
éramos llamados, as	fuéramos llamados, as
### PAST	### IMPERFECT (*second form*)
I was called, etc.	*I might be called, etc.*
fuí llamado, a	fuese llamado, a
fuimos llamados, as	fuésemos llamados, as
### FUTURE	### FUTURE
I shall be called, etc.	*I should be called, etc.*
seré llamado, a	fuere llamado, a
seremos llamados, as	fuéremos llamados, as

Indicative Mood

CONDITIONAL

I should be called, etc.
sería llamado, a
seríamos llamados, as

Compound Tenses

### PRESENT PERFECT	### PRESENT PERFECT
I have been called, etc.	*I may have been called, etc.*
he sido llamado, a	haya sido llamado, a
hemos sido llamados, as	hayamos sido llamados, as

PAST PERFECT	PAST PERFECT (*first form*)
I had been called, etc.	*I might have been called, etc.*
había sido llamado, a	hubiera sido llamado, a
habíamos sido llamados, as	hubiéramos sido llamados, as

PAST ANTERIOR	PAST PERFECT (*second form*)
I had been called, etc.	*I might have been called, etc.*
hube sido llamado, a	hubiese sido llamado, a
hubimos sido llamados, as	hubiésemos sido llamados, as

FUTURE PERFECT	FUTURE PERFECT
I shall have been called, etc.	*I should have been called, etc.*
habré sido llamado, a	hubiere sido llamado, a
habremos sido llamados, as	hubiéremos sido llamados, as

PAST CONDITIONAL

I should have been called, etc.
habría sido llamado, a
habríamos sido llamados, as

Remarks on the Passive

1. The past participle must, in the passive voice, agree in gender and number with the subject of the sentence, as:

Estos niños son amados.	*These children are loved.*
Estas señoras han sido siempre muy estimadas.	*These ladies have always been very much esteemed.*

2. **By,** after passive verbs or participles, is rendered by **por,** except when the verb denotes feeling or emotion, when it is rendered by **de,** as:

Este libro fué escrito por Castelar.	*This book was written by Castelar.*
Este cuadro fué pintado por Murillo.	*This picture was painted by Murillo.*
Este escritor es estimado de muchos.	*This writer is esteemed by many.*

3. Active verbs are often used passively with the pronoun **se** in the third person singular or plural, as:

Estas manzanas se venden a precios muy altos.	*These apples are sold at very high prices.*
Esta casa se alquiló hace más de un mes.	*This house was let more than a month ago.*
No se puede ver nada.	*Nothing can be seen.*

TRANSLATION EXERCISE

¿Cómo está V.? Tengo mucho gusto en ver a V. — Estoy muy
bien, gracias. ¿Y V.? — Para servir a V., gracias. — ¿Viene V. a
pasar mucho tiempo en Nueva York? — No, señor, vengo solamente
por algunos días. — ¿Tiene V. relaciones comerciales con países
españoles? — Sí, tenemos negocios con la América del Sur. — ¿Desearía V. importar algo en los Estados Unidos? — Desearía importar
café, tabaco, azúcar, madera de cedro,[1] lana y algunas frutas. —
¿Desea V. vender al contado[2] o a plazos?[3] — A algunos comerciantes
les venderé a un corto plazo, o cambiaré mis productos por efectos
americanos. — ¿Cómo piensa V. hacer esas importaciones? — Mi
idea es establecer aquí una sucursal[4] de mi casa de Valparaíso, a cuyo
frente[5] estará un hermano mío.[6] — El necesitará un poder[7] para hacer
legales[8] esas transacciones. — ¿Quién tiene que firmar[9] un poder para
que sea válido? — Un poder para ser válido tiene que ser firmado
ante un notario público y por dos testigos.[10] — Tengo que ir al correo
ahora pues espero algunas cartas. ¿No quiere V. venir conmigo? —
Pues, bien vamos al centro.[11]

The Reflexive Verb

Reflexive or pronominal verbs are conjugated with two personal
pronouns, the first (expressed or understood) being the subject, and
the second the object, as:

Yo me divierto *or* me divierto.   *I amuse myself.*
Él se engaña *or* se engaña.   *He deceives himself.*

Pronouns Accompanying the Reflexive Verb

me,	*myself*	nos,	*ourselves*
te,	*thyself*	os,	*yourselves*
se	*himself, herself* / *itself, yourself*	se	*themselves* / *yourselves*

Almost any verb may be used reflexively in Spanish, with, sometimes, a slight modification in its meaning, as:

Dormir; dormirse   *To sleep; to go to sleep*
Ir; irse   *To go; to go away*
Caer; caerse   *To fall; to fall down*

[1] Cedar-wood.—[2] For cash.—[3] Plazo corresponds to our English expression
terms, a plazos, *on credit;* a largo plazo, *on long credit;* a corto plazo, *on short
credit.*—[4] A branch.—[5] At the head of which.—[6] One of my brothers.—[7] A power
of attorney.—[8] To legalize.—[9] To sign.—[10] Witnesses.—[11] *downtown.*

Model Verb: Alabarse, to Praise Oneself
SIMPLE TENSES

INFINITIVE

alabarse, *to praise oneself*

GERUND

alabándose, *praising oneself*

Indicative Mood

PRESENT

I praise myself, etc.
me alabo
te alabas
se alaba
nos alabamos
os alabáis
se alaban

Subjunctive Mood

PRESENT

I may praise myself, etc.
me alabe
te alabes
se alabe
nos alabemos
os alabéis
se alaben

IMPERFECT

I praised myself, etc.
me alababa
te alababas
se alababa, *etc.*

IMPERFECT (*first form*)

I might praise myself, etc.
me alabara
te alabaras
se alabara, *etc.*

PAST

I praised myself, etc.
me alabé
te alabaste
se alabó, *etc.*

IMPERFECT (*second form*

I might praise myself, etc.
me alabase
te alabases
se alabase, *etc.*

FUTURE

I shall praise myself, etc.
me alabaré
te alabarás
se alabará, *etc.*

FUTURE

I should praise myself, eic
me alabare
te alabares
se alabare, *etc.*

Indicative Mood

CONDITIONAL

I should praise myself, etc.
me alabaría
te alabarías
se alabaría, *etc.*

Imperative Mood

alábate, *praise thyself*
alábese, *let him praise himself*
alábese, *praise yourself*

alabémonos, *let us praise ourselves*
alabaos, *praise yourselves*
alábense, *let them praise themselves*

COMPOUND TENSES

Indicative Mood	Subjunctive Mood

PRESENT PERFECT

I have praised myself, etc.
me he alabado
te has alabado
se ha alabado
nos hemos alabado
os habéis alabado
se han alabado

PRESENT PERFECT

I may have praised myself, etc.
me haya alabado
te hayas alabado
se haya alabado
nos hayamos alabado
os hayáis alabado
se hayan alabado

PAST PERFECT

I had praised myself, etc.
me había alabado, etc.

PAST PERFECT (*first form*)

I might have praised myself, etc.
me hubiere alabado, etc.

PAST ANTERIOR

I had praised myself, etc.
me hube alabado, etc.

PAST PERFECT (*second form*)

I might have praised myself, etc.
me hubiese alabado, etc.

FUTURE PERFECT

I shall have praised myself, etc.
me habré alabado, etc.

FUTURE PERFECT

I should have praised myself, etc.
me hubiere alabado, etc.

PAST CONDITIONAL

I should have praised myself, etc.
me habría alabado, etc.

Observations on the Reflexive and the Passive Verb

1. The pronouns which are generally placed before the verb may also stand after it, forming but one word with the verb, as:

Divertímonos.	*We amuse ourselves.*
Equivoquéme.	*I made a mistake.*
Equivocóse.	*He made a mistake.*
Heme equivocado.	*I have made a mistake.*

2. The **s** of the first person plural and the **d** of the second person plural are dropped in the Imperative, as:

Figurémonos (*for* figurémosnos).	*Let us imagine.*
Amémonos (*for* amémosnos).	*Let us love each other.*
Figuraos (*for* figurados).	*Imagine (you)!*

3. The number of essentially reflexive verbs is small, but accidentally almost any verb can be used reflexively in Spanish.

4. Many verbs are reflexive in Spanish which are not so in English, as:

alegrarse, *to rejoice*	equivocarse, *to be mistaken*
figurarse, *to imagine*	engañarse, *to be deceived*
disgustarse, *to be displeased*	burlarse, *to laugh at*

5. Essentially reflexive verbs may be conjugated impersonally with **se** (the dative of the pronoun serving to distinguish the person, etc.).

PERSONAL INFLECTION   IMPERSONAL INFLECTION

me figuro		se me figura		*I imagine*
te figuras		se te figura		*thou imaginest*
se figura	*I imagine (myself), etc.*	se le figura	*I imagine (myself) (it figures itself to me,) etc.*	*he imagines*
V. se figura		se le figura a V.		*you imagine*
nos figuramos		se nos figura		*we imagine*
os figuráis		se os figura		*you imagine*
se figuran		se les figura		*they imagine*
Vds. se figuran		se les figura a Vds.		*you imagine*

6. The passive voice is less common in Spanish than in English. Unless the agent is expressed (with **por** or **de**), the reflexive is preferred, as:

El dinero se perdió.	*The money was lost.*
Las casas se han vendido.	*The houses have been sold.*
Eso no se puede decir.	*That cannot be said.*
Se prohibe fijar carteles.	*"Post no bills."*
Aquí se habla español.	*Spanish spoken here.*

7. Reflexive verbs, when used in the plural, express sometimes a mutual or reciprocal action, as:

Se han escrito muchas cartas.	*They have written many letters to each other.*
Todos los individuos de esta familia se quieren.	*All the members of this family are fond of one another.*

8. In such cases **uno a otro** or **mutuamente** is frequently added for the sake of accuracy, as:

Se aman el uno al otro.	*They love each other.*
Nos amamos mutuamente.	*We love each other.*

9. The reflexive pronoun is used in Spanish when the object of the verb is a part of the body or an article of dress, as:

Me pongo el sombrero.   *I put on my hat.*
El se lava la cara.   *He washes his face.*
Me quito los guantes.   *I take off my gloves.*

TRANSLATION EXERCISE

La mesa está servida. Pasemos al comedor. — ¿Encontraremos coches en la estación? — Sí, señor; se ha establecido un servicio de ómnibus para todos los pueblos a veinte kilómetros a la redonda. — La lengua alemana se habla en una gran parte de Europa. El idioma español se habla en España, en Méjico, en la América central y del sur, y en muchas colonias del Asia y del Africa. — Yo acostumbro levantarme temprano y acostarme tarde. — Este paño se vende en la tienda del señor Palma. — ¿Qué se dice en la ciudad? Se dice que el azúcar se venderá muy bien este año. — La hacienda ha sido vendida después de la muerte del dueño. ¿Por qué no se sienta V.? — No estoy cansado, prefiero quedarme de pie. — ¿Se levanta V. temprano? — Me levanto tan pronto como me despierto. — ¿Por qué no va V. al jardín a divertirse con las muchachas? — No me siento bien, quiero ir a acostarme. — ¿Se acuerda V. de lo que dijo este hombre? — Me acuerdo de todo lo que dijo.

Impersonal Verbs

Impersonal verbs are employed in the third person singular, without any pronoun.

Impersonal verbs are inflected according to the conjugation indicated by their infinitive.

1. Nevar, nevando, nevado, **to snow.**

INDICATIVE MOOD	SUBJUNCTIVE MOOD
nieva, *it snows*	nieve, *it may snow*
nevaba, *it was snowing*	nevara, *it might snow*
nevó, *it snowed*	nevase, *it might snow*
nevará, *it will snow*	nevare, *it should snow*
nevaría, *it would snow*	haya nevado, *it may have snowed*
ha nevado, *it has snowed*	hubiera nevado, *it might have snowed*
había nevado, *it had snowed*	hubiese nevado, *it might have snowed*
hubo nevado, *(when) it had snowed*	hubiere nevado, *it should have snowed*
habrá nevado, *it will have snowed*	
habría nevado, *it would have snowed*	

2. Llover, lloviendo, llovido, **to rain.**

INDICATIVE MOOD	SUBJUNCTIVE MOOD
llueve, *it rains*	llueva, *it may rain*
llovía, *it was raining*	lloviera, *it might rain*
llovió, *it rained*	lloviese, *it might rain*
lloverá, *it will rain*	lloviere, *it should rain*
llovería, *it would rain*	

3. Amanecer, amaneciendo, amanecido, **to dawn.**

INDICATIVE MOOD	SUBJUNCTIVE MOOD
amanece, *it dawns*	amanezca, *it may dawn*
amanecía, *it was dawning*	amaneciera, *it might dawn*
ameneció, *it dawned*	amaneciese, *it might dawn*
amanecerá, *it will dawn*	amaneciere, *it should dawn*
amanecería, *it would dawn*	

4. List of the most common Impersonal Verbs.

INFINITIVE	INDICAT. PRESENT	PARTICIPLE
amanecer, *to dawn*	amanece	amanecido
anochecer, *to grow dark*	anochece	anochecido
oscurecer, *to grow dark*	oscurece	oscurecido
granizar, *to hail*	graniza	granizado
helar, *to freeze*	hiela	helado
deshelar, *to thaw*	deshiela	deshelado
llover, *to rain*	llueve	llovido
lloviznar, *to drizzle*	llovizna	lloviznado
nevar, *to snow*	nieva	nevado
relampaguear, *to lighten*	relampaguea	relampagueado
tronar, *to thunder*	truena	tronado

5. Some personal verbs are used impersonally, as:

Bastar, *to suffice*	Basta que V. lo diga, *it is sufficient that you say so*
Convenir, *to agree; to suit*	Conviene hacer esto, *it is expedient to do it* Juan me conviene, *John suits me*
Gustar, *to please*	Me gusta comer a la una, *I like to dine at one*
Disgustar, *to displease*	Me disgusta oír tal cosa, *it displeases me to hear such a thing*
Fastidiar, *to vex*	Me fastidia guardar cama, *it vexes me that I have to keep abed*
Importar, *to be of importance*	Importa decírselo, *it is important to tell it to him*

Parecer, *to seem*	Parece hacer frío hoy, *u seems to be cold to-day*
Placer, *to please*	Me place, *it pleases me; I like to*
Displacer, *to displease*	Me displace, *it displeases me; I dislike to*
suceder, *to happen*	Sucede muchas veces que . . ., *it happens often that . . .*
valer, *to be worth*	Más vale tarde que nunca, *better late than never*

6. The English impersonal expression "it is" is variously rendered:

a. By **es** with adjectives, adverbs, or nouns, as:

Es cierto; así es.	*It is certain; so it is.*
Es menester; es preciso.	*It is necessary.*
Es de día.	*It is daylight.*

b. By **está** to denote accidental state, as:

Está lloviendo.	*It is raining.*

c. By **hace,** with reference to the weather, as:

¿Qué tiempo hace?	*What kind of weather is it?*
Hace buen tiempo.	*It is fine weather.*

d. By **hay** with reference to distance.

¿Cuánto hay de aquí al banco?	*How far is it from here to the bank?*

Government of Verbs

1. The object of a transitive verb stands in the accusative (objective) case without a preposition when it denotes things.

2. When persons or animals are designated, the preposition **a** is used before the object.

Conozco a este hombre.	*I know this man.*

3. When the personal object is preceded by a cardinal number, **a** is generally omitted.

He visto cuatro mujeres.	*I saw four women.*

4. **A** is also left out when the personal object is unknown or indeterminate:

Busca una criada.	*She is looking for a servant girl.*

5. After **tener** in the sense of to have, to possess, **a** is omitted:

Tengo un buen hijo.	*I have a good son.*

But when **tener** is used idiomatically in the sense of to be, **a** is used:

Tengo a mi hijo enfermo.	*My son is ill.*

264

6. After the verb **querer, a** is used in the sense of to love, to like:

Quiero a esta muchacha.   *I like this girl.*

Querer without **a** means to want, to wish:

Quiero un hombre honrado que hable inglés.   *I want an honest man who speaks English.*

7. **A** is omitted after **perder,** to lose (**perder a,** means to ruin):

He perdido mi padre.   *I have lost my father.*

8. Many verbs are followed in Spanish by **a, de, con, por, para, sobre,** etc., where in English no preposition is used. Some of these verbs may, without changing their meaning, govern different prepositions.

9. Most reflexive verbs, and those expressing conditions of the mind, abundance, want, separation, deprivation, blame, etc., are generally followed by the preposition **de.** Such verbs are:

Abusar de, *to abuse*
acordarse de, *to remember*
admirarse de, *to wonder at*
alegrarse de, *to rejoice at*
aprovecharse de, *to use*
avergonzarse de, *to be ashamed of*
burlarse de, *to laugh at*
carecer de, *to want, to be without*
compadecerse de, *to pity*
condolerse de, *to pity*
desconfiar de, *to distrust*
dudar de, *to doubt*
fiarse de, *to trust*
gozar de, *to enjoy*
jactarse de, *to boast*
lamentarse de, *to lament*
mofarse de, *to scoff at*
necesitar de, *to need*
olvidarse de, *to forget*
preciarse de, *to boast*
prescindir de, *to do without*
privarse de, *to deprive*
reírse de, *to laugh at*
renegar de, *to abominate*
servirse de, *to use*
tener lástima de, *to pity*
tener vergüenza de, *to be ashamed of*
usar de, *to use*
valerse de, *to avail one's self of*
zafarse de, *to get rid of*

IRREGULAR VERBS

In our conversational lessons we have given the principal irregular verbs. The Spanish language contains a very large number of irregularly inflected verbs, but as these irregularities occur in certain moods, tenses and persons only, they may easily be reduced to a few classes.

Observe that in the following tables only deviations from the three model regular conjugations are printed in **heavy type.**

A long mark (–) has been placed over the vowel of the stressed syllable.

First Class

a. E Stems—(First Conjugation)

The characteristic of this class is that **i** is inserted before the stem-vowel **e = ie** throughout the singular and in the third person plural of the present indicative and subjunctive, and in the same persons in the imperative. To this class belong numerous verbs of the first and second conjugation.

1. Pensar, pensando, pensado, **to think.**

Pres Ind:	**piens-o**	**piens-as**	**piens-a**	pens-āmos	pens-áis	**piens-an**
Pres Subj:	**piens-e**	**piens-es**	**piens-e**	pens-ēmos	pens-éis	**piens-en**
Imperat:	———	**piens-a**	**piens-e**	pens-ēmos	pens-ād	**piens-en**

Note.—All other forms are regular:

pensāba, pensé, pensāra, pensāse, pensāre, pensaré, pensaría

2. Acertar, acertando, acertado, **to hit the mark, to guess.**

Pres Ind:	**acierto**	**aciertas**	**acierta**	acertāmos	acertáis	**aciertan**
Pres Subj:	**acierte**	**aciertes**	**acierte**	acertēmos	acertéis	**acierten**
Imperat:	———	**acierta**	**acierte**	acertēmos	acertād	**acierten**

Reg: acertāba, acerté, acertāra, acertāse, acertāre, acertaré, acertaría

3. Alentar, alentando, alentado, **to encourage, to cheer; to breathe.**

Pres Ind:	**aliento**	**alientas**	**alienta**	alentāmos	alentáis	**alientan**
Pres Subj:	**aliente**	**alientes**	**aliente**	alentēmos	alentéis	**alienten**
Imperat:	———	**alienta**	**aliente**	alentēmos	alentād	**alienten**

Reg: alentaba, alenté, alentara, alentase, alentare, alentaré, alentaría

4. Apretar, apretando, apretado, **to grasp tightly.**

Pres Ind:	**aprieto**	**aprietas**	**aprieta**	apretāmos	apretáis	**aprietan**
Pres Subj:	**apriete**	**aprietes**	**apriete**	apretēmos	apretéis	**aprieten**
Imperat:	———	**aprieta**	**apriete**	apretēmos	apretād	**aprieten**

Reg: apretaba, apreté, apretara, apretase, apretare, apretaré, apretaría

5. Atestar, atestando, atestado, **to crowd, to attest.**

Pres Ind:	**atiesto**	**atiestas**	**atiesta**	atestāmos	atestáis	**atiestan**
Pres Subj:	**atieste**	**atiestes**	**atieste**	atestēmos	atestéis	**atiesten**
Imperat:	———	**atiesta**	**atieste**	atestēmos	atestād	**atiesten**

Reg: atestaba, atesté, atestara, atestase, atestare, atestaré, atestaría

6. Cerrar, cerrando, cerrado, **to shut, to close.**

Pres Ind:	**cierro**	**cierras**	**cierra**	cerrāmos	cerráis	**cierran**
Pres Subj:	**cierre**	**cierres**	**cierre**	cerrēmos	cerréis	**cierren**
Imperat:	———	**cierra**	**cierre**	cerrēmos	cerrād	**cierren**

Reg: cerraba, cerré, cerrara, cerrase, cerrare, cerraré, cerraría

7. Empezar, empezando, empezado, to begin.

Pres Ind: **empiezo empiezas empieza** empezāmos empezáis **empiezan**
Pres Subj: **empiece empieces empiece** empecēmos empecéis **empiecen**
Imperat: —— **empieza empiece** empecēmos empezād **empiecen**
Reg: empezaba, empecé, empezara, empezase, etc.

8. Helar, helando, helado, to freeze.

Pres Ind: **hielo hielas hiela** helāmos heláis **hielan**
Pres Subj: **hiele hieles hiele** helēmos heléis **hielen**
Imperat: —— **hiela hiele** helēmos helād **hielen**
Reg: helaba, helé, helara, helase, etc.

9. Negar, negando, negado, to deny.

Pres Ind: **niego niegas niega** negāmos negáis **niegan**
Pres Subj: **niegue niegues niegue** neguēmos neguéis **nieguen**
Imperat: —— **niega niegue** neguēmos negād **nieguen**
Reg: negaba, negué, negara, negase, etc.

10. Sembrar, sembrando, sembrado, to sow.

Pres Ind: **siembro siembras siembra** sembrāmos sembráis **siembran**
Pres Subj: **siembre siembres siembre** sembrēmos sembréis **siembren**
Imperat: —— **siembra siembre** sembrēmos sembrād **siembren**
Reg: sembraba, sembré, sembrara, sembrase, etc.

11. Errar, errando, errado, to err.

This verb may be included in this class. It takes **y** in the same tenses and persons where the other verbs of this class insert **i** before the stem-vowel.

Pres Ind: **yerro yerras yerra** errāmos erráis **yerran**
Pres Subj: **yerre yerres yerre** errēmos erréis **yerren**
Imperat: —— **yerra yerre** errēmos errad **yerren**
Reg: erraba, erré, errara, errase, etc.

b. E Stems—(Second Conjugation)

12. Perder, perdiendo, perdido, to lose.

Pres Ind: **pierdo pierdes pierde** perdēmos perdéis **pierden**
Pres Subj: **pierda pierdas pierda** perdāmos perdáis **pierdan**
Imperat: —— **pierde pierda** perdāmos perdēd **pierdan**
Reg: perdía, perdí, perdiera, perdiese, perdiere, perderé, perdería

13. Entender, entendiendo, entendido, **to understand.**

Pres Ind:	**entiendo**	**entiendes**	**entiende**	entendēmos	**entendéis**
					entienden
Pres Subj:	**entienda**	**entiendas**	**entienda**	entendāmos	entendáis
					entiendan
Imperat:	——	**entiende**	**entienda**	entendēmos	entendēd
					entiendan

Reg: entendía, entendí, entendiera, entendiese, entendiere, etc.

c. O Stems—(First Conjugation)

The characteristic of this class is that the stem-vowel **o** is changed into **ue** throughout the singular and in the third person plural of the present indicative and subjunctive, and in the same persons in the imperative. Many verbs of the first and second conjugation belong to this class.

14. Acordar, acordando, acordado, **to agree, to remind, to remember.**

Pres Ind:	**acuerdo**	**acuerdas**	**acuerda**	acordāmos	acordáis	**acuerdan**
Pres Subj:	**acuerde**	**acuerdes**	**acuerde**	acordēmos	acordéis	**acuerden**
Imperat:	——	**acuerda**	**acuerde**	acordēmos	acordād	**acuerden**

Reg: acordaba, acordé, acordara, acordase, acordare, etc.

15. Contar, contando, contado, **to count.**

Pres Ind:	**cuento**	**cuentas**	**cuenta**	contāmos	contáis	**cuentan**
Pres Subj:	**cuente**	**cuentes**	**cuente**	contēmos	contéis	**cuenten**
Imperat:	——	**cuenta**	**cuente**	contēmos	contād	**cuenten**

Reg: contaba, conté, contara, contase, contare, contaré, contaría

16. Costar, costando, costado, **to cost.**

Pres Ind:	**cuesto**	**cuestas**	**cuesta**	costāmos	costáis	**cuestan**
Pres Subj:	**cueste**	**cuestes**	**cueste**	costēmos	costéis	**cuesten**
Imperat:	——	**cuesta**	**cueste**	costēmos	costād	**cuesten**

Reg: costaba, costé, costara, costase, costare, costaré, costaría

17. Hollar, hollando, hollado, **to trample.**

Pres Ind:	**huello**	**huellas**	**huella**	hollāmos	holláis	**huellan**
Pres Subj:	**huelle**	**huelles**	**huelle**	hollēmos	holléis	**huellen**
Imperat:	——	**huella**	**huelle**	hollēmos	hollād	**huellen**

Reg: hollaba, hollé, hollara, hollase, hollare, hollaré, hollaría

18. Probar, probando, probado, **to prove.**

Pres Ind:	pruebo	pruebas	**prueba**	probāmos	probáis	**prueban**
Pres Subj:	pruebe	pruebes	**pruebe**	probēmos	probéis	**prueben**
Imperat:	——	**prueba**	**pruebe**	probēmos	probād	**prueben**

Reg: probaba, probé, probara, probase, probare, probaré, probaría

19. Sonar, sonando, sonado, **to sound.**

Pres Ind:	sueno	suenas	**suena**	sonāmos	sonáis	**suenan**
Pres Subj:	suene	suenes	**suene**	sonēmos	sonéis	**suenen**
Imperat:	——	**suena**	**suene**	sonēmos	sonād	**suenen**

Reg: sonaba, soné, sonara, sonase, sonare, sonaré, sonaría

20. Volar, volando, volado, **to fly.**

Pres Ind:	vuelo	vuelas	vuela	volāmos	voláis	**vuelan**
Pres Subj:	vuele	vueles	vuele	volēmos	voléis	**vuelen**
Imperat:	——	**vuela**	**vuele**	volēmos	volād	**vuelen**

Reg: volaba, volé, volara, volase, volare, volaré, volaría

21. Forzar, forzando, forzado, **to force, to compel.**

Pres Ind:	fuerzo	fuerzas	fuerza	forzāmos	forzáis	**fuerzan**
Pres Subj:	fuerce	fuerces	fuerce	forcēmos	forcéis	**fuercen**
Imperat:	——	**fuerza**	**fuerce**	forcēmos	forzād	**fuercen**

Reg: forzaba, forcé, forzara, forzase, forzare, forzaré, forzaría

22. Rogar, rogando, rogado, **to request, to beg.**

Pres Ind:	ruego	ruegas	**ruega**	rogāmos	rogáis	**ruegan**
Pres Subj:	ruegue	ruegues	**ruegue**	roguēmos	roguéis	**rueguen**
Imperat:	——	**ruega**	**ruegue**	roguēmos	rogād	**rueguen**

Reg: rogaba, rogué, rogara, rogase, rogare, rogaré, rogaría

23. Trocar, trocando, trocado, **to barter.**

Pres Ind:	trueco	truecas	**trueca**	trocāmos	trocáis	**truecan**
Pres Subj:	trueque	trueques	**trueque**	troquēmos	troquéis	**truequen**
Imperat:	——	**trueca**	**trueque**	troquēmos	trocād	**truequen**

Reg: trocaba, troqué, trocara, trocase, trocare, trocaré, trocaría

24. Jugar,[1] jugando, jugado, **to play, to gamble.**

Pres Ind:	juego	juegas	**juega**	jugāmos	jugáis	**juegan**
Pres Subj:	juegue	juegues	**juegue**	juguēmos	juguéis	**jueguen**
Imperat:	——	**juega**	**juegue**	juguēmos	jugād	**jueguen**

Reg: jugaba, jugué, jugara, jugase, jugare, jugaré, jugaría

---

[1] Jugar was formerly jogar; that is why it is included among o-stem verbs and undergoes the same changes as these.

25. Agorar, agorando, agorado, **to divine.**

Pres Ind: agüero   **agüeras**   **agüera**   agorāmos   agoráis   **agüeran**
Pres Subj: agüere   **agüeres**   **agüere**   agorēmos   agoréis   **agüeren**
Imperat: ———   **agüera**   **agüere**   agorēmos   agorād   **agüeren**
Reg: agoraba, agoré, agorara, agorase, agorare, agoraré, agoraría

d. O Stems—(Second Conjugation)

26. Moler, moliendo, molido, **to grind.**

Pres Ind: **muelo**   **mueles**   **muele**   molēmos   moléis   **muelen**
Pres Subj: **muela**   **muelas**   **muela**   molāmos   moláis   **muelan**
Imperat: ———   **muele**   **muela**   molāmos   molēd   **muelan**
Reg: molía, molí, moliera, moliese, moliere, moleré, molería

27. Mover, moviendo, movido, **to move.**

Pres Ind: **muevo**   **mueves**   **mueve**   movēmos   movéis   **mueven**
Pres Subj: **mueva**   **muevas**   **mueva**   movāmos   mováis   **muevan**
Imperat: ———   **mueve**   **mueva**   movāmos   movēd   **muevan**
Reg: movía, moví, moviera, moviese, moviere, moveré, movería

28. Morder, mordiendo, mordido, **to bite.**

Pres Ind: **muerdo**   **muerdes**   **muerde**   mordēmos   mordéis   **muerden**
Pres Subj: **muerda**   **muerdas**   **muerda**   mordāmos   mordáis   **muerdan**
Imperat: ———   **muerde**   **muerda**   mordāmos   mordēd   **muerdan**
Reg: mordía, mordí, mordiera, mordiese, mordiere, morderé, mordería

29. Volver, volviendo, **vuelto, to return.**

Pres Ind: **vuelvo**   **vuelves**   **vuelve**   volvēmos   volvéis   **vuelven**
Pres Subj: **vuelva**   **vuelvas**   **vuelva**   volvāmos   volváis   **vuelvan**
Imperat: ———   **vuelve**   **vuelva**   volvāmos   volvēd   **vuelvan**
Reg: volvía, volví, volviera, volviese, volviere, volveré, volvería

30. Cocer, cociendo, cocido, **to boil, to cook.**

Pres Ind: **cuezo**   **cueces**   **cuece**   cocēmos   cocéis   **cuecen**
Pres Subj: **cueza**   **cuezas**   **cueza**   cozāmos   cozáis   **cuezan**
Imperat: ——   **cuece**   **cueza**   cozāmos   cocēd   **cuezan**
Reg: cocía, cocí, cociera, cociese, cociere, coceré, cocería

31. Torcer, torciendo, torcido, **to twist.**

Pres Ind: **tuerzo**   **tuerces**   **tuerce**   torcēmos   torcéis   **tuercen**
Pres Subj: **tuerza**   **tuerzas**   **tuerza**   torzāmos   torzáis   **tuerzan**
Imperat: ———   **tuerce**   **tuerza**   torzāmos   torcēd   **tuerzan**
Reg: torcía, torcí, torciera, torciese, torciere, torceré, torcería

32. Oler, oliendo, olido, **to smell, to scent.**

Pres Ind:	huelo	hueles	huele	olēmos	oléis	huelen
Pres Subj:	huela	huelas	huela	olāmos	oláis	huelan
Imperat:	——	huele	huele	olāmos	olēd	huelan

Reg: olía, olí, oliera, oliese, oliere, oleré, olería

Second Class

This class contains verbs of the THIRD CONJUGATION only with the stem-vowels e and o.

a. E STEMS

Verbs of this class insert **i** before the stem-vowel **e** throughout the singular and in the third person plural of the present indicative and subjunctive, and in the same persons in the imperative (**siento, sientes,** etc.).

In the first and second persons plural of the present subjunctive, and in the first person plural of the imperative, the stem-vowel **e** is changed into **i** (**sintāmos, sintáis**).

In the past stem, including the gerund, the stem-vowel **e** is changed into **i** whenever the inflection contains the diphthongs **ie** or **io.**

33. Sentir, **sintiendo,** sentido, **to feel, to perceive.**

Pres Ind:	sient-o	sient-es	sient-e	sent-īmos	sent-ís	sient-en
Pres Subj:	sient-a	sient-as	sient-a	sint-āmos	sint-áis	sient-an
Imperat:	——	sient-e	sient-a	sint-āmos	sent-īd	sient-an
Imperf:	sent-ía	-ías	-ía	-íamos	-íais	-ían

PAST STEM—sint (before ie or io)

Gerund:	sintiendo					
Past:	sent-í	-iste	sintió	sentīmos	-isteis	sintieron
¹*Imp Subj:*	sint-iēra	-iēras	-iēra	-iéramos	-ierais	-iēran
²*Imp Subj:*	sint-iēse	-iēses	-iēse	-iésemos	-ieseis	-iēsen
Fut Subj:	sint-iēre	-iēres	-iēre	-iéremos	-iereis	-iēren

FUTURE STEM—REGULAR

Future:	sentir-é	-ás	-á	-emos	-éis	-án
Condit:	sentir-ía	-ías	-ía	-íamos	-íais	-ían

34. Advertir, **advirtiendo,** advertido, **to observe, to advise.**

Pres Ind:	advierto	adviertes	advierte	advertīmos	advertís	advierten
Pres Subj:	advierta	adviertas	advierta	advirtāmos	advirtáis	adviertan
Imperat:	——	advierte	advierta	advirtāmos	advertīd	adviertan
Imperf:	advert-ía	-ías	-ía	-íamos	-íais	-ían
Gerund:	advirtiendo					

Past:	advert-í	-iste	**advirtió**	advert-īmos	-isteis	**-advirtieron**
[1]*Imp Subj:*	**advirt-iēra**	-iēras	-iēra	-iéramos	-ierais	-iēran
[2]*Imp Subj:*	**advirt-iese**	-iēses	-iēse	-iésemos	-ieseis	-iēsen
Fut Subj:	**advirt-iēre**	-iēres	-iēre	-iéremos	-iereis	-iēren
Future:	advertir-é	-ás	-á	-emos	-éis	-án
Condit:	advertir-ía	-ías	-ía	-íamos	-íais	-ían

35. Herir, **hiriendo,** herido, **to wound, to strike.**

Pres Ind:	**hiero**	**hieres**	**hiere**	herīmos	herís	**hieren**
Pres Subj:	**hiera**	**hieras**	**hiera**	hirāmos	hiráis	**hieran**
Imperat:	———	**hiere**	**hiera**	hirāmos	herīd	**hieran**
Imperf:	her-ía	-ías	-ía	-íamos	-íais	-ían
Past:	her-í	-iste	**hirió**	her-īmos	-ísteis	**hirieron**
[1]*Imp Subj:*	**hir-iera**	-ieras	-iera	-iéramos	-ierais	-ieran
[2]*Imp Subj:*	**hir-iese**	-ieses	-iese	-iésemos	-ieseis	-iesen
Fut Subj:	**hir-iere**	-ieres	-iere	-iéremos	-iereis	-ieren
Future:	herir-é	-ás	-á	-emos	-éis	-án
Condit:	herir-ía	-ías	-ía	-íamos	-íais	-ían

36. Hervir, **hirviendo,** hervido, **to boil.**

Pres Ind:	**hiervo**	**hierves**	**hierve**	hervīmos	hervís	**hierven**
Pres Subj:	**hierva**	**hiervas**	**hierva**	hirvāmos	hirváis	**hiervan**
Imperat:	———	**hierve**	**hierva**	hirvāmos	hervīd	**hiervan**
Past:	herv-í	-iste	**hirvió**	herv-īmos	-isteis	**hirvieron**
[1]*Imp Subj:*	**hirv-iera**	-ieras	-iera	-iéramos	-ierais	-ieran
[2]*Imp Subj:*	**hirv-iese**	-ieses	-iese	-iésemos	-ieseis	-iesen
Fut Subj:	**hirv-iere**	-ieres	-iere	-iéremos	-iereis	-ieren
Future:	hervir-é	-ás	-á	-emos	-éis	-án
Condit:	hervir-ía	-ías	-ía	-íamos	-ías	-ían

37. Erguir, **irguiendo,** erguido, **to raise, to swell with pride.**

This verb is conjugated like **sentir.** The stem being initial, the vowel **i** may either be consonantized or may replace the diphthong in the present tenses:—

Pres Ind:	**yergo**	**yergues**	**yergue**	erguīmos	erguís	**yerguen**
	irgo	**irgues**	**irgue**			**irguen**
Pres Subj:	**yerga**	**yergas**	**yerga**	irgāmos	irgáis	**yergan**
	irga	**irgas**	**irga**			**irgan**
Imperat:	——	**yergue**	**yerga**	irgāmos	erguīd	**yergan**
	——	**irgue**	**irga**			**irgan**
Past:	erguí	erguiste	**irguió**	erguīmos	erguisteis	irguieron
[1]*Imp Subj:*	irguiera	irguieras	irguiera	irguiéramos	irguierais	irguieran

[2]*Imp Subj:*	irguiese	irguieses	irguiese	irguiésemos	irguieseis	irguiesen
Fut Subj:	irguiere	irguieres	irguiere	irguiéremos	irguiereis	irguieren
Future:	erguir-é	-ás	-á	-emos	-éis	-án
Condit:	erguir-ía	-ías	-ía	-íamos	-íais	-ían

38. Adquirir, adquiriendo, adquirido, to obtain, to acquire.

Verbs in **-quirir**, which are derived from the Latin *quaerere*, have the diphthong **ie** in the present stem (when stressed), but preserve their characteristic **i** in all other tenses.

Pres Ind:	**adquiero**	**adquieres**	**adquiere**	adquirimos	adquirís
					adquieren
Pres Subj:	**adquiera**	**adquieras**	**adquiera**	adquirāmos	adquiráis
					adquieran
Imperat:	———	**adquiere**	**adquiera**	adquirāmos	adquirid
					adquieran

Reg: adquiría, adquirí, adquiriera, adquiriese, adquiriere, adquiriré, adquiriría

O STEMS

The stem-vowel **o** is changed into **ue** in the singular, and in the third person plural of the present indicative and subjunctive, and also of the imperative.

Observe, furthermore, that **o** is changed into **u** in the first and second persons plural of the present subjunctive, and in the first person plural of the imperative.

In the preterite stem, including the gerund, **o** is changed into **u** as often as the ending contains the diphthong **ie** or **io**.

39. Dormir, durmiendo, dormido, to sleep.

Pres Ind:	**duermo**	**duermes**	**duerme**	dormīmos	dormís	**duermen**
Pres Subj:	**duerma**	**duermas**	**duerma**	durmāmos	durmáis	**duerman**
Imperat:	———	**duerme**	**duerma**	durmāmos	dormid	**duerman**
Imperf:	dorm-ía	-ías	-ía	-íamos	-íais	-ían
Past:	dorm-í	-iste	**durmió**	dorm-īmos	-īsteis	**durmieron**
[1]*Imp Subj:*	**durm-iera**	-ieras	-iera	-iéramos	-ierais	-ieran
[2]*Imp Subj:*	**durm-iese**	-ieses	-iese	-iésemos	-ieseis	-iesen
Fut Subj:	**durm-iere**	-ieres	-iere	-iéremos	-iereis	-ieren
Future:	dormir-é	-ás	-á	-emos	-éis	-án
Condit:	dormir-ía	-ías	-ía	-íamos	-íais	-ían

40. Morir, muriendo, muerto, to die.

Pres Ind:	**muero**	**mueres**	**muere**	morīmos	morís	**mueren**
Pres Subj:	**muera**	**mueras**	**muera**	murāmos	muráis	**mueran**

Imperat:	——	muere	muera	murámos	morīd	mueran
Imperf:	mor-ía	-ías	-ía	-íamos	-íais	-ían
Past:	mor-í	-iste	murió	mor-īmos	-isteis	murieron
¹Imp Subj:	mur-iera	-ieras	-iera	-iéramos	-ierais	-ieran
²Imp Subj:	mur-iese	-ieses	-iese	-iésemos	-ieseis	-iesen
Fut Subj:	mur-iere	-ieres	-iere	-iéremos	-iereis	-ieren
Future:	morir-é	-ás	-á	-emos	-éis	-án
Condit:	morir-ía	-ías	-ía	-íamos	-íais	-ían

Third Class

Only verbs of the third conjugation with the stem-vowel **e** belong to this class. The gerund belongs generally to the preterite stem.

In the present stem, the vowel **e** is changed into **i** throughout the present indicative, subjunctive, and the imperative, except the first and second persons plural of the indicative, and the second person plural of the imperative.

In the preterite stem, the vowel **e**—as in **e** stems of the preceding class—is changed into **i** when the personal ending contains the diphthong **ie** or **io**.

41. Pedir, **pidiendo,** pedido, **to ask.**

Pres Ind:	pīdo	pīdes	pīde	pedīmos	pedís	pīden
Pres Subj:	pīda	pīdas	pīda	pidāmos	pidáis	pīdan
Imperat:	——	pīde	pīda	pidāmos	pedīd	pīdan
Imperf:	ped-ía	-ías	-ía	-íamos	-íais	-ían
Past:	ped-í	-iste	pidió	ped-imos	-isteis	pidieron
¹Imp Subj:	pid-iera	-ieras	-iera	-iéramos	-ierais	-ieran
²Imp Subj:	pid-iese	-ieses	-iese	-iésemos	-ieseis	-iesen
Fut Subj:	pid-iere	-ieres	-iere	-iéremos	-iereis	-ieren
Future:	pedir-é	-ás	-á	-emos	-éis	-án
Condit:	pedir-ía	-ías	-ía	-íamos	-íais	-ían

42. Servir, **sirviendo,** servido, **to serve.**

Pres Ind:	sirvo	sirves	sirve	servīmos	servís	sirven
Pres Subj:	sirva	sirvas	sirva	sirvāmos	sirváis	sirvan
Imperat:	——	sirve	sirva	sirvamos	servīd	sirvan
Imperf:	serv-ía	-ías	-ía	-íamos	-íais	-ían
Past:	serv-í	-iste	sirvió	serv-imos	-isteis	sirvieron
¹Imp Subj:	sirv-iera	-ieras	-iera	-iéramos	-ierais	-ieran
²Imp Subj:	sirv-iese	-ieses	-iese	-iésemos	-ieseis	-iesen
Fut Subj:	sirv-iere	-ieres	-iere	-iéremos	-iereis	-ieren
Future:	servir-é	-ás	-á	-emos	-éis	-án
Condit:	servir-ía	-ías	-ía	-íamos	-íais	-ían

43. Regir, **rigiendo**, regido, **to rule.**[1]

Pres Ind:	rījo	rīges	rīge	regīmos	regís	rīgen
Pres Subj:	rīja	rījas	rīja	rijāmos	rijáis	rījan
Imperat:	———	rīge	rīja	rijāmos	regīd	rījan
Imperf:	reg-ía	-ías	-ía	-íamos	-íais	-ían
Past:	reg-í	-iste	rigió	reg-imos	-isteis	rigieron
[1]Imp Subj:	rig-iera	-ieras	-iera	-iéramos	-ierais	-ieran
[2]Imp Subj:	rig-iese	-ieses	-iese	-iésemos	-ieseis	-iesen
Fut Subj:	rig-iere	-ieres	-iere	-iéremos	-iereis	-ieren
Future:	regir-é	-ás	-á	-emos	-éis	-án
Condit:	regir-ía	-ías	-ía	-íamos	-íais	-ían

44. Seguir, **siguiendo**, seguido, **to follow.**[2]

Pres Ind:	sigo	sigues	sigue	seguīmos	seguís	siguen
Pres Subj:	siga	sigas	siga	sigāmos	sigáis	sigan
Imperat:	———	sigue	siga	sigāmos	seguīd	sigan
Imperf:	segu-ía	-ías	-ía	-íamos	-íais	-ían
Past:	segu-í	-iste	siguió	segu-īmos	-isteis	siguieron
[1]Imp Subj:	sigu-iera	-ieras	-iera	-iéramos	-ierais	-ieran
[2]Imp Subj:	sigu-iese	-ieses	-iese	-iésemos	-ieseis	-iesen
Fut Subj:	sigu-iere	-ieres	-iere	-iéremos	-iereis	-ieren
Future:	seguir-é	-ás	-á	-emos	-éis	-án
Condit:	seguir-ía	-ías	-ía	-íamos	-íais	-ían

45. Reír, **riendo**, reído, **to laugh.**[3]

Pres Ind:	río	ríes	ríe	reímos	reís	ríen
Pres Subj:	ría	rías	ría	riamos	riáis	rían
Imperat:	———	ríe	ría	riāmos	reíd	rían
Imperf:	re-ía	-ías	-ía	-íamos	-íais	-ían
Past:	re-í	-íste	rió	re-ímos	-ísteis	rieron
[1]Imp Subj:	ri-era	-eras	-era	-éramos	-erais	-eran
[2]Imp Subj:	ri-ese	-eses	-ese	-ésemos	-eseis	-esen
Fut Subj:	ri-ere	-eres	-ere	-éremos	-ereis	-eren
Future:	reir-é	-ás	-á	-emos	-éis	-án
Condit:	reir-ía	-ías	-ía	-íamos	-íais	-ían

---

[1] Verbs of this class, ending in *gir*, must change g into j before **a** or **o**.

[2] Verbs of this class, ending in *guir*, lose the u before **a** and **o**.

[3] Verbs of this class, ending in **eír**, lose the **i** of the diphthongs **ie** and **ió** throughout the preterite stem.

46. Ceñir, ciñendo, ceñido, to gird.[2]

Pres Ind:	ciño	ciñes	ciñe	ceñimos	ceñís	ciñen
Pres Subj:	ciña	ciñas	ciña	ciñamos	ciñáis	ciñan
Imperat:	———	ciñe	ciña	ciñamos	ceñíd	ciñan
Imperf:	ceñ-ía	-ías	-ía	-íamos	-íais	-ían
Past:	ceñ-í	-iste	ciñó	ceñ-īmos	-isteis	ciñeron
[1]Imp Subj:	ciñ-era	-eras	-era	-éramos	-erais	-eran
[2]Imp Subj:	ciñ-ese	-eses	-ese	-ésemos	-eseis	-esen
Fut Subj:	ciñ-ere	-eres	-ere	-éremos	-ereis	-eren
Future:	ceñir-é	-ás	-á	-emos	-éis	-án
Condit:	ceñir-ía	-ías	-ía	-íamos	-íais	-ían

Fourth Class

All verbs ending in **uir**, including those in **güir** (but not those in **guir**), belong to this class.

The gerund uniformly belongs to the preterite stem.

The consonant **y** is inserted throughout the present indicative, subjunctive and the imperative, except in the first and second persons plural of the indicative, and in the second person plural of the imperative.

In the preterite stems, including the gerund, the diphthongs **ie** and **ió** are consonantized throughout = **ye, yó.**

47. Atribuir, atribuyendo, atribuido, to ascribe.

Pres Ind:	atribuyo	atribuyes	atribuye	atribuímos	atribuís	atribuyen
Pres Subj:	atribu-ya	-yas	-ya	-yāmos	-yáis	-yan
Imperat:	———	atribu-ye	-ya	-yāmos	atribuíd	atribuyan
Imperf:	atribu-ía	-ías	-ía	-íamos	-íais	-ían
Past:	atribu-í	-iste	-yó	-īmos	-isteis	-yeron
[1]Imp Subj:	atribu-yēra	-yēras	-yēra	-yéramos	-yerais	-yēran
[2]Imp Subj:	atribu-yēse	-yēses	-yēse	-yésemos	-yeseis	-yēsen
Fut Subj:	atribu-yēre	-yēres	-yēre	-yéremos	-yereis	-yēren
Future:	atribuir-é	-ás	-á	-emos	-éis	-án
Condit:	atribuir-ía	-ías	-ía	-íamos	-íais	-ían

---

[2] Verbs of this class, ending in **ñir**, drop the **i** of the diphthongs **ie** and **ió** in the gerund, in the third persons singular and plural of the past and in the derivative tenses.

48. Huir, **huyendo,** huido, **to flee.**

Pres Ind:	huyo	huyes	huye	huīmos	huís	huyen
Pres Subj:	huya	huyas	huya	huyāmos	huyáis	huyan
Imperat:	———	huye	huya	huyāmos	huīd	huyan
Imperf:	hu-ía	-ías	-ía	-íamos	-íais	-ían
Past:	hu-í	-iste	-yó	-īmos	-īsteis	-yēron
¹Imp Subj:	hu-yēra	-yēras	-yēra	-yéramos	-yerais	-yēran
²Imp Subj:	hu-yēse	-yēses	-yēse	-yésemos	-yeseis	-yēsen
Fut Subj:	hu-yēre	-yēres	-yēre	-yéremos	-yereis	-yēren
Future:	huir-é	-ás	-á	-emos	-éis	-án
Condit:	huir-ía	-ías	-ía	-íamos	-íais	-ían

49. Instituir, **instituyendo,** instituido, **to establish.**

Pres Ind:	institu-yo	-yes	-ye	-īmos	-ís	institu-yen
Pres Subj:	institu-ya	-yas	-ya	-yāmos	-yáis	institu-yan
Imperat:	———	institu-ye	-ya	-yāmos	-īd	institu-yan
Imperf:	institu-ía	-ías	-ía	-íamos	-íais	-ían
Past:	institu-í	-īste	-yó	-īmos	-īsteis	-yēron
¹Imp Subj:	institu-yēra	-yēras	-yēra	-yéramos	-yerais	-yēran
²Imp Subj:	institu-yēse	-yēses	-yēse	-yésemos	-yeseis	-yēsen
Fut Subj:	institu-yēre	-yēres	-yēre	-yéremos	-yereis	-yēren
Future:	instituir-é	-ás	-á	-emos	-éis	-án
Condit:	instituir-ía	-ías	-ía	-íamos	-íais	-ían

50. Argüir, **arguyendo,** argüido, **to argue.**[1]

Pres Ind:	argu-yo	-yes	-ye	argü-īmos	-ís	argu-yen
Pres Subj:	argu-ya	-yas	-ya	argu-yāmos	-yáis	argu-yan
Imperat:	———	-ye	-ya	argu-yāmos	argü-īd	argu-yan
Imperf:	argü-ía	-ías	-ía	-íamos	-íais	-ían
Past:	argü-í	-īste	arguyó	argü-īmos	-īsteis	arguyēron
¹Imp Subj:	argu-yēra	-yēras	-yēra	-yéramos	-yerais	-yēran
²Imp Subj:	argu-yēse	-yēses	-yēse	-yésemos	-yeseis	-yēsen
Fut Subj:	argu-yēre	-yēres	-yēre	-yéremos	-yereis	-yēren
Future:	argüir-é	-ás	-á	-emos	-éis	-án
Condit:	argüir-ía	-ías	-ía	-íamos	-íais	-ían

Fifth Class

All verbs belonging to this class have irregular preterite stems. The stress is on the radical in the first and third persons singular of the past tense.

Their present and future stems are mostly irregular.

---

[1] Verbs in güir lose the diaeresis as often as the consonant **y** is used.

FIRST CONJUGATION

51. Andar, andando, andado, to go.[1]

PRESENT STEM—Regular

Pres Ind:	ando	andas	anda	andāmos	andáis	āndan
Pres Subj:	ande	andes	ande	andēmos	andéis	ānden
Imperat:	———	anda	ande	andēmos	andād	ānden
Imperf:	and-aba	-abas	-aba	-ábamos	-abais	-āban

PAST STEM—anduv (Irregular)

Past:	anduve	anduvīste	anduvo	anduv-īmos	-isteis	-iēron
[1]*Imp Subj:*	anduv-iēra	-ēras	-iēra	-iéramos	-ierais	-iēran
[2]*Imp Subj:*	anduv-iēse	-iēses	-iēse	-iésemos	-ieseis	-iēsen
Fut Subj:	anduv-iēre	-iēres	-iēre	-iéremos	-iereis	-iēren

FUTURE STEM—Regular

Future:	andar-é	-ás	-á	-emos	-éis	-án
Condit:	andar-ía	-ías	-ía	-íamos	-íais	-ían

SECOND CONJUGATION

52. Caber, cabiendo, cabido, to be contained in (en), to hold.[2]

PRESENT STEMS—quep (strong); cab (weak)

Pres Ind:	**quepo**	cabes	cabe	cabēmos	cabéis	caben
Pres Subj:	**quepa**	**quepas**	**quepa**	**quepāmos**	**quepais**	**quepan**
Imperat:	———	cabe	**quepa**	**quepāmos**	cabēd	**quepan**

PAST STEM—cup (Irregular)

Past:	cupe	cupīste	cupo	cup-imos	-isteis	-iēron
[1]*Imp Subj:*	cup-iēra	-iēras	-iēra	-iéramos	-ierais	-iēran
[2]*Imp Subj:*	cup-iēse	-iēses	-iēse	-iésemos	-ieseis	-iēsen
Fut Subj:	cup-iēre	-iēres	-iēre	-iéremos	-iereis	-iēren

FUTURE STEM—cabr

Future:	cabr-é	-ás	-á	-emos	-éis	-án
Condit:	cabr-ía	-ías	-íá	-íamos	-íais	-ían

---

[1] **Andar** expresses the manner of going, or going for an indefinite purpose; **ir** means to go in a specific direction. **Andar** is therefore used of machines, watches, and inanimate objects, or animals generally, while **ir** is used of persons.

[2] Cabe is used impersonally, in the sense of *it is possible;* si cabe, *if it is possible, if it may be;* no cabe duda, *there is no possible doubt.*

53. Hacer, haciendo, **hecho, to make, to do.**

PRESENT STEMS—hag (strong); hac (weak)

Pres Ind:	hago	haces	hace	hacēmos	hacéis	hacen
Pres Subj:	haga	hagas	haga	hagāmos	hagáis	hagan
Imperat:	——	haz	haga	hagāmos	hacēd	hagan
Imperf:	hacía	hacías	hacía	hacíamos	hacíais	hacían

PAST STEM—hic (Irregular)

Past:	hice	hicīste	hizo	hicīmos	hicīsteis	hiciēron
[1]*Imp Subj:*	hic-iēra	-iēras	-iēra	-iéramos	-ierais	-iēran
[2]*Imp Subj:*	hic-iēse	-iēses	-iēse	-iésemos	-ieseis	-iēsen
Fut Subj:	hic-iēre	-iēres	-iēre	-iéremos	-iereis	-iēren

FUTURE STEM—har

Future:	har-é	-ás	-á	-emos	-éis	-án
Condit:	har-ía	-ías	-ía	-íamos	-íais	-ían

54. Satisfacer, satisfaciendo, **satisfecho, to satisfy.**

	satis-			satis-		
Pres Ind:	fago	faces	face	facēmos	facéis	facen
Pres Subj:	faga	fagas	faga	fagāmos	fagáis	fagan
Imperat:	——	face *or* faz	faga	fagāmos	facēd	fagan
Imperf:	fac-ía	-ías	-ía	-íamos	-íais	-ían
Past:	fice	ficīste	fizo	ficīmos	ficisteis	ficiēron
[1]*Imp Subj:*	fic-iera	-ieras	-iera	-iéramos	-ierais	-ieran
[2]*Imp Subj:*	fic-iese	-ieses	-iese	-iésemos	-ieseis	-iesen
Fut Subj:	fic-iere	-ieres	-iere	-iéremos	-iereis	-ieren
Fut:	faré, etc.			*Condit:* faría, etc.		

55. Poder, **pudiendo,** podido, **to be able.**

PRESENT STEMS—pued and pod

Pres Ind:	**puedo**	**puedes**	**puede**	podemos	podéis	**pueden**
Pres Subj:	**pueda**	**puedas**	**pueda**	podamos	podáis	**puedan**
Imperat:	——	——	——	——	——	——
Imperf:	pod-ía	-ías	-ía	-íamos	-íais	-ían

PAST STEM—pud (Irregular)

Past:	pude	pudīste	pudo	pud-imos	-isteis	-ieron
[1]*Imp Subj:*	pud-iera	-ieras	-iera	-iéramos	-ierais	-ieran
[2]*Imp Subj:*	pud-iese	-ieses	-iese	-iésemos	-ieseis	-iesen
Fut Subj:	pud-iere	-ieres	-iere	-iéremos	-iereis	-ieren

FUTURE STEM—podr

Future:	podr-é	-ás	-á	-emos	-éis	-án
Condit:	podr-ía	-ías	-ía	-íamos	-íais	-ían

56. Poner, poniendo, **puesto, to put, to place.**

Pres Ind:	pongo	pones	pone	ponémos	ponéis	ponen
Pres Subj:	ponga	pongas	ponga	pongámos	pongáis	pongan
Imperat:	———	pon	ponga	pongámos	ponéd	pongan
Imperf:	pon-ía	-ías	-ía	-íamos	-íais	-ían

PAST STEM—pus (Irregular)

Past:	puse	pusíste	puso	pus-ímos	-isteis	-ieron
[1]*Imp Subj:*	pus-iera	-ieras	-iera	-iéramos	-ierais	-ieran
[2]*Imp Subj:*	pus-iese	-ieses	-iese	-iésemos	-ieseis	-iesen
Fut Subj:	pus-iere	-ieres	-iere	-iéremos	-iereis	-ieren

FUTURE STEM—pondr

Future:	pondr-é	-ás	-á	-emos	-éis	-án
Condit:	pondr-ía	-ías	-ía	-íamos	-íais	-ían

57. Querer, queriendo, querido, **to will, to wish.**

PRESENT STEMS—quier and quer

Pres Ind:	**quiero**	**quieres**	**quiere**	querémos	queréis	**quieren**
Pres Subj:	**quiera**	**quieras**	**quiera**	querámos	queráis	**quieran**
Imperat:	———	**quiere**	**quiera**	querámos	queréd	**quieran**
Imperf:	quer-ía	-ías	-ía	-íamos	-íais	-ían

PAST STEM—quis (Irregular)

Past:	quíse	quisíste	quíso	quis-ímos	-isteis	-ieron
[1]*Imp Subj:*	quis-iera	-ieras	-iera	-iéramos	-ierais	-ieran
[2]*Imp Subj:*	quis-iese	-ieses	-iese	-iésemos	-ieseis	-iesen
Fut Subj:	quis-iere	-ieres	-iere	-iéremos	-iereis	-ieren

FUTURE STEM—querr

Future:	querr-é	-ás	-á	-emos	-éis	-án
Condit:	querr-ía	-ías	-ía	-íamos	-íais	-ían

58. Saber, sabiendo, sabido, **to know** (*things*).

PRESENT STEMS—sep and sab

Pres Ind:	**sé**	sabes	sabe	sabémos	sabéis	saben
Pres Subj:	**sepa**	**sepas**	**sepa**	**sepámos**	**sepáis**	**sepan**
Imperat:	———	sabe	**sepa**	**sepámos**	sabéd	**sepan**
Imperf:	sab-ía	-ías	-ía	-íamos	-íais	-ían

Past Stem—sup (Irregular)

Past:	supe	supíste	supo	sup-ímos	-isteis	-ieron
¹Imp Subj:	sup-iera	-ieras	-iera	-iéramos	-ierais	-ieran
²Imp Subj:	sup-iese	-ieses	-iese	-iésemos	-ieseis	-iesen
Fut Subj:	sup-iere	-ieres	-iere	-iéremos	-iereis	-ieren

Future Stem—sabr

Future:	sabr-é	-ás	-á	-emos	-éis	-án
Condit:	sabr-ía	-ías	-ía	-íamos	-íais	-ían

59. Traer, **trayendo**, traído, **to bring.**

Present Stems—traig and tra

Pres Ind:	trāigo	traes	trae	traēmos	traéis	trāen
Pres Subj:	trāiga	traigas	traiga	traigāmos	traigáis	traigan
Imperat:	———	trae	traiga	traigāmos	traed	traigan
Imperf:	tra-ía	-ías	-ía	-íamos	-íais	-ían

Past Stem—traj

Past:	trāje	trajíste	trājo	traj-ímos	-isteis	-eron
¹Imp Subj:	traj-era	-eras	-era	-éramos	-erais	-eran
²Imp Subj:	traj-ese	-eses	-ese	-ésemos	-eseis	-esen
Fut Subj:	traj-ere	-eres	-ere	-éremos	-ereis	-eren

Future Stem—Regular

Future:	traer-é	-ás	-á	-emos	-éis	-án
Condit:	traer-ía	-ías	-ía	-íamos	-íais	-ían

Third Conjugation

60. Conducir, conduciendo, conducido, **to conduct.**

Present Stems—conduzc and conduc (Irregular)

Pres Ind:	conduzco	conduces	conduce	conducímos	conducís
					conducen
Pres Subj:	conduzca	conduzcas	conduzca	conduzcāmos	conduzcáis
					conduzcan
Imperat:	———	conduce	conduzca	conduzcāmos	conducíd
					conduzcan
Imperf:	conduc-ía	-ías	-ía	-íamos	-íais	-ían

Past Stem—conduj (Irregular)

Past:	conduje	condujíste	condujo	conduj-ímos	-isteis	-eron
¹Imp Subj:	conduj-era	-eras	-era	-éramos	-erais	-eran
²Imp Subj:	conduj-ese	-eses	-ese	-ésemos	-eseis	-esen
Fut Subj:	conduj-ere	-eres	-ere	-éremos	-ereis	-eren

Future Stem—Regular

Future:	conducir-é	-ás	-á	-emos	-éis	-án
Condit:	conducir-ía	-ías	-ía	-íamos	-íais	-ían

61. Decir, diciendo, dicho, to say, to tell.

Present Stems—dig, dic and dec

Pres Ind:	digo	dices	dice	decímos	decís	dicen
Pres Subj:	diga	digas	diga	digámos	digáis	digan
Imperat:	——	dí	diga	digámos	decíd	digan
Imperf:	dec-ía	-ías	-ía	-íamos	-íais	-ían

Past Stem—dij (Irregular)

Past:	dīje	dijīste	dījo	dij-īmos	-isteis	-eron
[1]*Imp Subj:*	dij-era	-eras	-era	-éramos	-erais	-eran
[2]*Imp Subj:*	dij-ese	-eses	-ese	-ésemos	-eseis	-esen
Fut Subj:	dij-ere	-eres	-ere	-éremos	-ereis	-eren

Future Stem—dir

Future:	dir-é	-ás	-á	-emos	-éis	-án
Condit:	dir-ía	-ías	-ía	-íamos	-íais	-ían

62. Bendecir, bendiciendo, bendecido (and bendito), to bless.

	ben-			ben-		
Pres Ind:	digo	dices	dice	decímos	decís	dicen
Pres Subj:	diga	digas	diga	digamos	digáis	digan
Imperat:	——	dice	diga	digamos	decíd	digan
Imperf:	decía	-ías	-ía	-íamos	-íais	-ían
Past:	dije	dijiste	dijo	dij-īmos	-isteis	-eron
[1]*Imp Subj:*	dij-era	-eras	-era	-éramos	-erais	-eran
[2]*Imp Subj:*	dij-ese	-eses	-ese	-ésemos	-eseis	-esen
Fut Subj:	dij-ere	-eres	-ere	-éremos	-ereis	-eren
Future:	decir-é	-ás	-á	-emos	-éis	-án
Condit:	decir-ía	-ías	-ía	-íamos	-íais	-ían

63. Venir, viniendo, venido, to come.

Present Stems—veng, ven, and vien

Pres Ind:	vengo	vienes	viene	venímos	venís	vienen
Pres Subj:	venga	vengas	venga	vengámos	vengáis	vengan
Imperat:	——	ven	venga	vengámos	veníd	vengan
Imperf:	ven-ía	-ías	-ía	-íamos	-íais	-ían

PAST STEM—vin (Irregular)

Past:	vine	viniste	vino	vin-imos	-isteis	-ieron
[1]Imp Subj:	vin-iera	-ieras	-iera	-iéramos	-ierais	-ieran
[2]Imp Subj:	vin-iese	-ieses	-iese	-iésemos	-ieseis	-iesen
Fut Subj:	vin-iere	-ieres	-iere	-iéremos	-iereis	-ieren

FUTURE STEM—vendr

Future:	vendr-é	-ás	-á	-emos	-éis	-án
Condit:	vendr-ía	-ías	-ía	-íamos	-íais	-ían

Sixth Class

This class contains a few verbs not reducible to any of the foregoing

FIRST CONJUGATION

64. Dar, dando, dado, to give.

PRESENT STEM—Regular

Pres Ind:	**doy**	das	da	damos	dais	dan
Pres Subj:	**dé**	des	dé	demos	deis	den
Imperat:	——	da	dé	demos	dad	den
Imperf:	daba	dabas	daba	dábamos	dabais	daban

PAST STEM—SECOND CONJUGATION—Irregular

Past:	di	diste	dió	dimos	disteis	dieron
[1]Imp Subj:	diera	dieras	diera	diéramos	dierais	dieran
[2]Imp Subj:	diese	dieses	diese	diésemos	dieseis	diesen
Fut Subj:	diere	dieres	diere	diéremos	diereis	dieren

FUTURE STEM—Regular

Future:	dar-é	-ás	-á	-emos	-éis	-án
Condit:	dar-ía	-ías	-ía	-íamos	-íais	-ían

SECOND CONJUGATION

65. Caer, **cayendo,** caído, to fall.

PRESENT STEMS—caig and ca

Pres Ind:	caigo	caes	cae	caemos	caéis	caen
Pres Subj:	caiga	caigas	caiga	caigamos	caigáis	caigan
Imperat:	——	cae	caiga	caigamos	caed	caigan
Imperf:	ca-ía	-ías	-ía	-íamos	-íais	-ían

Past Stem—Regular

Past:	caí	caíste	cayó	ca-ímos	-ísteis	-yéron
¹Imp Subj:	ca-yera	-yeras	-yera	-yéramos	-yerais	-yeran
²Imp Subj:	ca-yese	-yeses	-yese	-yésemos	-yeseis	-yesen
Fut Subj:	ca-yere	-yeres	-yere	-yéremos	-yereis	-yeren

Future Stem—Regular

Future:	caer-é	-ás	-á	-emos	-éis	-án
Condit:	caer-ía	-ías	-ía	-íamos	-íais	-ían

66. Valer, valiendo, valido, **to be worth.**

Present Stems—valg and val

Pres Ind:	valgo	vales	vale	valēmos	valéis	vălen
Pres Subj:	valga	valgas	valga	valgāmos	valgáis	valgan
Imperat:	———	val *or* vale	valga	valgāmos	valēd	valgan
Imperf:	val-ía	-ías	-ía	-íamos	-íais	-ían

Past Stem—Regular

Past:	val-í	-iste	-ió	-īmos	-isteis	-ieron
¹Imp Subj:	val-iera	-ieras	-iera	-iéramos	-ierais	-ieran
²Imp Subj:	val-iese	-ieses	-iese	-iésemos	-ieseis	-iesen
Fut Subj:	val-iere	-ieres	-iere	-iéremos	-iereis	-ieren

Future Stem—valdr

Future:	valdr-é	-ás	-á	-emos	-éis	-án
Condit:	valdr-ía	-ías	-ía	-íamos	-íais	-ían

67. Ver, viendo, **visto, to see.**

Present Stems—ve

Pres Ind:	veo	ves	ve	vēmos	vēis	ven
Pres Subj:	vea	veas	vea	veāmos	veáis	vean
Imperat:	———	ve	vea	veāmos	ved	vean
Imperf:	ve-ía	-ías	-ía	íamos	-íais	-ían

Past Stem—Irregular

Past:	ví	vīste	vió	vīmos	vīsteis	viēron
¹Imp Subj:	viera	vieras	viera	viéramos	vierais	vieran
²Imp Subj:	viese	vieses	viese	viésemos	vieseis	viesen
Fut Subj:	viere	vieres	viere	viéremos	viereis	vieren

Future Stem—Regular

Future:	ver-é	-ás	-á	-emos	-éis	-án
Condit:	ver-ía	-ías	-ía	-íamos	-íais	-ían

68. Proveer, **proveyendo,** proveído or **provisto, to provide.**

Pres Ind:	provēo	provēes	provēe	proveēmos	proveéis	provēen
Pres. Subj:	provēa	provēas	provēa	proveāmos	proveáis	provēan
Imperat:	———	provēe	provēa	proveāmos	proveēd	provēan
Imperf:	prove-ía	-ías	-ía	-íamos	-íais	-ían
Past:	prove-í	-iste	-yó	-ímos	-ísteis	-yēron
[1]*Imp Subj:*	prove-yēra	-yēras	-yēra	-yéramos	-yerais	-yēran
[2]*Imp Subj:*	prove-yēse	-yēses	-yēse	-yésemos	-yeseis	-yēsen
Fut Subj:	prove-yēre	-yēres	-yēre	-yéremos	-yereis	-yēren
Future:	proveer-é	-ás	-á	-emos	-éis	-án
Condit:	proveer-ía	-ías	-ía	-íamos	-íais	-ían

69. Creer, **creyendo,** creído, **to believe.**

Pres Ind:	creo	crees	cree	creemos	creéis	creen
Pres Subj:	crea	creas	crea	creāmos	creáis	crean
Imperat:	———	cree	crea	creāmos	creēd	crean
Imperf:	cre-ía	-ías	-ía	-íamos	-íais	-ían
Past:	cre-í	-íste	-yó	-ímos	-ísteis	-yēron
[1]*Imp Subj:*	cre-yera	-yeras	-yera	-yéramos	-yerais	-yeran
[2]*Imp Subj:*	cre-yese	-yeses	-yese	-yésemos	-yeseis	-yesen
Fut Subj:	cre-yere	-yeres	-yere	-yéremos	-yereis	-yeren
Future:	creer-é, etc.			*Condit:* creer-ía, etc.		

70. Poseer, **poseyendo,** poseído, **to possess.**

Pres Ind:	posēo	posēes	posēe	poseēmos	poseéis	posēen
Pres Subj:	posēa	posēas	posēa	poseāmos	poseáis	posēan
Imperat:	———	posēe	posēa	poseāmos	poseēd	posēan
Imperf:	pose-ía	-ías	-ía	-íamos	-íais	-ían
Past:	pose-í	-íste	-yó	-ímos	-ísteis	-yēron
[1]*Imp Subj:*	pose-yēra	-yēras	-yēra	-yéramos	-yerais	-yēran
[2]*Imp Subj:*	pose-yēse	-yēses	-yēse	-yésemos	-yeseis	-yēsen
Fut Subj:	pose-yēre	-yēres	-yēre	-yéremos	-yereis	-yēren
Future:	poseer-é, etc.			*Condit:* poseer-ía, etc.		

71. Yacer, yaciendo, yacido, **to be situated, to lie in the grave.**

Pres Ind:	yazco / yazgo / yago	yaces	yace	yacēmos	yacéis	yacen
Pres Subj:	yazca / yazga / yaga	yazcas / yazgas / yagas	yazca / yazga / yaga	yazcāmos / yazgāmos / yagāmos	yazcáis / yazgáis / yagáis	yazcan / yazgan / **yagan**
Imperat:	yace *or* yaz			yaced		

yacía yací yaciēra yaciēse yaciēre yaceré yacería

Third Conjugation

72. Asir, asiendo, asido, to lay hold of.

Present Stems—asg and as

Pres Ind:	asgo	ases	ase	asīmos	asís	āsen
Pres Subj:	asga	asgas	asga	asgámos	asgáis	asgan
Imperat:	——	ase	asga	asgámos	asíd	asgan
	asía así	asiēra	asiēse	asiēre asiré asiría		

73. Ir, yendo, ido, to go (*for a definite purpose*).

Pres Ind:	voy	vas	va	vamos	vais	van
Pres Subj:	vaya	vayas	vaya	vayāmos	vayáis	vayan
Imperat:	——	ve	vaya	vayāmos	id	vayan
Imperf:	iba	ibas	iba	íbamos	ibais	iban
Past:	fuí	fuíste	fué	fuímos	fuisteis	fuēron
[1]*Imp Subj:*	fuēra	fuēras	fuēra	fuéramos	fuerais	fuēran
[2]*Imp Subj:*	fuēse	fuēses	fuēse	fuésemos	fueseis	fuēsen
Fut Subj:	fuēre	fuēres	fuēre	fuéremos	fuereis	fuēren
Future:	ir-é	-ás	-á	-emos	-éis	-án
Condit:	ir-ía	-ías	-ía	-íamos	-íais	-ían

74. Oír, oyendo, oído, to hear.

Present Stems—oig, oy, and o

Pres Ind:	ōigo	ōyes	ōye	oímos	oís	ōyen
Pres Subj:	ōiga	ōigas	ōiga	oigāmos	oigáis	ōigan
Imperat:	——	ōye	ōiga	oigāmos	oíd	ōigan
Imperf:	o-ía	-ías	-ía	-íamos	-íais	-ían

Past Stem—o (Diphthongs *ie* and *ió* consonantized)

Past:	oí	oíste	oyó	oímos	oísteis	oyēron
[1]*Imp Subj:*	oyēra	oyēras	oyēra	oyéramos	oyērais	oyēran
[2]*Imp Subj:*	oyēse	oyēses	oyēse	oyésemos	oyeseis	oyēsen
Fut Subj:	oyēre	oyēres	oyēre	oyéremos	oyereis	oyēren

Future Stem—Regular

Future:	oir-é	-ás	-á	-emos	-éis	-án
Condit:	oir-ía	-ías	-ía	-íamos	-íais	-ían

75. Salir, saliendo, salido, to go out.

Present Stems—salg and sal

Pres Ind:	salgo	sales	sale	salīmos	salís	salen
Pres Subj:	salga	salgas	salga	salgāmos	salgáis	salgan
Imperat:	——	sal	salga	salgāmos	salid	salgan
Imperf:	sal-ía	-ías	-ía	-íamos	-íais	-ían

PAST STEM—Regular

Past:	sal-í	-íste	-ió	-ímos	-ísteis	-iéron
[1]*Imp Subj:*	sal-iera	-ieras	-iera	-iéramos	-ierais	-ieran
[2]*Imp Subj:*	sal-iese	-ieses	-iese	-iésemos	-ieseis	-iesen
Fut Subj:	sal-iere	-ieres	-iere	-iéremos	-iereis	-ieren

FUTURE STEM—saldr

Future:	saldr-é	-ás	-á	-emos	-éis	-án
Condit:	saldr-ía	-ías	-ía	-íamos	-íais	-ían

Moods and Tenses

INDICATIVE MOOD

PRESENT TENSE

1. The present indicative expresses an action occurring or a state existing at the present time:

Yo escribo y ella dibuja.	*I write and she draws.*
Estoy escribiendo una carta.	*I am writing a letter.*
¿Qué está V. haciendo?	*What are you doing?*

2. It sometimes replaces the past, especially in lively narration:

Apenas dada la orden, avanza la caballería, ataca al enemigo, que presto queda completamente derrotado.	*Hardly was the order given, when the cavalry advanced, attacked the enemy, who soon was completely routed.*

3. It sometimes replaces the future:

El barco sale mañana.	*The boat will leave tomorrow.*
La primavera que viene hay una feria en Málaga.	*Next spring there will be a fair in Malaga.*

4. It is used after **hace, it is,** when expressing time:

¿Cuánto tiempo hace que está V. en Méjico?	*How long have you been in Mexico?*
Hace mucho tiempo que no le veo.	*It is a long time since I saw him.*

IMPERFECT TENSE

1. The imperfect indicative is employed to express an action or event which was going on or existing, when another past action took place:

Yo estaba escribiendo cuando mi amigo Carlos entró.	*I was writing when my friend Charles came in.*

2. It denotes customary or habitual action, and may in such cases be translated by "used to":

Cuando era joven me alegraba de cosas que no me gustan ahora.

When I was young, I used to take pleasure in things which do not please me now.

Past Tense

1. The past tense of the indicative denotes what occurred within a period of time wholly elapsed. It may have happened yesterday, a few weeks before or ages ago:

Fuí a verle ayer.

I went to see him yesterday.

Murió hace dos meses.

He died two months ago.

Cervantes nació a mediados del siglo dieciséis, y murió en Madrid a principios del siglo diecisiete.

Cervantes was born in the middle of the sixteenth century, and died at Madrid in the beginning of the seventeenth century.

2. It is therefore called the historical tense, and is used especially in narration:

Entregaron la ciudad a los enemigos, pero éstos no se atrevieron al principio a entrar en ella.

They delivered the town to the enemies, but the latter did not venture at first to enter it.

Present Perfect Tense

1. The present perfect tense of the indicative denotes what is past without stating a specific period:

He comprado un caballo.

I have bought a horse.

2. It denotes an action in the past belonging to a period of time (day, week, month, year, etc.), not entirely elapsed:

He estado aquí dos horas.

I have been here for two hours.

Muchas cosas nuevas han sido inventadas en el siglo presente.

Many new things have been invented during the present century.

Past Perfect Tense

The past perfect tense denotes an action which is not only past in itself, but also past with reference to some other past action expressed or implied:

Había acabado de almorzar antes que él viniese.

I had breakfasted before he came.

Past Anterior

The past anterior is used in the same manner as the past perfect, but is always preceded by a conjunction of time, as **cuando,** when; **después que,** after; **luego que, así que, tan pronto como,** as soon as; **no bien,** no sooner; **apenas,** hardly, scarcely, etc.:

Tan pronto como hube leído el libro lo devolví.   *When I had read the book, I returned it.*

Future Tense

1. The future denotes future time:

Él vendrá mañana.   *He will come to-morrow.*

2. It is frequently used in questions, especially when the interrogator is convinced that his query cannot be denied:

¿Habrá desgracia mayor que la mía?   *Can there be a greater misfortune than mine?*

¿Se habrá visto cosa más primorosa?   *Has ever anything more beautiful been seen?*

Future Perfect

This tense is used in the same manner as the corresponding English form:

Ya habré terminado la tarea cuando llegue el invierno.   *I shall have finished my task when the winter comes.*

Conditional

1. The conditional is used chiefly in conditional sentences of which it forms the conclusions, while the clause with **si, if,** forms the condition:

Compraría libros si tuviese (*or* tuviera) dinero.   *I should buy books if I had money.*

2. In the conditional clauses with **si,** the forms in **-se** and **-ra** are interchangeable:

Habríamos ido a ver los fuegos artificiales, **si** hubiésemos (*or* hubiéramos) sabido que los había.   *We should have gone to see the fireworks if we had known that there were any.*

3. The conditional is used to express a wish or modest request:

Desearía que mis hijos aprendiesen (*or* aprendieran) algunas lenguas.   *I would desire my children to learn some languages.*

4. It denotes an uncertain and approximate statement in narrations:

Las once y media serían cuando nos acostamos anoche.	*It may have been (it was about) half-past eleven when we went to bed last night.*

5. It expresses possibility or fitness:

¿Sería verdad eso?	*Could that be true?*
Él podría venir.	*He might come.*

The Use of the Subjunctive Mood

1. The subjunctive mood expresses possibility, doubt, apprehension, prohibition, entreaty, surprise, necessity, advice, etc. It is chiefly used in dependent clauses connected with the principal clause by the conjunction **que, that.**

2. The tense of the subjunctive mood, being subordinate to the verb in the principal clause, is regulated by it.

3. The subjunctive mood is used in principal clauses to supply the negative form of the imperative:

No me lo diga, *do not tell it me!*	No se vaya V., *do not go away.*

It also supplies the affirmative form of the imperative in the first and third persons:

Sea yo, *let me be.*	Sea él, *let him be.*

4. The subjunctive mood must be used after verbs expressive of wish, desire, entreaty, command, permission, expectation, hope, doubt, fear, apprehension, joy, grief, vexation, and surprise:

Temo que no vengan a tiempo para ir al teatro.	*I am afraid they will not arrive in time to go to the theatre.*
Quiere que lo haga yo.	*He wants me to do this.*
Todos desean que vuelva hoy.	*Everyone desires him to return to-day.*
Me alegro que lo sepa.	*I am glad you know it.*
Espero que llegue mi hermano.	*I hope my brother will arrive.*
Me alegro que llueva.	*I am glad it rains.*
Le mandaron que fuese a Chihuahua.	*They ordered him to go to Chihuahua.*
Permítame V. que le haga una pregunta.	*Allow me to ask you a question.*
Siento que no hayamos podido venir.	*I regret we could not come.*

5. The subjunctive mood is employed after impersonal expressions, unless they denote positive certainty:

Conviene que lo sepa.	*It is proper for him to know it.*
Es justo que sea V. premiado por su obra.	*It is right you should be rewarded for your work.*
Es lástima que no venga.	*It is a pity that he does not come.*
Es menester que vaya V. a buscar al médico.	*You must go for the physician.*

But:

Es seguro que viene.	*It is certain that he will come.*

6. The subjunctive mood is used in relative sentences when the relative refers to persons, objects, or ideas mentioned in an uncertain or indefinite sense:

Venga lo que viniere.	*Come what will.*
Quien quiera que sea.	*Whoever he may be.*
¡Haga V. lo que más le gustare!	*Do what you like best!*

7. The subjunctive is also used when a future, possible, or contingent effect is expressed:

Lo compraré cuando tenga dinero.	*I will buy it when I have money.*

8. After verbs of saying, thinking, believing, etc., the subjunctive mood is used in negative or interrogative sentences:

No crea V. que mi amigo haya hecho esto.	*Do not believe that my friend did this!*
¿Piensa V. que ella salga hoy?	*Do you think she will go out to-day?*

a. In affirmative sentences, however, the indicative mood must be used after these verbs:

La criada dice que la sopa está en la mesa.	*The maid says that the soup is on the table.*

Correspondence of Tenses

1. The present subjunctive is generally employed when the verb in the principal clause stands in the present, present perfect, future indicative, or in the imperative:

Me alegro que el tiempo favorezca la fiesta.	*I am glad the weather is favorable to the festival.*
Sentiré que no llegue mañana.	*I shall be sorry if he does not arrive tomorrow.*
Dígale que entre.	*Tell him to come in.*

2. The imperfect subjunctive in either form is employed after verbs in any past tense in the indicative:

Quise que viniese (*or* viniera).	*I wished him to come.*
Le rogaba que se fuera.	*He begged him to go away.*

3. The present perfect subjunctive is used after verbs in the present or the future Indicative:

No volveré hasta que me haya restablecido.	*I shall not return till I am well.*

4. The past perfect subjunctive in either form is used after verbs of any past tense in the indicative:

Creíamos que ya hubiera (*or* hubiese) dado este libro a Juanita.	*We thought he had already given this book to little Jane.*

5. The future and future perfect subjunctive may be used after **si, if; cuando, when; mientras, while;** or after a relative pronoun or adverb in sentences denoting future contingency:

Si hiciere mal tiempo, se aplazará la función.	*If the weather is bad, the performance will be postponed.*
Yo traeré a V. los libros que me dieren.	*I will bring you the books they may give me.*

Except in proverbs and legal phrases, the future subjunctive is rarely used today. Its place is taken by the present subjunctive or, in conditional clauses, by the present indicative:

Yo traeré a V. los libros que me den.	*I will bring you the books they may give me.*
Si hace mal tiempo, se aplazará la función.	*If the weather is bad, the performance will be postponed.*

Use of the Infinitive

1. The infinitive may be used like a noun. As such, it may be preceded by an article:

Hablar mucho es un vicio.	*To talk much is a bad habit.*
El escribir bien necesita gran esfuerzo.	*To write well demands a great effort.*

2. The infinitive stands after all prepositions:

Después de oír a ambas partes, es como se puede juzgar.	*After hearing both parties, one is able to judge.*
Para aprender algo es preciso estudiar.	*In order to learn anything, one must study.*

3. The infinitive with **a** or **al** corresponds to English sentences beginning with **when, after, as,** or **if**:

Al salir de casa me encontré con mi agente.	*When I left the house I met my agent.*
A saber yo que había venido, no hubiera salido.	*If I had known he had come, I should not have gone out.*

4. The infinitive without any preposition is used after verbs denoting fear, doubt, wish, desire, need, duty, thought, etc., when both verbs have the same subject:

Temíamos dormir demasiado.	*We were afraid to sleep too long.*
Necesitaba salir en seguida.	*I needed to go out at once.*

After verbs of command, or forbidding, causing, preventing, etc., either the infinitive or subjunctive may follow:

Le mandé venir Le mandé que viniera $\Big\}$	*I ordered him to come.*

Verbs requiring no Preposition before a following Infinitive

aconsejar, *to advise*
acostumbrar, *to accustom*
afirmar, *to affirm*
agradar, *to be agreeable*
concebir, *to conceive*
confesar, *to confess*
contar, *to relate*
conviene, *it is convenient to*
creer, *to believe*
deber, *to owe, must*
declarar, *to declare*
dejar, *to let, to leave*
desear, *to desire*
determinar, *to resolve to*
esperar, *to hope, to expect to*
gustar, *to like to*
hacer, *to make, to cause to*
imaginar, *to imagine*
impedir, *to prevent from*
intentar, *to intend*
mandar, *to order*
manifestar, *to manifest*

más vale, *it is better to*
necesitar, *to want to*
negar, *to deny*
oír, *to hear*
osar, *to dare, to venture to*
parecer, *to appear*
pensar, *to think, to intend*
poder, *to be able*
preferir, *to prefer*
presumir, *to presume*
pretender, *to pretend, to claim*
procurar, *to try to*
prohibir, *to forbid to*
prometer, *to promise*
proponer, *to propose*
protestar, *to protest*
querer, *to wish*
saber, *to know how, to be able*
sentir, *to feel, to regret*
soler, *to be accustomed to*
temer, *to fear to*
ver, *to see*

5. Verbs of motion, destination, encouragement, inclination, habit, or reflexive verbs expressive of strong moral decision or effort, require the preposition **a** before the infinitive of the verb they govern.

Verbs requiring a before a following Infinitive

animar a, *to encourage to*

aprender a, *to learn to*

aspirar a, *to aspire to*

autorizar a, *to authorize to*

atreverse a, *to dare to*

ayudar a, *to help to*

comenzar a, *to commence to*

condenar a, *to condemn to*

consentir a, *to consent to*

convidar a, *to invite to*

dar a, *to give to*

decidirse a, *to resolve to*

echar a ⎱
empezar a ⎰ *to begin to*

enseñar a, *to teach to*

enviar a, *to send to*

esforzarse a, *to try*

habituar a, *to accustom to*

inclinar a, *to incline to*

invitar a, *to invite to*

ir a, *to go to*

negarse a, *to refuse to*

obligar a, *to compel to*

pasar a, *to go to, to come to*

ponerse a, *to begin to*

resistirse a, *to resist*

salir a, *to start for*

tender a, *to aim at*

venir a, *to come to*

volver a, *to return to*

6. The preposition **a** before the infinitive is used in a number of elliptical phrases, as:

A decir la verdad	*to speak truly*
A saber	*namely*

7. The preposition **de** is used before the infinitive after nouns and adjectives:

Hágame V. el favor de venir conmigo.	*Do me the favor to come with me.*
No tengo el gusto de conocer a V.	*I have not the pleasure of knowing you.*
Es difícil de aprender.	*It is difficult to learn.*

8. Verbs requiring de before a following Infinitive

acabar de, *to have just*

acordarse de, *to be glad to*

alegrarse de, *to be glad to*

arrepentirse de, *to repent of*

cesar de, *to cease to*

dejar de, *to fail to, to leave off*

desistir de, *to cease from*

disuadir de, *to dissuade from*

encargar de, *to commission to*

excusar de, *to excuse from*

eximir de, *to free from*

haber de, *to be about to*

ocuparse de, *to busy one's self with*

olvidarse de, *to forget to*

tratar de, *to try to*

9. **De** must be used after **ser, to be,** when used impersonally:

Es de esperar.	*It is to be hoped.*
Es de desear que no venga.	*It is desirable he should not come.*

10. The preposition **en** is required before the infinitive after verbs denoting occupation or insistence:

Se ocupa en leer, en escribir.   *He occupies himself with reading, with writing.*

11. The preposition **con** is required before the infinitive after verbs which signify diversion or amusement:

Le entretengo con leerle algo gracioso.   *I entertain him by reading some witty piece to him.*

The gerund is generally used in such cases:

Divierto a mi hermana tocándole algunas arias al piano.   *I entertain my sister by playing some airs on the piano to her.*

The Gerund

1. The **gerund** is invariable in gender and number. As in English, it is used in connection with the verb **estar** to form the progressive conjugation, which denotes that the action of the verb is continuing or unfinished:

Estoy comiendo.   *I am eating.*
Estaba leyendo.   *He was reading.*
Estará escribiendo.   *He will be writing.*

Observe that **estar** cannot be used with the Gerund of **ser, to be; ir, to go;** and **venir, to come.** Thus we say **voy, I am going; vengo, I am going.**

2. The gerund is used when it denotes the state of the subject:

Habla durmiendo.   *He speaks in his sleep (while he is asleep).*

3. The gerund is frequently used for the sake of brevity where we have to employ **while, whilst, as, since, if, although,** or **by:**

Estando escribiendo una carta a mi agente, entró él mismo en mi cuarto.   *Whilst writing a letter to my agent, he himself entered into my room.*

Teniendo malo el pie no puede levantarse.   *He cannot rise as he has a sore foot.*

4. The gerund is also used with the preposition **en.** It is to be observed that the gerund with or without **en** may have an indefinite personal subject:

En diciendo esto, se marchó.   *Having said so, he went away.*
El llegando a Veracruz, escribiré.   *As soon as I arrive in Vera-Cruz, I shall write.*

5. The gerund naturally partakes of the nature of the verb from which it is derived, and governs the same cases:

Gozando de buena salud	*Enjoying good health*
Olvidándose de lo pasado	*Forgetting the past*

The Past Participle

1. The past participle of all verbs joined to the auxiliary **haber** is invariable:

Hemos visto dos señoritas.	*We have seen two young ladies.*
Las señoritas que hemos visto son muy lindas.	*The young ladies we saw are very pretty.*

2. **Llevar** or **tener,** when used as substitutes of **haber,** require the past participles accompanying them to agree in number and gender with their object:

Tengo escrita una carta.	*I have written a letter.*
Llevan escritas dos cartas.	*They have written two letters.*

3. In the tenses of the passive voice the past participle is inflected and agrees in gender and number with its subject. It is also inflected when joined to the verbs **ser** or **estar, to be:**

Estos hombres están cansados.	*These men are tired.*
Estas mujeres están cansadas.	*These women are tired.*

4. Separated from the auxiliary, the past participle is inflected like any adjective, agreeing in gender and number with the noun qualified:

Una mujer casada	*A married woman*
Un hombre perdido	*A lost man*
Se vieron vencidos del enemigo.	*They saw themselves defeated by the enemy.*

5. The past participle may be used absolutely:

Muerta la reina, su hijo tomó el título de rey.	*The queen having died, her son took the title of king.*
Concluído este negocio, se despidió.	*The business concluded, he took leave.*

The Imperative

1. There are only two forms in the imperative, viz., the second person singular and plural. All the others are simply taken from the subjunctive:

habla, *speak (thou)*	hablad, *speak (you)*

2. The Imperative proper can **never** be used negatively. In its place the corresponding subjunctive forms must be employed:

No hable, *let him not speak*   No hable V., *do not speak*
No hablemos, *let us not speak*   No hablen Vds., *do not speak*

THE ADJECTIVE

1. Adjectives agree in number and gender with the noun they qualify, as:

El libro nuevo, *the new book*   Una casa nueva, *a new house*
Libros nuevos, *new books*   Casas nuevas, *new houses*

2. The plural of adjectives is formed like the plural of nouns, viz., by adding s to vowel-endings, and es to consonant or accented vowel-endings, always changing z into c before **es,** as:

SINGULAR		PLURAL		
fresco	fresca	frescos	frescas	*fresh*
feliz	feliz	felices	felices	*happy*

Formation of the Feminine

1. The feminine of adjectives is generally formed by changing the final o into a, or by adding a to the consonant terminations **an, on,** and **or,** as:

Bueno, buena, *good*   Holgazán, holgazana, *lazy*

Mayor, **greater,** menor, **smaller,** and anterior, **anterior,** form an exception to this rule; they have the same form for both genders.

2. Adjectives referring to nationality and ending in a consonant add **a** for the feminine, as:

Francés, francesa, *French*   Inglés, inglesa, *English*

3. Adjectives ending in any other letter remain unchanged in the feminine, as:

Un hombre cortés   *A polite man*
Una mujer cortés   *A polite woman*

4. When an adjective refers to two or more nouns in the singular, it must be placed in the plural, and in the masculine plural when the nouns are of different genders, as:

El padre y su hijo son buenos.   *The father and his son are good.*
El padre y la madre son buenos.   *The father and the mother are good.*

Peculiarities of some Adjectives

1. The following adjectives lose the final o when standing before a masculine noun singular, as:

Bueno, *good*	Tercero, *third*
Malo, *bad*	Uno, *one*
Postrero, *latter, last*	Alguno, *some, any*
Primero, *first*	Ninguno, *none, not any*

Examples

Un buen hombre, *a good man*	El tercer día, *the third day*
Un mal caballo, *a bad horse*	Un perro, *one dog*

2. Grande, **great, large,** santo, **holy,** and ciento, **a hundred,** lose the last syllable:

Un gran peligro, *a great peril*	San Pedro, *St. Peter*
Una gran casa, *a great house*	Cien soldados, *a hundred soldiers*

Note.—**Santo** is not abbreviated before the following four names of Saints:

Santo Domingo, *St. Dominic*	Santo Toribio, *St. Toribius*
Santo Tomé, *St. Timothy*	Santo Tomás, *St. Thomas*

Position of the Adjective

1. The adjective stands generally after the noun qualified, as:

El hombre prudente	*The prudent man*
La planta venenosa	*The poisonous plant*

2. There are many cases in which the adjective is placed before the noun, though a satisfactory reason cannot always be adduced for them. It is almost entirely a matter of style.

The following rules will be found useful:

a. Numeral adjectives are generally placed before the noun:

La tercera casa	*The third house*
El primer tomo	*The first volume*

b. Adjectives which are used in a figurative sense, or when used in an explanatory manner, are usually placed before the noun, as:

Un delicioso viaje	*A delightful journey*
¡Admirable acción!	*Admirable action!*

3. All adjectives denoting color, nationality, taste, or shape, and all participles used adjectively are placed after the noun, as:

El músico alemán	*The German musician*
Una madre amada	*A beloved mother*
Una posición perdida	*A lost position*

4. Some adjectives have different meanings according to their position, as:

Una buena noche, *a good night*	Noche buena, *Christmas*
Negra acción, *dark deed*	Un vestido negro, *a black dress*
Varios papeles, *various papers*	Papeles varios, *miscellaneous papers*
Pobre autor, *a miserable writer*	Autor pobre, *a poor author*
Cierta época, *a certain period*	Noticia cierta, *reliable news*

These rules may serve merely to guide the student. By placing the adjectives before the nouns more weight and emphasis is given.

Comparison of Adjectives

1. The comparative is formed by placing **más, more,** or **menos, less,** before the positive, as:

caro, *dear*   más caro, *dearer*   menos caro, *less dear*

2. The superlative is formed, either by placing **el, lo, la más** or **menos** before the positive, or by adding **ísimo, ísima** to the positive with the elision of its last vowel, as:

Caro, *dear*   el más caro, *the dearest*
carísimo, *very dear*

The former is called the relative superlative, and the latter the absolute superlative.

The superlative is also formed by placing before the adjective the adverbs **muy, grandemente, enormemente, sumamente,** etc., and in a few cases by using the prefix **archi,** as:

muy grande, very large   *enormemente rico,* enormously rich
archimillonario, multimillionaire

Positive	Comparative
docto, doctos } *learned*	más docto, más doctos } *more learned*
docta, doctas	más docta, más doctas

Relative Superlative	Absolute Superlative
el *or* lo más docto } *the most learned*	doctísimo } *very learned*
la más docta	doctísima
los más doctos	doctísimos
las más doctas	doctísimas

3. The comparative is followed by **que, than,** as:

Tengo menos libros que V.   *I have fewer books than you.*

NOTE.—After **más** and **menos, than** is rendered by **de** when a numeral follows, as:

Tenía más de cien duros.   *I had more than a hundred dollars.*

4. If the sentence which contains the comparison is followed by a verb, **de lo que** must be employed in place of **que,** as:

Don Felipe es mayor de lo que parece.   *Don Philip is older than he seems.*

Este comerciante tiene menos dinero de lo que V. cree.   *This merchant has less money than you think.*

5. The comparative of equality—as—as—is given by **tan—como** with adjectives or adverbs, and by **tanto (tantos, tanta, tantas)—como** with nouns (or **tanto—cuanto** when a verb follows), as:

Él es tan instruído como V.   *He is as educated as you.*

Juan tiene tantos libros como yo.   *John has as many books as I.*

6. Four adjectives have, besides their regular comparatives and superlatives, an irregular form. They are:

POSITIVE	COMPARATIVE
bueno, a, *good*	mejor *better*
malo, a, *bad, poor*	peor *worse, poorer*
grande, *great, large*	mayor *greater, larger*
pequeño, a, *small, little*	menor *smaller, less*

RELATIVE SUPERLATIVE

el, la, lo { mejor / peor / mayor / menor }   los, las { mejores, *the best* / peores, *the worst, poorest* / mayores, *the greatest, largest, oldest* / menores, *the smallest, least, youngest* }

ABSOLUTE SUPERLATIVE

bonísimo, a, *or* muy bueno, a (*rarely* óptimo, a), *very good*

malísimo, a, *or* muy malo, a (*rarely* pésimo, a), *very bad, poor*

grandísimo, a, *or* muy grande (*rarely* máximo, a), *very large, great*

pequeñísimo, a, muy pequeño, a (*rarely* mínimo, a), *very small, little*

The Absolute Superlative

Observe that

1. Adjectives ending in **co** or **go** form their superlative in **quísimo** and **guísimo** to preserve the original sounds of **c** and **g,** as:

> rico, *rich;* riquísimo, *very rich*
> vago, *vague;* vaguísimo, *very vague*

2. Adjectives ending in **z** change **z** into **c,** as:

> feliz, *happy;* felicísimo, *very happy*

3. Adjectives ending in **io** drop these letters, so that the repetition of **i** may be avoided in the superlative, as:

> limpio, *clean;* limpísimo, *very clean*
> necesario, *necessary;* necesarísimo, *very necessary*

Exceptions are:

> agrio, *sour;* agriísimo, *very sour*
> frío, *cold;* friísimo, *very cold*
> pío, *pious;* piísimo, *very pious*

4. Adjectives ending in **ble** change it into **bilísimo,** as:

> afable, *affable;* afabilísimo, *very affable*
> noble, *noble;* nobilísimo, *very noble*

5. Adjectives which have **ie** in the syllable before the last elide the **i,** as:

> cierto, *certain;* certísimo, *very certain*
> tierno, *tender;* ternísimo, *very tender*

6. A few superlatives in **érrimo** and **ísimo** are of Latin derivation, as:

acre, *acrimonious;* acérrimo
áspero, *harsh;* aspérrimo
célebre, *celebrated;* celebérrimo
libre; *free;* libérrimo
pobre, *poor;* paupérrimo
salubre, *healthful;* salubérrimo
fuerte, *strong;* fortísimo
nuevo, *new;* novísimo
pío \
piadoso / *devoted;* pientísimo

antiguo, *ancient;* antiquísimo
benévolo, *benevolent;* benevolentísimo
fiel, *faithful;* fidelísimo
magnífico, *magnificent;* magnificentísimo
bueno, *good;* bonísimo
sabio, *wise;* sapientísimo
sacro \
sagrado / *sacred;* sacratísimo

7. The superlative in ísimo is always stronger and more emphatic than that formed with **muy.** If the superlative is preceded by the indefinite article, the form in ísimo is employed for elegance's sake, as: es un valentísimo hombre, **he is a very brave man** (not: es un hombre muy valiente).

THE PRONOUNS

I. Personal Pronouns

There are two classes of personal pronouns, viz.: **pronombres absolutos** or absolute pronouns and **pronombres subjuntivos** or conjunctive pronouns. The latter are used in the **dative** and **accusative** only.

Singular

FIRST PERSON

	ABSOLUTE	DISJUNCTIVE	CONJUNCTIVE	
Nom:	yo			*I*
Gen:		de mí		*of me*
Dat:		a mí	me	*to me*
Acc:			me	*me*

SECOND PERSON

Nom:	tú			*thou*
Gen:		de ti		*of thee*
Dat:		a ti	te	*to thee*
Acc:			te	*thee*

THIRD PERSON (*masculine*)

Nom:	él			*he, it*
Gen:		de él		*of him, of it*
Dat:		a él	le	*to him, to it*
Acc:			le	*him, it*

THIRD PERSON (*feminine*)

Nom:	ella			*she, it*
Gen:		de ella		*of her, of it*
Dat:		a ella	le	*to her, to it*
Acc:			la	*her, it*

Second Person (*address*)

(*When there is no familiarity between the person who speaks and the one spoken to.*)[1]

Nom:	V.			*you*
Gen:		de V.		*of you*
Dat:		a V.	le	*to you*
Acc:			le, la	*you*

THIRD PERSON (*neuter*)

Nom:	ello			*it*
Gen:		de ello		*of it*
Dat:		a ello	le	*to it*
Acc:			lo	*it*

Plural

First Person

	ABSOLUTE	DISJUNCTIVE	CONJUNCTIVE	
Nom:	nosotros			*we*
Gen:		de nosotros		*of us*
Dat:		a nosotros	nos	*to us*
Acc:			nos	*us*

Second Person

Nom:	vosotros			*you*
Gen:		de vosotros		*of you*
Dat:		a vosotros	os	*to you*
Acc:			os	*you*

Third Person (*masculine*)

Nom:	ellos			*they*
Gen:		de ellos		*of them*
Dat:		a ellos	les	*to them*
Acc:			los	*them*

Third Person (*feminine*)

Nom:	ellas			*they*
Gen:		de ellas		*of them*
Dat:		a ellas	les	*to them*
Acc:			las	*them*

---

[1] The word usted (abbreviated Vd., or V.) derives from the respectful expression **vuestra merced**, your mercy, your worship, which, of course, governed the third person singular; afterwards that expression was contracted first in **usarced** and, at last, in usted.

SECOND PERSON (*address*)

(When there is no familiarity between the person who speaks and the one spoken to.)[1]

Nom:	Vds.		you
Gen:		de Vds.	of you
Dat:		a Vds.	les	to you
Acc:			los, las	you

REFLEX. SUB. OF THIRD PERSON

Nom:	se		oneself, themselves, itself
Gen:		de sí	of himself, herself, themselves
Dat:		a sí	se	to himself, herself, themselves
Acc:			se	himself, herself, themselves

Remarks on the Personal Pronouns

1. The nominative of the personal pronouns **yo, tú, él, ella,** etc., is generally omitted.

It must, however, be expressed in questions, in cases of ambiguity and for the purpose of emphasis or contrast, as:

¿Pago yo o paga él?	*Do I pay, or he?*
¿Qué he de hacer yo?	*What have I to do?*
Él estudia y ella escribe.	*He studies and she writes.*

2. The absolute personal pronouns must be used when governed by a preposition or when standing alone in answer to questions, as:

¿Quién manda aquí?	*Who commands here?*
¿Él, ella, V., o quién?	*He, she, you, or who?*
¿A quién llama V.?	*Whom are you calling?*
¿A mí, a él, a nosotros?	*Me, him, us?*

3. The conjunctive forms **me, te, le, la, lo, se** and their plurals **nos, os, les, las, los,** are placed before the verb in Spanish, except in affirmative imperative sentences, or if the verb stands in the infinitive or in the present participle (gerund), or at the beginning of the sentence.

In the latter four cases the pronouns are placed after the verb, and merged into one word with it.

Ella me paga.	*She pays me.*
Él nos dió la noticia.	*He gave us the news.*
Yo le he escrito la carta.	*I have written the letter to him.*
Voy a darle la carta.	*I am going to give him the letter*
Enséñeme V. el libro.	*Show me the book.*
Preguntaránme acaso.	*They perhaps will ask me.*

4. The English expressions **it is I, it is he,** etc., are given by **soy yo, es él,** etc.:

¿Quién llama? Soy yo.	*Who is knocking? It is I.*
Es él quien lo hizo.	*It is he who did it.*

5. When **mí, ti, sí** are governed by the preposition **con, with,** they form **conmigo, with me; contigo, with thee; consigo, with himself, with itself, with them.**

Pleonastic Construction

1. To give emphasis to the phrase, the conjunctive and disjunctive pronouns are used together. The disjunctive forms are often placed first to give greater intensity to the meaning, as:

Me pagan a mí.	⎱ *They pay me.*
A mí me pagan.	⎰
¿A mí qué me importa?	*What do I care?*
Yo le escribí a él con preferencia.	*I preferred to write to him.*

2. Any noun may replace the disjunctive pronoun while the pleonastic construction with the conjunctive pronoun remains unchanged, as:

A nosotros los españoles nos gusta charlar.	*We Spaniards like to gossip,* or: *It pleases us Spaniards to gossip.*
Le aseguro al comerciante.	*I assure the merchant.*

Inflection and Use of "Usted"

1. **Usted** is inflected like any noun.

2. The datives and accusatives of **él** and **ella,** together with the reflexive pronoun of the third person, are frequently substituted for **usted.** This is done to avoid repetition, as:

Oigo a V. mas no le veo.	*I hear you, but I do not see you.*
Vengo a ver a V. y a hablarle.	*I come to see you and to talk to you.*

	SINGULAR	PLURAL
Nom:	usted, *you*	ustedes, *you*
Gen:	de usted, *of you*	de ustedes, *of you*
Dat:	a usted, le (subst.) *to you*	a ustedes, les (subst.) *to you*
Acc:	(a) usted, le, la, *you*	(a) ustedes, los, las, (*les*), *you*
Nom:	——	——
Gen:	de sí, *of yourself*	de sí, *of yourselves*
Dat:	se, a sí, *to yourself*	se, a sí, *to yourselves*
Acc:	se, a sí, *yourself*	se, a sí, *yourselves*[1]

3. The substitutes of **usted** follow the general rules of position laid down for conjunctive pronouns:

Le digo.	*I tell you* (singular).
Les digo.	*I tell you* (plural).
Voy a decirles.	*I am going to tell you.*
Yo se lo ruego.	*I beg you for it.*

4. **Usted** and its substitutes are used in the pleonastic construction, as:

Le diré a V.	*I shall tell you*
¿Qué le pasa a V.?	*What is the matter with you?* (singular).
¿Qué les pasa a Vds.	*What is the matter with you?* (plural).
¿Puedo pedirle a V. un favor?	*May I ask a favor of you?*
¿Le parece a V. que yo deba ir al banco?	*Do you think that I must go to the bank?*

5. The genitive and dative of **usted** may take the place of the possessive adjective:

A los pies de V., señora.	*At your feet, lady.*[2]
Beso a V. la mano, caballero.	*I kiss your hand, sir.*[2]

6. **Usted,** as subject, may stand before or after the verb:

V. no sabe, *or,* no sabe V.	*You do not know.*
¿Ha recibido V. la carta?	*Have you received the letter?*

---

[1] Properly speaking, the inflections **de sí, se, a sí,** etc., mean *of himself, to himself, himself, of yourselves, to yourselves,* and *yourselves.* They, however, may be used in connection with **usted.**

[2] These are formal, but very frequently used, modes of salutation.

The Reflexive Pronoun

1. The conjunctive pronouns of the first and second **persons have a** reflexive meaning when they refer to the same person as the **subject:**

Nos preguntamos.	*We ask ourselves.*
Me hallo ocupado.	*I find myself (= I am) busy.*

2. Conjunctive pronouns of the third person, including **usted,** refer to a different person (or thing) from the subject. Each gender employs the regular substitute **se** to express reflexive or reciprocal action on the subject:

Le engaña.	*He deceives him.*
Se engaña.	*He deceives himself.*
V. la engaña.	*You deceive her.*
V. se engaña.	*You deceive yourself.*

3. The translation of **se** is generally omitted as superfluous in English:

Lléveselo.	*Take it.*
Se rompe.	*It breaks.*
Se abre.	*It opens.*
Se cierra.	*It shuts.*

Two Objective Pronouns

1. When a verb governs two objective pronouns, the dative must precede the accusative, with the exception of the reflexive pronoun **se,** which always stands first, whatever may be its case, as:

V. me lo dará.	*You will give it to me.*
Él nos lo ha dado.	*He has given it to us.*
¿Me lo dará V.?	*Will you give it to me?*
Se lo escribiré esta tarde.	*I will write him so this afternoon.*

2. For the sake of euphony, Spaniards never say **le lo, le le, le la, le les, le los, le las, les lo, les le, les la,** etc., but change it into **se lo, se le, se la,** etc.

There are, therefore, the following:

Le le	*and* les le	become	**se le**
le la	" les la	"	**se la**
le lo	" les lo	"	**se lo**
le les	" les les	"	**se les**
le los	" les los	"	**se los**
le las	" les las	"	**se las**

3. The pleonastic construction is the same for two objectives as for one:

Se lo doy a V. ⎫
Se lo doy a Vds. ⎬ *I give it to you* (sing. and plural).

A mí me lo han escrito. *They wrote me so.*

Él se lo había dicho a mi hermana. ⎫
A mi hermana se lo había dicho. ⎬ *He had said so to my sister.*

Possessive Adjectives and Pronouns

1. Possessive adjectives are either short or long. The short forms stand before the noun they qualify, while the long stand after it. They are inflected like adjectives.

2. They are as follows:

SINGULAR		PLURAL		
SHORT	LONG	SHORT	LONG	
mi	mío, mía	mis	míos, mías	*my*
tu	tuyo, tuya	tus	tuyos, tuyas	*thy*
su	suyo, suya	sus	suyos, suyas	{ *her* *his* *its* *your*
nuestro, -a	nuestro, nuestra	nuestros, -as	nuestros, nuestras	*our*
vuestro, -a	vuestro, vuestra	vuestros, -as	vuestros, vuestras	*your*
su	suyo, suya	sus	suyos, suyas	{ *their* *your*

3. Since **su, sus** can mean **his, her, its, their,** and **your** and may therefore be ambiguous in meaning, the genitive case of the appropriate personal pronoun is frequently added. Instead of **su** or **sus, el, la, los,** or **las** may be used, as:

Su libro de él *His book*
Su libro de ella *Her book*
El libro de él, de ella *His book, her book*
Su libro de ellos, de ellas ⎫
El libro de ellos, de ellas ⎬ *Their book*

4. **Your** is expressed by **su, sus** when the sense of the sentence sufficiently indicates to what person **su** refers. It can also be expressed pleonastically by **su (sus) de V.** or **de Vds.,** as:

Tengo su libro de V. ⎫
Tengo el libro de V. ⎬ *I have your book.*
¿Tiene V. su libro? *Have you your book?*

5. When parts of the body or articles of dress are mentioned, the definite article is employed instead of the possessive adjective, as:

¿Qué tiene V. en la mano?	*What have you in your hand?*
Me duele la cabeza.	*My head aches.*
Se quita los zapatos.	*He takes his shoes off.*

6. The long forms **mío, tuyo, suyo,** etc., stand always after the the noun. They are used to express greater intensity or rhetorical effect, as:

| Es culpa suya y no mía. | *It is his fault, and not mine.* |
| Es costumbre suya de pagar al contado. | *It is a habit of his to pay cash.* |

7. The long forms are used in direct address and when used with nouns in an indeterminate sense (with a, an, or some, of mine, of thine, etc.), as:

¡Padre mío!	*My father!*
¡Madre mía!	*My mother!*
¡Pobre muchacho mío!	*My poor boy!*
¡Querido amigo mío!	*My dear friend!*
Carlos es amigo mío.	*Charles is a friend of mine.*

8. It is mine, thine, etc., or it belongs to me, to thee, etc., are expressed by **ser, to be,** with the possessive pronoun, as:

Esta casa es mía.	*This house is mine; [belongs to me].*
Este cuadro es suyo.	*This picture belongs to him.*
Estos papeles son míos y no de V.	*These papers are mine and not yours.*

Demonstrative Adjectives and Pronouns

1. The demonstrative adjectives agree in gender and number with the noun they limit, except the neuter forms, as:

SINGULAR			PLURAL		
MASC.	FEM.		MASC.	FEM.	
este	esta	*this*	estos	estas	*these*
ese	esa	*that*	esos	esas	*those*
aquel	aquella	*that yonder*	aquellos	aquellas	*those yonder*

When the demonstrative adjectives do not modify a noun, they have the value of pronouns, and take the written accent: **éste, ése, aquél, éstos, ésos, aquéllos,** etc. The neuter forms **esto, eso, aquello** are used only as pronouns and bear no accent. They refer to an idea or an object to which gender cannot be attributed.

2. **Este, esta,** designates the person or object nearest to the speaker, **ese, esa,** that which is near the person addressed; **aquel, aquella,** that which is remote from both:

Este libro que estoy leyendo . . .	*This book which I am reading . . .*
Ese tratado que tiene V. en la mano . . .	*That treatise which you have in your hand . . .*
Aquel folleto que está sobre la mesa . . .	*That pamphlet which lies upon the table . . .*
Esta pluma es mejor que ésa.	*This pen is better than that one.*

3. The demonstrative adjective must be repeated before each noun, as:

Este hombre, esta mujer, y este muchacho están malos.	*This man, this woman, and this child are ill.*

4. Although the demonstrative adjectives naturally precede the nouns, they are placed after them to express sarcasm and contempt, as:

El hombre este.	*This man here.*

5. The words **ciudad, city,** and **plaza, market,** are usually omitted with **esta** and **esa** after the preposition **en, in. En ésta** means, therefore, **here,** and **en ésa, there:**

En ésta no hay novedad.	*There is nothing new here (with us).*
¿Cómo van los negocios en ésa?	*How is business there (with you)?*

6. In reference to time, **este** denotes the present; **ese,** a past period within our recollection; **aquel,** the past generally:

Este es el siglo del progreso.	*This is the age of progress.*
Me acuerdo bien de ese día.	*I remember that day well.*
Aquéllos eran tiempos de mucha barbarie.	*Those were days of great barbarism.*

7. The neuter forms are **esto, this** (what is near to the person who speaks); **eso, that** (what is near to the person to whom one speaks); **aquello, that** (what is remote from the one who speaks and from the one spoken to), as:

Esto es verdad.	*This is the truth.*
Eso es increíble.	*That is incredible.*
Aquello fué una lástima.	*That was a pity.*

8. The definite article is often used as a demonstrative pronoun, assuming the gender and number of the noun it replaces:

Este caballo y el de mi amigo.	*This horse and that of my friend.*
Esta casa y la de mi vecino.	*This house and that of my neighbor.*

Relative Pronouns

The relative pronouns are:

que, *who, whom, which, that, what*
quien (sing.), quienes (plur.), *who, whom, whoever, whomsoever*
el cual, la cual, los cuales, las cuales } *who; which*
el que, la que, los que, las que
lo cual *or* lo que, *that, which, what*
cuyo, cuya, cuyos. cuyas, *whose, of which, which*
aquel que, aquella que, *the one who, the one which*
aquellos que, aquellas que, *the ones who, those who*

Que

1. **Que** refers to persons or things in the nominative and accusative only; in the other cases it usually refers to things:

El hombre que viene es mi tío.	*The man who comes is my uncle.*
Es una mujer que sabe mucho.	*She is a woman who knows many things.*
Los libros que leemos son buenos.	*The books we are reading are good.*
La ciudad de que le hablo.	*The city of which I am talking to you.*

2. **Que** relating to an accusative does not require the preposition **a,** even when referring to a person. Observe that the relative must always be expressed in Spanish, as:

He visto al niño que V. espera.	*I have seen the boy (whom) you expect.*

1. **Quien, quienes**—for both genders—is used after prepositions and refers only to persons:

El caballero con quien hablé ha partido.	*The gentleman with whom I talked has left.*
Las señoras a quienes vimos son inglesas.	*The ladies whom we saw are English.*

2. If the noun is immediately followed by the relative pronoun, it is preferable to use **que** even of persons, as:

Este es el hombre que me dió el libro.	*This is the man who gave me the book.*

El cual, el que

1. **El cual, la cual, lo cual, los cuales,** and **las cuales; el que,**
la que, lo que, los que and **las que,** are substitutes for **quien** and **que,**
and relate, therefore, both to persons and things. They are employed
to avoid ambiguity. Observe that they take the preposition **a** in the
accusative when they refer to persons:

La hija de nuestro vecino, la que (*or*, la cual) nos habló ayer, ha muerto hoy.	*Our neighbor's daughter, who spoke to us yesterday, died today.*
Este es el criado de doña Juana del cual (*or*, del que) hemos oído cosas muy malas.	*This is Doña Jane's servant, of whom we have heard very bad things.*
La esposa de Juan, a la que (*or*, a la cual) vi ayer, se va hoy.	*John's wife, whom I saw yesterday, leaves today.*

Lo que

Lo que, that which, what, and **todo lo que, all that,** relate to an
idea, not to a word:

Lo que él dice no es lo que V. piensa.	*What he says is not what you think.*
No creo nada de todo lo que Pedro nos ha dicho.	*I do not believe anything of all that Peter has told us.*

Cuyo, cuya

Cuyo, cuya, whose, of whose, which, refers to both persons and
things, and takes the gender and the number of the noun which it
precedes:

El hombre cuyas desgracias V. conoce, es amigo mío.	*The man whose misfortunes you know, is a friend of mine.*
La señora N. es mujer de cuya nobleza hay mucho que dudar.	*Mrs. N. is a woman whose nobility of spirit may be strongly doubted.*

Interrogative Pronouns

1. The interrogative pronouns are distinguished from the relatives
by being written with an acute accent. They are used in direct and
indirect questions. They are:

quién, pl. quiénes, *who?*		qué, *what?*
cúyo, cúya		cuál
cuyos, cúyas	*whose?*	cuáles
de quién, de quiénes		*which? what?*

2. Quién, quiénes, who? is used only in connection with persons:

¿Quién llama a la puerta?	*Who is knocking at the door?*
¿De quién habla V.?	*Of whom are you speaking?*

3. Cuál, cuáles, which, is used where one or several objects in a group are referred to. It is more definite than **que**:

¿Cuál es mi sombrero?	*Which (one) is my hat?*
No sé cuál es el mío.	*I do not know which (one) is mine.*
¿Cuáles son mis lápices?	*Which (ones) are my pencils?*

4. Whose, used interrogatively, is expressed by **cúyo** (rarely) **or** by **de quién**:

¿Cúyo es este libro?	
¿Cúyo libro es éste?	*To whom does this book belong?*
¿De quién es este libro?	
¿Cúyos zapatos son éstos?—De mi padre.	*Whose shoes are these?—My father's.*

5. Qué, what? can refer to persons or things and can be used with or without a noun:

¿Qué hombre es éste?	*What kind of a man is this?*
¿A qué mujer ha visto V.?	*Which woman have you seen?*
¿Qué hay de nuevo?	*What is the news?*

NOTE.—**Qué** is also used in exclamations:

¡Qué de burlas!	*What fun!*
¡Qué bella vista!	*What a beautiful view!*

Indefinite Adjectives and Pronouns

The indefinite pronouns are in fact adjectives. When used as pronouns they stand without nouns and may be preceded by a preposition. They are:

1. Ajeno, ajena, another's, of other's, other people's. The neuter, **lo ajeno**, signifies **other people's property**:

Debemos respetar lo ajeno.	*We must respect other people's property.*

Ajeno de signifies **foreign to,** as:

Esto es ajeno de mi carácter.	*This is foreign to my character.*

2. **Alguien, someone, anyone, somebody, anybody,** can be used of persons only, as:

Alguien ha estado aquí.	*Someone has been here.*
Alguien preguntó por V.	*Someone inquired for you.*
¿Lo ha visto alguien?	*Has anyone seen it?*

3. **Alguno, alguna,** as relating to persons, means **somebody, someone, anybody, anyone, some, any, a few :**

Alguno ha estado aquí.	*Someone has been here.*
Algunos han venido, los otros no.	*Some (a few) came, but not the others.*

Alguno, as relating to things, signifies **some, any, a few :**

Necesito algún dinero y algunas letras de cambio.	*I need some money and some bills of exchange.*

Observe that the final **o** in **alguno** is dropped before masculine nouns.

4. **Algo** or **alguna cosa, something, anything.**

Tengo algo (*or* alguna cosa) que decirle.	*I have something to tell you.*
¿Le falta a V. algo?—Sí, me falta algo.	*Do you want anything?—Yes, I want something.*

Algo is frequently employed as an adverb and signifies **somewhat, rather :**

Esta carne es algo cara.	*This meat is rather dear.*

5. **Ambos, ambas, both,** is used either as a pronoun or as an adjective. It refers to persons or things, and can be replaced by **los dos, las dos :**

Es menester oír ambas partes.	*One must hear both parties.*

Entrambos, entrambas, are used in the same sense:

Los ví a entrambos.	*I saw both of them.*

6. **Cada, each, every,** is only employed in the singular and is an invariable adjective:

Cada país tiene sus costumbres.	*Every country has its customs.*
Cada hombre; cada mujer	*Every man; every woman*

a. **Cada** may be used before plural nouns when accompanied by numerals:

Cada dos días	*Every two days*
Cada tres años	*Every three years*

b. **Cada** is often accompanied by **uno** or **cual**, forming **cada uno.** (cada una), cada cual:

Cada uno tiene sus quehaceres.	*Everyone has his occupations.*
Cada una de estas señoritas es muy rica y muy amable.	*Each of these young ladies is very rich and very amiable.*
Cada cual sabe lo que le duele.	*Everyone knows what ails him.*

c. **Every** may also be expressed by **todos los** (fem. **todas las)** agreeing with a plural noun, referring to a period of time, as:

Todos los años	*Every year*
Todos los días	*Every day*
Todas las semanas	*Every week*
Todas las veces	*Every time*

7. **Cierto, cierta, a certain, ciertos, ciertas, certain,** is used with nouns without article, as:

Cierto hombre	*A certain man*
Cierta señora	*A certain lady*
Bajo ciertas condiciones	*Under certain conditions*

a. **Cierto,** if standing after a noun, means **sure, authentic, certain.**

Noticias ciertas	*Authentic news*
La noticia es cierta.	*The news is certain* (*true*).

8. **Cosa** is used meaning **something, anything;** and with a negative, **nothing.**

Es cosa muy de ver.	*It is something well worth seeing.*
No quiero otra cosa.	*I do not want anything else.*
Esta es otra cosa.	*That is something quite different.*

9. **Fulano, fulana,** means **so and so, such a one.** It is also used of persons whose names we do not know, remember, or care to give. If used alone, it commonly takes the form of **fulano de tal;** of two persons, **fulano y mengano;** of three, **fulano, mengano y zutano** = "Tom, Dick and Harry," as:

¿Quién lo dijo? ¿Qué sé yo? Fulano de tal.	*Who said so? How do I know? So and so.*
V. dijo que fulano y zutano ya lo sabían.	*You said that so and so knew it already.*

10. **Mismo,** standing before a noun, means **the same.** It is accompanied either by the definite or indefinite article, or by a demon-

strative or possessive pronoun; after a noun, however, it serves to emphasize some idea:

El mismo día	*The same day*
La misma noche	*The same night*
Mis mismos enemigos	*My very enemies*
Hoy mismo	*This very day*
Aquí mismo	*In this very place*
But:	
Yo mismo	*I myself*
V. mismo	*You yourself*
El rey mismo lo ordenó.	*It was ordered by the king himself.*

11. **Nada, nothing, not anything,** stands either before a positive verb, or after a negative verb:

Nada tengo *or* no tengo nada.	*Nothing is the matter with me.*
Nada vale *or* no vale nada.	*It is worth nothing or it is not worth anything.*

a. Instead of **nada,** the forms **ninguna cosa** or **cosa alguna** are frequently used: **Cosa alguna** must always be employed in connection with a negative verb:

Ninguna cosa tengo.
No tengo ninguna cosa. } *I have not anything.*
No tengo cosa alguna.

12. **Nadie, no one, nobody,** is the negative of **alguien.** It is invariable, referring to persons only. It stands either before a positive, or after a negative, verb:

Nadie ha venido todavía.
No ha venido nadie todavía. } *Nobody has come as yet.*
Nadie lo sabe. *No one knows it.*

a. After the prepositions **sin** and **antes de,** and the conjunctions **sin que** and **antes que,** the forms **nadie** and **nada** must be used instead of **alguien** and **algo:**

Salió sin que nadie le viese.	*He went out without anybody seeing him.*
Antes de decir nada	*Before saying anything*

13. **Ninguno, ninguna, nobody, no one, none, no,** is used of persons and things and may be employed as a pronoun or an adjective. Unlike **nadie,** it may be followed by **de.** It stands either before a positive, or after a negative, verb. The final **o** is dropped before masculine nouns:

Ninguna mujer es más hermosa.	*No woman is handsomer.*
No lo he dicho a ninguno.	*I have told it to no one.*
Ninguno de los que V. conoce está aquí.	*None of those whom you know here.*

14. English **no, not any,** is translated by a negative verb, followed by a noun without an article:

No tengo tiempo.	*I have no time.*
No tengo dinero conmigo.	*I have no money with me.*

15. **Otro, otra, another, other,** is used of persons and things, and may be employed as a pronoun or as an adjective. It does not take the indefinite article as in English, but requires the definite article whenever a distinct person or thing is specified:

Déme V. otro libro.	*Give me another book.*
Quiero otro	*I want another one.*
Hablo del otro.	*I speak of the other one.*

a. **Otro** signifies frequently **a second, more, additional**:

Es otro Don Juan.	*He is a second Don Jaun.*

b. Observe the following expressions:

El otro día	*The other day*
Al otro día	*The next day*
Otro día	*Another day*
Una y otra vez	*Repeatedly*
Yo haría otro tanto.	*I should do the same thing.*
He ganado otro tanto.	*I have made (gained) as much.*

c. **Ni uno, ni otro, neither one**:

Ni uno ni otro me gusta.	*Neither pleases me.*

16. **Propio, propia, self, own,** is used like **mismo**:

Este dinero es suyo propio.	*This money is his own.*

17. **Quienquiera, whoever, anyone whatever,** relates only to persons:

Puede hablar con quienquiera que V. guste.	*You may speak with whomsoever you please.*

18. **Cualquiera,** plur. **cualesquiera, any (whatever), any (you please),** is used both as an adjective or as a pronoun, relating to persons or things:

Cualquiera lo creería.	*Anyone would believe it.*

a. **Cualquiera** followed by **que,** requires the verb in the subjunctive:

Cualquier cosa que V. diga   *Whatever you may say*

b. **Cualquiera que** may be replaced by **sea el (la) que quiera** plur. **sean los (las) que quieran,** with a noun and the verb in the subjunctive:

Sea el que quiera el motivo que se presente.   *Whatever reason may be assigned.*

c. **Whatever,** as an indefinite pronoun, is rendered by **por más que** with the subjunctive:

Por más que diga, no lo creo.   *Whatever he may say, I do not believe it.*

19. **Tal,** plur. **tales, such, such a,** is used both as a pronoun and an adjective referring to persons and things:

Tal hombre   *Such a man*
Tal mujer   *Such a woman*
No creo tal.   *I do not believe such a thing.*

a. **Un tal, una tal** means a **certain (indefinite) person.**

Un tal me lo ha dicho.   *A certain person told me so.*
Una tal me lo ha contado.   *A certain woman related it to me.*

b. **Con tal que** means **on condition**:

Lo haré con tal que V. no lo diga a mi hermano.   *I will do it on condition that you do not tell my brother.*

20. **Todo, toda, all, whole, every, anything,** is used either as an adjective, or an indefinite pronoun. As an adjective it is followed by the definite article or a possessive or a demonstrative:

Todo el día   *The whole day; all day*
Toda su fortuna   *His whole fortune*
Todos estos hombres   *All these men*

a. **Todo,** in the singular, when not followed by the definite article, or a possessive, or a demonstrative, denotes the entire class represented by the noun; it is then the equivalent of **every**:

Toda mujer le odia.   *Every woman hates him.*
Todo ciudadano debe obedecer las leyes.   *Every citizen must obey the laws.*

b. As a neuter pronoun, in the singular, **todo** means **everything, all**:

Todo tiene su fin.   *Everything has its end.*

c. The neuter expression **todo lo que** corresponds to the English **all that**:

Me dijo todo lo que pasó.   *He told me all that happened.*

21. **Uno, una,** is an adjective and a pronoun, signifying in the singular **a, one, each other**; and in the plural, **some, each other, one another**:

Si V. quiere una pluma, puedo darle una.   *If you want a pen, I can give you one.*

a. **Uno a otro, each other**:

Se aman uno a otro.   *They love each other.*

b. **Uno y otro** means **both** when the identity of each of the two nouns is to be preserved:

Uno y otro son culpables de tal acción.   *Both are guilty of such an action.*

c. **Uno u otro** denotes **either** of two persons or things:

¿Vino blanco o tinto? Uno u otro.   *White or red wine? Either one.*

d. **Uno, one; se, they, you; gente, people,** are used in the vague sense of **someone, anyone**:

¿Qué pudo uno hacer en tal caso?
Llama gente
No se sabe qué hacer.
     What could one do in such a case?
Somebody knocks
One does not know what to do.

THE ADVERB

1. The adverbs are divided into simple and derivatives.

2. Simple adverbs are expressed by a single word, as: más, menos, bien, mal.

a. Observe that many simple adverbs are really neuter adjectives used adverbially, as: alto, **aloud**; bajo, **low**; sólo, **only**; poco, **little;** mucho, **much.**

3. Derivative adverbs are formed by adding **-mente** to the feminine form of the adjective:

antiguo, *old*   antiguamente, *in olden times*
franco, *frank*   francamente, *frankly*
común, *common*   comúnmente, *commonly*
constante, *constant*   constantemente, *constantly*

fácil, *easy*	fácilmente, *easily*
fuerte, *strong*	fuertemente, *vehemently*
feliz. *happy*	felizmente, *happily*
mayor, *greater*	mayormente, *for the greater part*

4. Some neuter adjectives are used adverbially, their **derivative** adverbs in **-mente** being employed in a different sense, as:

ADJETIVOS	ADVERBIOS	DERIVADOS
alto, *high*	alto, *loud*	altamente, *proudly, highly*
bajo, *low*	bajo, *softly*	bajamente, *meanly*
bueno, *good*	bueno, *well*	buenamente, *willingly, ready*
caro, *dear*	caro, *dearly*	caramente, *exceedingly*
claro, *clear*	claro, *clearly*	claramente, *openly, conspicuously*
cierto, *certain*	cierto, *certainly*	ciertamente, *surely*
demasiado, *bold, excessive*	demasiado, *excessively*	demasiadamente, *too*
derecho, *right*	derecho, *rightly*	derechamente, *directly, expressly*
fuerte, *strong*	fuerte, *strongly*	fuertemente, *vehemently*
malo, *bad, ill*	malo, *badly*	malamente, *wickedly*
primero, *first*	primero, *firstly*	primeramente, *in the first place, mainly*
pronto, *quick*	pronto, *soon*	prontamente, *promptly, nimbly*
recio, *strong*	recio, *powerfully*	reciamente, *stoutly, forcibly*

5. Adverbial expressions are formed in the following manner:

a. With the article:

a la verdad, *truly*	a la derecha, *to the right*
al contado, *cash, in cash*	a la izquierda, *to the left*
al momento, *instantly*	al vivo, *vividly*
al punto, *immediately*	en el acto, *instantly*
por lo más, *at most*	por lo menos, *at least*

b. Without the article:

a caballo, *on horseback*	de lance, *at a bargain*
a escape, *in haste*	de noche, *by night*
a pie, *on foot*	de nuevo, *anew*
a una, *together*	de prisa, *in haste*
con todo, *notwithstanding*	de pronto, *quickly*
de continuo, *continually*	de propósito, *purposely*
de día, *by day*	de seguro, *surely*
de golpe, *suddenly*	de suyo, *of one's own accord*
de hecho, *truly, in fact*	de todo punto, *wholly*

Comparison of Adverbs

1. Adverbs have three degrees of comparison (but without variation for gender and number):

cerca, *near;* más cerca, *nearer;* (lo) más cerca, *the nearest;* cerquísima, *very near.*

2. Four adverbs have an irregular comparison:

Positive	Comparative	Superl. (relative)
mucho, *much*	más, *more*	(lo) más, *the most*
poco, *little*	menos, *less*	(lo) menos, *the least*
bien, *well*	mejor, *better*	(lo) mejor, *the best*
mal, *badly*	peor, *worse*	(lo) peor, *the worst*

Superl. (absolute)

muchísimo, *very much*	—— ——
poquísimo, *very little*	malísimo, *very badly*

Adverbs of Affirmation and Negation

1. After verbs of saying, believing, declaring, suspecting, etc., **yes** and **no** are expressed by **que sí, que no,** as:

Yo digo que sí, él dice que no.   *I say yes, he says no.*

2. **No, not,** stands always before the verb:

No lo tengo.—V. no la ama.   *I have it not.—You do not love her.*

3. A double negative is used to render the negation stronger:

No quiero nada.	*I do not want anything.*
No lo sabe nadie.	*Nobody knows it.*
No lo he visto jamás.	*I have never seen it.*
No tengo ni pluma, ni papel.	*I have neither pen nor paper.*

No is omitted when these negatives stand at the beginning of the sentence:

Nada quiero.	*I do not want anything.*
Nadie lo sabe.	*Nobody knows it.*
Jamás lo he visto.	*I have never seen it.*
Ni pluma, ni papel tengo.	*I have neither pen nor paper.*

4. **Jamás** and **nunca** have the same meaning, and are often placed at the beginning of sentences:

Jamás ⎫
Nunca ⎬ vi tal cosa.   *I never saw such a thing.*

No lo he oído nunca.   *I have never heard it.*

5. Jamás, in connection with **por siempre** or **para siempre,** means **forever:**

Me acordaré de él por siempre jamás, (*or* para siempre jamás).	*I shall remember him forever.*

6. Jamás, placed after a positive interrogative verb, means **ever:**

¿Ha visto V. jamás tal proceder?	*Did you ever see such behavior?*

7. No is sometimes used after comparatives, losing thereby its negative quality:

Mejor es el trabajo que no la ociosidad.	*Work is better than idleness.*

8. Ya, already, now; but with a negative, **no longer, not any more, not now:**

Lo sabía ya.	*I knew it already.*
¿Me entiende V. ya?	*Do you understand me now?*
Ya no lo veo.	*I do not see it any longer.*
Nadie le escribe ya.	*No one writes to him any more.*

PREPOSITIONS

1. The simple prepositions are:

a, *to, at*	hasta, *till, until, up to, to*
ante, *before, in presence of*	mediante, *through, by means of*
bajo, *under*	menos, *except, but*
con, *with*	no obstante, *notwithstanding*
contra, *against*	para, *for, to, in order to*
de, *of, from*	por, *by, through, for*
desde, *from, since*	según, *according to, as*
durante, *during*	sin, *without*
en, *in, at, on*	so, *under*
entre, *between, among*	sobre, *on, upon, about, above*
excepto, *except*	tras, *after, behind, besides*
hacia, *towards*	

2. The compound prepositions requiring **de** after them are:

acerca de, *concerning, about*	dentro de, *within, in, into*
además de, *beside*	después de, *after (time or order)*
alrededor de, *around*	detrás de, *behind (place)*
antes de, *before (time or order)*	encima de, *on, over*
cerca de, *near, about*	fuera de, *outside, beyond*
debajo de, *under (place)*	lejos de, *far from*
delante de, *before (place)*	

3. Compound prepositions requiring **a** after them are:

conforme a, *according to*
contrario a, *contrary to*
frente a, *opposite, in front of*

junto a, *near, close by*
con respecto a, *with respect to*
tocante a, *touching*

4. Prepositional expressions followed by **de** are:

a casa de, *to the house of*
a causa de, *on account of*
a excepción de, *with the exception of*
a fuerza de, *by dint of*
a la vista de, *within sight of*
al cabo de, *at the expiration of*
al lado de, *at the side of*
en medio de, *in the midst of*
en vez de, *instead of*
en virtud de, *by virtue of*
en vista de, *in view of*
más allá de, *beyond*

en casa de, *at the house of*
en frente de, *opposite*
en lugar de, *instead of*
a través de, *across, through*
a pesar de, *in spite of*
a razón de, *at the rate of*
de casa de, *from the house of*
de parte de, *on the part of*
por causa de, *on account of*
por el lado de, *on the side of*
por razón de, *by reason of*
sin embargo de, *notwithstanding*

5. Prepositional expressions followed by **a** are:

en cuanto a, *with respect to*

en orden a, *with respect to*

Use of Certain Prepositions

1. A is used after transitive verbs to mark the personal object, as.

Amo a Juan.

I love John.

2. A signifies motion toward a given locality, while **en** refers to rest in a given place:

Voy a Inglaterra.
Está en casa.

I am going to England.
He is at home.

3. A is used in reference to time, price, or rate:

Vendrá a la noche.
A veinte centavos la vara.

He will come in the evening.
At twenty cents a yard.

4. A is used after certain verbs to show purpose or aim:

Voy a leer.

I am going to read.

5. A signifies distance off or from, or rest after motion:

Se sientan a la mesa.
Le cogieron a la puerta.
He venido de Cádiz a Madrid.

They sit at the table.
They caught him at the door.
I came from Cadiz to Madrid.

6. **A** between two infinitives signifies the difference of their results:

Va mucho de decir a hacer, de prometer a cumplir ¿no es verdad?	*There is a great difference between saying and doing, between promising and fulfilling, is there not?*

Ante

1. Ante signifies in the presence of:

Compareció ante le juez.	*He appeared before the judge.*

2. Ante is used in regard to order or preference:

Nuestro deber es ante todo.	*Our duty comes first of all.*

3. Antes de is used instead of **ante** when denoting priority of order, rank, or time:

Antes de los condes van los marqueses.	*Marquises go before counts.*
Antes de la comida	*Before dinner*

Bajo

Bajo, under, below, underneath, beneath, denotes location; figuratively it signifies guarantee, protection, or subordination:

La puerta está bajo la ventana.	*The door is under the window.*
Estoy bajo sus órdenes.	*I am under his orders.*

Con

1. Con, with, denotes accompaniment or means:

Salió con su padre.	*He went out with his father.*
Le hirió con una espada.	*He wounded him with a sword.*

2. Con, in connection with **dar,** forms idiomatic meanings:

Dió con ella en la calle.	*He met her in the street.*
Le dió con la puerta en la cara.	*He shut the door in his face.*

3. Con, with the infinitive, means **by** or **although:**

Con enseñar se aprende.	*One learns by teaching.*
Con ser tan listo, se ha equivocado.	*Although he is so clever, he has made a mistake.*

De

1. De signifies **of** or **from:**

Lo he recibido de él.	*I received it from him.*

2. It expresses the material of which a thing is made, the use to which a thing is put, or a restriction imposed on a general term:

Un reloj de oro	*A gold watch*
Un buzón de correos	*A letter-box*
El tren del norte	*The northern train*

3. **De** denotes cause—**for, with, from**:

No podía moverme de frío.	*I could not move on account of the cold.*

4. **De** is used especially after a number of adjectives and participles to express a physical or moral peculiarity, the way of dressing, or abundance and scarcity:

Está ciego de furor.	*He is blind with fury.*
Estaba vestido de luto.	*He was dressed in mourning.*
Este país es pobre de agua.	*This country is poor in water.*
Es sordo de un oído.	*He is deaf in one ear.*
La niña de los ojos negros.	*The girl with the black eyes.*

5. **De** must be used with the passive instead of **por** when a feeling or mental action is expressed:

Es amado de sus amigos y odiado de sus enemigos.	*He is beloved by his friends and hated by his enemies.*

6. **De** is used in exclamations:

¡Infeliz de mí!	*What an unhappy man I am!*

7. **De** is used as a connective between a finite verb and an infinitive:

Ha de venir.	*He must come.*
Acabo de llegar.	*I just arrived.*
Es de esperar.	*It is to be hoped.*

8. **De** signifies office or profession:

Papá es médico de profesión.	*My father is a physician by profession.*
Está de embajador de Suiza en París.	*He is ambassador of Switzerland in Paris.*

Desde

Desde signifies **from** as a starting-point—either place or time:

Me acompañó desde su casa hasta el teatro.	*He accompanied me from his house to the theatre.*

En

1. En signifies **in, at, on;** it relates to place or time:

Don Julio vive en Barcelona.	*Mr. Julius lives in Barcelona.*
Llegaré de hoy en ocho días.	*I shall arrive a week from to-day.*
Salimos en el mes de julio, y volveremos en octubre.	*We start in the month of July, and shall return in October.*

2. En refers to occupation:

Don Julio trabaja en relojes.	*Mr. Julius works in watches.*

3. En is used idiomatically:

De día en día	*From day to day*
De año en año	*From year to year*
De tiempo en tiempo	*From time to time*
De hoy en quince días	*A fortnight from to-day*
De cuando en cuando	*Sometimes. Every now and then*
En general	*Generally*
En particular	*Especially*

Hacia

Hacia, towards, denotes direction or proximity in time:

Voy hacia casa.	*I am going homewards.*
Hacia mediodía.	*Towards noon*

Hasta

Hasta, till, until, up to, as far as, in expressions of time, place, or degree:

Hasta mañana	*Till to-morrow*
Voy hasta Madrid.	*I go as far as Madrid.*
Hasta la vista ⎫ Hasta luego ⎭	*Till I see you again*

Para

1. Para, for, to, denotes direction or destination:

Esta carta es para Don Carlos.	*This letter is for Don Carlos.*
Pienso partir para Italia.	*I think of starting for Italy.*
Es hombre para mucho.	*He is a clever man.*
No es hombre para nada.	*He is good for nothing.*

2. Para denotes aim or purpose:

Estudio para aprender.	*I study in order to learn.*

3. Para con expresses moral direction:

Es bondadoso para con sus hijos.   *He is kind toward his children.*

4. Para, in connection with **estar,** denotes to be **on the point of.**

Estoy para partir.   *I am on the point of leaving.*

Estaba para decirle que callase.   *I was on the point of telling him to be silent.*

Por

1. Por, for, by, is used with passive verbs, denoting physical, not mental, actions:

Este cuadro fué pintado por Murillo.   *This picture was painted by Murillo.*

Mental actions are expressed by **de.** (See remarks on **de.**)

2. Por denotes the motive, aim, or manner of an action:

Lo hace por temor.   *He does it from fear.*

3. Por refers to local descriptions:

Fuimos por Cádiz a Madrid.   *We went to Madrid by way of Cadiz.*

Perdí mi sortija por la calle.   *I lost my ring in the street.*

4. Por denotes price, exchange, buying, selling, equality, etc.:

Prestan dinero a cinco o a seis por ciento.   *They loan money at five or six per cent.*

5. Por, in connection with **estar,** denotes an action which is **or** ought to be done:

Este cuarto está por alquilar.   *This room is (still) to be let.*

6. Por, in connection with an adjective and **que,** introduces the subjunctive and has the meaning of **although, though:**

Por rico que sea, no le puedo estimar.   *Rich though (however rich) he may be, I cannot esteem him.*

7. Observe the peculiar expressions:

Enviar por el médico   *To send for the physician*

Mandar por vino   *To send for wine*

Venir por algo, por alguien   *To call for something, for someone*

CONJUNCTIONS

The following are the original conjunctions:

y, *and*

o, *or*

pero, mas, sino, *but*

ni, *nor, neither*

que, *that*

si, *if, whether*

The following are derivative conjunctions, adverbial conjunctions, or conjunctive phrases:

además de, *besides*

a fin de que, *in order that*

a más de, *besides*

a no ser que ⎫

a menos que ⎭ *unless*

antes que, *before*

así como, *as*

así que, *so that, so*

aunque ⎫

bien que ⎭ *although*

caso que, *in case that*

como, *as*

como si, *as if*

como quiera que, *however*

con que, *so, therefore*

con motivo que, *so that*

con tal que, *provided that*

cuando, *when*

cuanto más que, *the more since*

dado que, *in case that*

dado caso que, *supposing that*

de manera que ⎫

de modo que ⎬ *so that*

de suerte que ⎭

desde que, *since*

en vez de que, *instead of*

entre tanto que, *while*

excepto que, *excepting*

hasta que, *until*

luego, *then, furthermore*

luego que, *as soon as*

mientras, *while*

mientras que, *while*

mientras tanto que, *while*

no obstante que, *notwithstanding*

para que, *in order that*

por—que, *however*

por consiguiente, *consequently*

por lo mismo, *therefore*

por lo tanto, *therefore*

por más que, *however much*

por menos que ⎫

por poco que ⎭ *however little*

porque, *because, in order that*

pues, *because, as, for*

pues que ⎫

puesto que ⎭ *since*

sea que, *whether, while*

según que, *as, according to*

siempre que, *wherever*

sin que, *without*

supuesto que, *since*

tal como, *as*

también, *also, too*

tampoco, *neither, not either*

tanto—como, *as well—as*

ya—ya, *whether—or*

ya que, *since*

Remarks on Certain Conjunctions

1. **Y, and,** is changed into **e** when followed by a word beginning with **i** or **hi** (but not **hie**):

Es hábil e ingenioso.

Padres e hijos

He is clever and ingenious.

Parents and children

But.

Plomo y hierro	*Lead and iron*

2. **O, or,** is changed into **u** before a word beginning with **o** or **ho**:

Uno u otro	*Either one (one or the other)*
Ayer u hoy	*Yesterday or today*

3. **Pero, mas,** and **sino** correspond to English **but**. **Sino**, however, is used only to introduce a positive statement in direct contrast to a preceding negative one:

No es blanco sino pardo.	*It is not white, but gray.*
Me dijo que lo sabía, pero (*or* mas) parece que no es verdad.	*He told me he knew it, but it does not seem to be true.*

4. After the following conjunctions the subjunctive is used when uncertainty, doubt, possibility, or an indefinite future time is expressed:

antes que, *before*	en caso de que, *in case that*
a menos que, *unless*	hasta que, *until*
a fin de que, *to the end that*	hasta donde, *as far as*
aunque, *although*	luego que, *as soon as*
bien que, *although*	mientras, *while*
como, *when, as*	no sea que, *lest*
como si ⎫ *as if* cual si ⎭	ojalá, *would that*
	para que, *in order that*
como quiera que, *notwithstanding*	por—que, *however*
con tal que, *provided that*	siempre que, *whenever*
cuando, *when*	sin que, *without*
dado que, *granted that*	supuesto que, *supposing that*

Examples

Aunque me lo haya dicho el otro día, no me acuerdo ya de ello.	*Although he may have told me so the other day, I do not remember it.*
No volveré hasta que me hayan entregado el dinero.	*I shall not return till they have handed me the money.*
Cuando sea tiempo le daré a V. los géneros.	*When the time comes I shall give you the goods.*
Iré aunque llueva.	*I shall go, though it may rain.*

INTERJECTIONS
Of Joy

¡Ah, Ah! *Ah, Ah!*	¡Gracias a Dios! *Thank God!*
¡Ah, qué alegría! ⎫ ¡Ay qué gozo! ⎭ *What joy!*	¡Bendito sea Dios! ⎫ ¡Alabado sea Dios! ⎭ *God be praised!*
¡Bueno! *Good!*	¡Vaya, vaya! *Well now!*

OF SADNESS

¡Ah, ay! *Ah, ay!*
¡Ay qué pena! *What an affliction!*
¡Ay de mí! *Poor me! Woe is me!*

¡Dios mío! *Good heavens!*
¡Válgame Dios! *May God help me!*
¡Virgen santísima! *Holy Virgin!*
¡Ave María! *God forbid!*

OF APPROBATION AND SURPRISE

¡Muy bien! *Very good!*
¡Bien hecho! *Well done!*
¡Es un pasmo! ⎫
¡Es una maravilla! ⎬ *Beautiful!*
¡Bravo! *Magnificent!*
¡Viva, viva! *Hurrah, hurrah!*

¡Cáspita! ⎫ *These words express*
¡Cáscaras! ⎪ *various emotional*
¡Caracoles! ⎬ *reactions to an event*
¡Fuego! ⎭ *awakening surprise.*
¡Bravo! *Bravo!*
¡Oiga! ¡calle! *Yoy don't say so!*
¡Hola! *Hallo!*
¡Caramba! *Hang it!*
¡Toma! *Indeed! (Ironically).*

OF CONTEMPT, BLAME, AND DISGUST

¡Dios mío! *Good heavens!*
¡Vaya, vaya! *Well, now!*
¡Qué asco! *How disgusting!*
¡Grande hazaña! *A great feat!*

¡Qué vergüenza! *What a shame!*
¡Quita allá! *Get away!*
¡Calle, que es bueno! *That is very fine!*

OF ANGER

¡Voto a! *Don't make me mad!*
¡Caramba! *The plague take you!*

¡Diantre! *Hang it!*
¡Vaya V. a paseo! ⎫
¡Anda enhoramala! ⎬ *Get away!*

OF EXHORTATION AND ENCOURAGEMENT

¡Vaya, vaya! *Bravely!*
¡Vamos, vamos! *Come on!*
¡Alerta! *Look out!*
¡Ea pues! *Well now!*
¡Ea, ánimo! *Courage!*

¡Basta, basta! *Enough!*
¡Cuidado! *Take care!*
¡Fuera, fuera! *Out with him!*
¡Fuego, fuego! *Fire!*

OF SILENCE

¡Que callen! *Quiet!*
¡Calla, calla! *Be silent!*

¡Silencio! *Silence!*
¡Chito, chitón! *Hush!*

VOCABULARY

abajo, under, below
abandonar, to leave, to forsake
abanico, *m.* fan
abeja, *f.* bee
abierto, open, clear
abril, *m.* April
abrir, to open
acabar, to finish
aceite, *m.* oil, olive oil
aceituna, *f.* olive
acero, *m.* steel
acogida, *f.* reception
adelantar, to advance
afeitar, to shave
agosto, *m.* August
agotar, to exhaust, to drain
agradecer, to appreciate
agrio, sour
agua, *f.* water, fluid
agudo, sharp
aguja, *f.* needle
ahora, now, at present
ahorrar, to save
ala, *f.* wing
albaricoque, *m.* apricot
alcance, *m.* reach
aldea, *f.* village
alegre, merry, joyful
alfiler, *m.* pin
algodón, *m.* cotton
almohada, *f.* pillow, cushion
almuerzo, *m.* breakfast
alto, high, elevated
altura, *f.* height
alzar, to raise
amanecer, to dawn
amarillo, yellow

amigo, *m.* friend
ancho, wide
andar, to walk
antes, before
añadir, to add
año, *m.* year
apenas, hardly, scarcely
araña, *f.* spider
árbol, *m.* tree, axle
arriba, above, over, up
arrojar, to throw, to fling
arroz, *m.* rice
así, so, thus, therefore
asiento, *m.* chair, seat
asunto, *m.* subject, affair
atar, to tie, to bind
atrás, behind, back
aún, yet, as yet
aunque, although
ayuda, *f.* help, aid
azúcar, *m.* sugar
azul, blue

bajar, to come down, to descend
bajo, low, short, humble
bandera, *f.* flag
bañar, to bathe
baño, *m.* bath
barato, cheap
barba, *f.* beard
bastante, enough
beber, to drink
besar, to kiss
bien, well, right
billete, *m.* ticket, note
blanco, white, blank
blando, soft

boca, *f.* mouth
bolsa, *f.* purse
bondad, *f.* kindness
bueno, good, kind
buzón, *m.* letter-box

caballero, *m.* gentleman
caballo, *m.* horse
cabeza, *f.* head, chief
cada, each, every
caer, to fall, to drop
caja, *f.* box, case, cash
calor, *m.* heat
callar, to be silent
cama, *f.* bed, couch
camarero, *m.* waiter
camino, *m.* road, path
camisa, *f.* shirt
campana, *f.* bell
campo, *m.* field, country
canción, *f.* song
cantar, to sing
capa, *f.* cloak, mantle
cara, *f.* face, visage
carne, *f.* flesh, meat
carrera, *f.* run, race, career
carta, *f.* letter, epistle
casa, *f.* house, home
casar, to marry, to wed
cazar, to hunt, to chase
cebolla, *f.* onion
cerrar, to close, to lock
ciego, blind
cielo, *m.* sky, heavens
cinta, *f.* ribbon
ciudad, *f.* city, town
cocer, to boil, to cook
cocina, *f.* kitchen
codo, *m.* elbow
comer, to eat, to dine

como, how, like
con, with
conocer, to know, to perceive
copa, *f.* cup, wine-glass
corazón, *m.* heart, core
corbata, *f.* necktie
correr, to run, to race
cortar, to cut, to sever
corto, short, curt
crecer, to grow, to increase
creer, to believe
cosa, *f.* thing, object
coser, to sew, to stitch
cual, which, who
cuando, when
cuanto, how much
cubrir, to cover
cuchara, *f.* spoon
cuchillo, *m.* knife
cuero, *m.* leather
cuerpo, *m.* body
cuidado, *m.* care

dar, to give, to grant
debajo, beneath
deber, duty, obligation
decir, to say, to tell
dedo, *m.* finger, toe
dejar, to leave, to let
delgado, thin
dentro, inside, within
derecha, right
despertar, to awaken
deuda, *f.* debt
día, *m.* day, daylight
diciembre, *m.* December
diente, *m.* tooth
dinero, *m.* money, currency
docena, *f.* dozen
dolor, *m.* pain, ache

domingo, *m.* Sunday
donde, where
dormir, to sleep
dueño, *m.* proprietor
dulce, sweet
duro, hard

echar, to throw, to cast
edad, *f.* age, era
edificio, *m.* building
empresa, *f.* enterprise
encender, to kindle, to light
encima, above, on top
enero, *m.* January
enfermo, ill, sick
entender, to understand
entero, whole, entire
entrada, *f.* entry, entrance
entrar, to enter
entregar, to deliver
enviar, to send, to remit
escalera, *f.* staircase
escaso, scant, scarce
escoba, *f.* broom
esconder, to hide, to conceal
escribir, to write
escritorio, *m.* office
escuchar, to listen
esfuerzo, *m.* effort
espalda, *f.* back, shoulders
espantar, to frighten
esperar, to expect, to wait
espeso, thick, dense
esponja, *f.* sponge
esposa, *f.* wife
esposo, *m.* husband
estación, *f.* railroad-station
estar, to be
estómago, *m.* stomach

estrecho, narrow, straight, tight
estrella, *f.* star

falda, *f.* skirt, lap
faltar, to fail, to lack
febrero, *m.* February
fecha, *f.* date
feliz, happy
feo, ugly
ferretería, *f.* hardware
ferrocarril, *m.* railroad
fiel, faithful
fiesta, *f.* feast, holiday
fijar, to fix, to fasten
firma, *f.* signature
firmar, to sign
flojo, mild, lax
flor, *f.* flower
fonda, *f.* inn, hotel
fósforo, *m.* match
frente, *f.* forehead
fresa, *f.* strawberry
fresco, fresh, cool
frío, *m.* cold
fruta, *f.* fruit
fuego, *m.* fire
fuera, out, outside, away
fuerza, *f.* strength, force
fumar, to smoke

gabán, *m.* overcoat
gallina, *f.* hen
gallo, *m.* rooster
gana, *f.* appetite
ganado, *m.* cattle
ganar, to gain, to profit
ganga, *f.* bargain
garbanzo, *m.* chick-pea
garganta, *f.* throat
gastar, to spend, to waste

gato, cat, tom-cat
gente, *f.* people
gobierno, *m.* government
golondrina, *f.* swallow
golpear, to strike, to beat
gordo, fat, stout
gorra, *f.* cap, bonnet
gota, *f.* drop
gracias, *f. pl.* thanks
grande, large, big, great
grito, *m.* cry, scream
guante, *m.* glove
guerra, *f.* war
guía, *f.* guide, guide-book
guisante, *m.* pea
gustar, to please, to taste
gusto, *m.* taste

haber, to have, to own
hablar, to speak, to talk
hacer, to do, to make
hacia, toward
hallar, to find
hasta, till, until
helar, to freeze
hermana, *f.* sister
hermano, *m.* brother
hervir, to boil
hielo, *m.* ice, frost
hierro, *m.* iron
hija, *f.* daughter
hijo, *m.* son
hilo, *m.* thread
hogar, *m.* hearth, home
hombre, *m.* man
hora, *f.* hour
hormiga, *f.* ant
hoy, to-day, now
hueso, *m.* bone

huevo, *m.* egg
huir, to flee

idioma, *f.* language
iglesia, *f.* church
intentar, to attempt
invierno, *m.* winter
ir, to go, to move
izquierda, left

jabón, *m.* soap
jamás, never
jamón, *m.* ham
jardín, *m.* garden
jefe, *m.* chief, leader
joven, young
joya, *f.* jewel
juego, *m.* play, game
jueves, *m.* Thursday
jugar, to play
juguete, *m.* toy
julio, *m.* July
junio, *m.* June
junto, near, close

lado, *m.* side, edge
ladrón, *m.* thief
lágrima, *f.* tear
lámpara, *f.* lamp
lana, *f.* wool
lápiz, *m.* pencil
largo, long, large
lástima, *f.* pity
lata, *f.* tin can
lavar, to wash
leche, *f.* milk
lechuga, *f.* lettuce
leer, to read, to peruse
lejos, far, far away
lengua, *f.* tongue, language

lento, slow
levantar, to raise, to lift
libre, free
libro, *m.* book
ligero, light, airy
limpiar, to clean
listo, ready
lobo, *m.* wolf
loco, *m.* mad, insane
lograr, to attain
lomo, *m.* loin
lucir, to shine, to glitter
lucha, *f.* struggle
luego, presently
lugar, *m.* place, site
luna, *f.* moon
lunes, *m.* Monday
luz, *f.* light, clarity

llama, *f.* flame
llamar, to call
llano, level, plain
llave, *f.* key
llegar, to arrive
llenar, to fill
lleno, full
llevar, to carry
llorar, to weep
llover, to rain
lluvia, rain

madera, *f.* wood
madre, *f.* mother
madrugada, *f.* dawn
maestro, *m.* teacher, master
maleta, *f.* suitcase
malo, bad
manchar, to stain, to soil
manga, *f.* sleeve
mano, *f.* hand

manta, *f.* blanket
mantequilla, *f.* butter
mañana, *f.* morning, (*adv.*) to-
  morrow
mar, *m.* sea
martes, *m.* Tuesday
martillo, *m.* hammer
marzo, *m.* March
más, more, moreover
mayo, *m.* May
mayor, greater, larger
medio, half, mid
medir, to measure
mejor, better, superior
mejorar, to improve
melocotón, *m.* peach
menor, smaller, minor
menos, less, least
mentir, to lie
merienda, *f.* lunch
mes, *m.* month
mesa, *f.* table
meter, to insert, to put into
miedo, *m.* fear
miel, *f.* honey
mientras, while
miércoles, *m.* Wednesday
milagro, *m.* wonder, miracle
mirar, to look, to behold
mismo, same
mitad, *f.* half, center
mosca, *f.* fly
mostaza, *f.* mustard
mozo, *m.* youth, waiter
muchacha, *f.* girl
muchacho, *m.* boy
mucho, much, plenty
mujer, *f.* woman
mundo, *m.* world

muñeca, *f.* doll
muy, very, greatly

nada, *f.* nothing
nadar, to swim
naranja, *f.* orange
nariz, *f.* nose
nata, *f.* cream
navaja, *f.* razor
negar, to deny
nevar, to snow
nido, *m.* nest
nieve, *f.* snow
ninguno, none
niño, *m.* child, infant
noche, *f.* night
nombre, *m.* name
nosotros, we, ourselves
noviembre, *m.* November
nuestro, our, ours
nuevo, new, fresh
nuez, *f.* walnut

obedecer, to obey
obrar, to work
octubre, *m.* October
oír, to hear
ojo, *m.* eye, sight
oler, to smell, to scent
olla, pot, kettle
oreja, *f.* ear
oro, *m.* gold
oso, *m.* bear
otoño, *m.* autumn
oveja, *m.* sheep

padre, *m.* father
pagar, to pay
paja, *f.* straw
palabra, *f.* word

paloma, *f.* pigeon
pan, *m.* bread
pañuelo, *m.* handkerchief
para, for, to, in order to
parar, to stop
pared, *f.* wall
pariente, *m.* relation, kinsman
partir, to depart, to sever
pasa, *f.* raisin
pasar, to pass
pasear, to take a walk
paso, *m.* pace, step
patata, *f.* potato
pato, *m.* duck
pavo, *m.* turkey
pecho, *m.* breast
pedir, to ask, to request
peine, *m.* comb
pelo, *m.* hair
pelota, *f.* ball
pensar, to think, to reflect
peor, worse
pequeño, small
perder, to lose
pero, but, except
perro, *m.* dog
pesado, heavy
pesar, to weigh
pescar, to fish
pie, *m.* foot
piedra, *f.* stone
piel, *f.* skin
pierna, *f.* leg
pintura, *f.* painting, picture
piso, *m.* floor, story
placer, *m.* pleasure
plata, *f.* silver
plato, *m.* dish, plate
pluma, *f.* feather
poco, little

polvo, *m.* dust
pollo, *m.* chicken
poner, to put, to place
por, by, through, across
porque, because
precio, *m.* price
preguntar, to ask, to question
primavera, *f.* spring
prisa, *f.* hurry, haste
pronto, quick, prompt, soon
propina, *f.* fee, tip
provecho, *m.* profit
prueba, *f.* test, trial
puente, *m.* bridge
puerta, *f.* door
pues, because, therefore
puño, *m.* fist

que, who, which, that
quedar, to stay, to remain
queja, *f.* complaint
quemar, to burn
querer, to desire, to love
queso, *m.* cheese
quien, who, whom
quitar, to take away

rabo, *m.* tail
rama, *f.* branch
rana, *f.* frog
rato, *m.* a little while
ratón, *m.* mouse
recado, *m.* message, errand
recibo, *m.* receipt
recoger, to gather, to pick
recordar, to remember
recuerdo, *m.* souvenir
redondo, round
regalo, *m.* gift, present
reír, to laugh

reloj, *m.* clock, watch
reñir, to quarrel, to fight
respuesta, *f.* reply, answer
retrato, *m.* portrait
risa, *f.* laughter
romper, to break
ropa, *f.* clothing
ruido, *m.* noise

sábado, *m.* Saturday
saber, to know
sabor, *m.* taste, flavor
sacar, to pull out, to draw
sala, *f.* parlor
salida, *f.* exit, departure
salir, to depart, to go out
saltar, to leap, to jump
salud, *f.* health
secar, to dry
sed, *f.* thirst
seda, *f.* silk
seguir, to follow
sello, *m.* postage-stamp
semana, *f.* week
sentir, to feel
señor, *m.* sir, mister
señora, *f.* lady, madam
señorita, *f.* young lady
señorito, *m.* young gentleman
septiembre, *m.* September
ser, to be
siempre, always
siglo, *m.* century
silla, *f.* chair, saddle
sin, without
sobre, *m.* envelope, (*adv.*) on, upon, over
sol, *m.* sun
sombra, *f.* shade
sombrero, *m.* hat

soplar, to blow
sordo, deaf
subir, to rise, to climb
sudor, *m.* perspiration
suelo, *m.* ground, soil
sueño, *m.* sleep
suspirar, to sigh

tal, such, so, as, thus
talón, *m.* heel
tanto, so much, as much
tapar, to cover, to hide
tarde, *f.* afternoon, evening
tarde, late, too late
tarjeta, *f.* card
tela, *f.* cloth, fabric
temporada, *f.* season
temprano, early
tener, to have, to hold
tiempo, *m.* time, era
tierra, *f.* earth, soil
tijeras, *pl. f.* scissors
tinta, *f.* ink
tirar, to throw, to cast
toalla, *f.* towel
tocar, to touch
todo, all, everything
tomar, to take, to seize
trabajar, to work, to labor
traer, to bring, to fetch
traje, *m.* suit of clothes
tren, *m.* railroad-train
trigo, *m.* wheat
triste, sad, mournful

último, last, latest
uña, *f.* finger-nail

usar, to use
uva, *f.* grape

vaca, *f.* cow
vacío, empty
valer, to be worth
vaso, *m.* drinking-glass
vela, *f.* candle, sail, wake
vender, to sell
venir, to come, to draw near
venta, *f.* sale
ventana, *f.* window
ver, to see, to look into
verano, *m.* summer
verdad, *f.* truth
verde, green
vestido, *m.* dress
vestir, to dress, to clothe
vez, *f.* turn, time
viajar, to travel
viaje, *m.* journey, trip
vida, *f.* life
viento, *m.* wind, air
viernes, *m.* Friday
vino, *m.* wine
vivir, to live, to dwell
volver, to return, to turn
vuelta, *f.* return

y, and
ya, already, now
yema, *f.* yolk of an egg

zanahoria, *f.* carrot
zanja, *f.* ditch
zapato, *f.* shoe
zorra, *f.* fox
zurcir, to darn

INDEX

340